VOLUME 523

SEPTEMBER 1992

THE ANNALS

of The American Academy *of* Political
and Social Science

RICHARD D. LAMBERT, *Editor*
ALAN W. HESTON, *Associate Editor*

AFFIRMATIVE ACTION REVISITED

Special Editors of this Volume

HAROLD ORLANS   JUNE O'NEILL

Chevy Chase   *Baruch College*
Maryland   *City University of New York*

Ⓢ SAGE PUBLICATIONS *NEWBURY PARK   LONDON   NEW DELHI*

THE ANNALS

© 1992 *by* The American Academy *of* Political *and* Social Science

Editorial Office: 3937 Chestnut Street, Philadelphia, PA 19104.

For information about membership* (individuals only) and subscriptions (institutions), address:

SAGE PUBLICATIONS, INC.
2455 Teller Road
Newbury Park, CA 91320

From India and South Asia,
write to:
SAGE PUBLICATIONS INDIA Pvt. Ltd.
P.O. Box 4215
New Delhi 110 048
INDIA

From the UK, Europe, the Middle
East and Africa, write to:
SAGE PUBLICATIONS LTD
6 Bonhill Street
London EC2A 4PU
UNITED KINGDOM

SAGE Production Staff: LINDA GRAY, LIANN LECH, and JANELLE LeMASTER
*Please note that members of The Academy receive THE ANNALS with their membership.
Library of Congress Catalog Card Number 91-67479
International Standard Serial Number ISSN 0002-7162
International Standard Book Number ISBN 0-8039-4685-6 (Vol. 523, 1992 paper)
International Standard Book Number ISBN 0-8039-4684-8 (Vol. 523, 1992 cloth)
Manufactured in the United States of America. First printing, September 1992.

The articles appearing in THE ANNALS are indexed in *Book Review Index, Public Affairs Information Service Bulletin, Social Sciences Index, Current Contents, General Periodicals Index, Academic Index, Pro-Views,* and *Combined Retrospective Index Sets.* They are also abstracted and indexed in *ABC Pol Sci, Historical Abstracts, Human Resources Abstracts, Social Sciences Citation Index, United States Political Science Documents, Social Work Research & Abstracts, Sage Urban Studies Abstracts, International Political Science Abstracts, America: History and Life, Sociological Abstracts, Managing Abstracts, Social Planning/Policy & Development Abstracts, Automatic Subject Citation Alert, Book Review Digest, Work Related Abstracts, Periodica Islamica,* and/or *Family Resources Database,* and are available on microfilm from University Microfilms, Ann Arbor, Michigan.

Information about membership rates, institutional subscriptions, and back issue prices may be found on the facing page.

Advertising. Current rates and specifications may be obtained by writing to THE ANNALS Advertising and Promotion Manager at the Newbury Park office (address above).

Claims. Claims for undelivered copies must be made no later than three months following month of publication. The publisher will supply missing copies when losses have been sustained in transit and when the reserve stock will permit.

Change of Address. Six weeks' advance notice must be given when notifying of change of address to ensure proper identification. Please specify name of journal. Send address changes to: THE ANNALS, c/o Sage Publications, Inc., 2455 Teller Road, Newbury Park, CA 91320.

The American Academy of Political and Social Science

3937 Chestnut Street Philadelphia, Pennsylvania 19104

Origin and Purpose. The Academy was organized December 14, 1889, to promote the progress of political and social science, especially through publications and meetings. The Academy does not take sides in controverted questions, but seeks to gather and present reliable information to assist the public in forming an intelligent and accurate judgment.

Meetings. The Academy occasionally holds a meeting in the spring extending over two days.

Publications. THE ANNALS is the bimonthly publication of The Academy. Each issue contains articles on some prominent social or political problem, written at the invitation of the editors. Also, monographs are published from time to time, numbers of which are distributed to pertinent professional organizations. These volumes constitute important reference works on the topics with which they deal, and they are extensively cited by authorities throughout the United States and abroad. The papers presented at the meetings of The Academy are included in THE ANNALS.

Membership. Each member of The Academy receives THE ANNALS and may attend the meetings of The Academy. Membership is open only to individuals. Annual dues: $42.00 for the regular paperbound edition (clothbound, $60.00). California residents must add 7.25% sales tax on all orders ($45.05 paperbound; $64.35 clothbound). Add $9.00 per year for membership outside the U.S.A. Members may also purchase single issues of THE ANNALS for $13.00 each (clothbound, $18.00). California residents: $13.94 paperbound, $19.31 clothbound. Add $1.50 for shipping and handling on all prepaid orders.

Subscriptions. THE ANNALS (ISSN 0002-7162) is published six times annually—in January, March, May, July, September, and November. Institutions may subscribe to THE ANNALS at the annual rate: $132.00 (clothbound, $156.00). California institutions: $141.57 paperbound, $167.31 clothbound. Add $9.00 per year for subscriptions outside the U.S.A. Institutional rates for single issues: $24.00 each (clothbound, $29.00). California institutions: $25.74 paperbound, $31.10 clothbound.

Second class postage paid at Thousand Oaks, California, and additional offices.

Single issues of THE ANNALS may be obtained by individuals who are not members of The Academy for $17.00 each (clothbound, $26.00). California residents: $18.23 paperbound, $27.89 clothbound. Add $1.50 for shipping and handling on all prepaid orders. Single issues of THE ANNALS have proven to be excellent supplementary texts for classroom use. Direct inquiries regarding adoptions to THE ANNALS c/o Sage Publications (address below).

All correspondence concerning membership in The Academy, dues renewals, inquiries about membership status, and/or purchase of single issues of THE ANNALS should be sent to THE ANNALS c/o Sage Publications, Inc., 2455 Teller Road, Newbury Park, CA 91320. Telephone: (805) 499-0721; FAX/Order line: (805) 499-0871. *Please note that orders under $30 must be prepaid.* Sage affiliates in London and India will assist institutional subscribers abroad with regard to orders, claims, and inquiries for both subscriptions and single issues.

Printed on recycled, acid-free paper

THE ANNALS

of The American Academy *of* Political *and* Social Science

RICHARD D. LAMBERT, *Editor*
ALAN W. HESTON, *Associate Editor*

——————————— FORTHCOMING ———————————

See page 3 for information on Academy membership and
purchase of single volumes of **The Annals.**

CONTENTS

BOOK DEPARTMENT CONTENTS

PREFACE

For the purpose of this issue of *The Annals*, "affirmative action" is defined as a conscious effort to increase the representation of women and other designated groups in particular organizations, occupations, programs, and a wide range of activities. Such activities include education and training; housing and transportation; and the award of contracts, grants, licenses, degrees, scholarships, honors, and appointments to governing boards and political or judicial posts.

The groups most commonly selected for affirmative action include women; four officially defined minority groups—blacks who are not Hispanic; white and black Hispanics; Asians and Pacific Islanders; and American Indians and Alaskan Natives—and persons with disabilities.

Affirmative action may be voluntary or mandated by court order, regulation, contract, or local law. It may aim to increase the representation of most, some, or one of the groups named previously. Representation is assessed by comparing the proportion of group members in the national or local population or in a population with stated educational or occupational qualifications with the proportion in a given activity, occupation, firm, or institution. However, opinion is sharply divided about the degree to which broad educational or occupational statistics can measure the composition of the qualified population or coincide with the qualifications required for particular positions.

Affirmative action programs may aim not merely to replicate the proportion of qualified group members in given positions and firms but to raise that proportion and improve the group's status to match that of white males, the principal group excluded from these programs. However, Butler reports, in his contribution to this volume, that efforts are being made to recruit more white males to counterbalance the "overrepresentation" of African Americans in the armed forces.

Current programs have many sources: presidential orders requiring affirmative hiring by federal contractors; court orders requiring affirmative measures to end segregation and remedy discrimination; legislation barring discrimination. Protests, political and economic pressure, and legal action by members and supporters of affected groups have prompted many affirmative measures, as have voluntary actions by individuals and organizations seeking social peace and justice.

Affirmative action is contentious. Supporters see it as a means to offset not only the damages that discrimination has inflicted on individuals but the institutionalized forms and processes that have perpetuated the low status of entire groups, even without any manifest discrimination against individuals. Opponents believe it attributes to discrimination differences in group status that have many causes, and that to award jobs and benefits by group statistics rather than individual merit or need is unjust, lowers standards and organizational effectiveness, and fosters social divisiveness.

The views of proponents and opponents can be irreconcilable, and no knowledgeable authority appears to be entirely neutral. Hence, though we have sought balance in this volume, it is less likely to be attained in every article than in the collection as a whole. In the articles discussing the law, the views of proponents (Taylor and Liss) and opponents (Reynolds) are explicitly juxtaposed. Hamilton provides a sympathetic review of basic principles, while Loury presents a formal model emphasizing unintended and undesirable consequences.

The variety of groups, programs, and agencies involved in affirmative action makes a comprehensive review impractical. Many studies focus on only one group—usually blacks or women—or on federal requirements or federal court rulings. This volume also considers, in Oi's article, disabled persons, the focus of 1990 legislation. It emphasizes employment (O'Neill and O'Neill), education (Thernstrom, Orlans, Williams), and politics (Lipset, Chavez) and recognizes the importance of state and local programs (LaNoue, Kellough, Thernstrom) and private initiatives (Orlans), as well as federal programs (Graham; O'Neill and O'Neill; Kellough).

Discussions of affirmative action often suffer from excessive abstraction and insufficient historical sense. Several of our contributors, especially Hamilton, Graham, and Butler, present a historical perspective; Lipset and Povall add an international dimension; case studies of a bank, the armed forces, and a university illustrate how the principles of affirmative action are implemented in specific institutions.

In the 1978 *Bakke* case, the Supreme Court declared quotas illegal but held it legal to take race into account as one but not the only factor in academic admissions. In his opinion, Justice Harry Blackmun declared that, "in order to get beyond racism, we must first take account of race." Thousands of affirmative action programs now take account—and a count—of race, minority status, sex, language and/or country of ancestry or origin, whether or not one is a veteran, and bodily ability and disability. Singling out members of one group for favorable attention evidently leads other groups to demand similar attention. There have been additions to affirmative action programs but few subtractions.

One subtraction occurred in the 1950s, when Jewish organizations concurred in the removal of Jews from the minority groups whose employment was reported by government contractors.[1] The University of California has removed most Asian students from its affirmative recruitment and admissions programs because they are statistically overrepresented; however, Filipinos are still included. Following the Supreme Court's 1989 *Croson* decision, a number of local governments have removed remote minorities like Alaskan Natives and Aleuts from those eligible for minority contract awards.

Even staunch proponents of affirmative action should favor such modifications of national guidelines, which are often used in local situations where they are plainly inapplicable.

1. Harold Orlans, "The Politics of Minority Statistics," *Society*, 26(4):24 (May-June 1989).

However, increasing the number of groups and individuals eligible for affirmative action has been more characteristic. In 1977, Pakistanis, Indians, and Sri Lankans were reclassified from white to Asian, that is, from beneficiaries to victims of discrimination. The City University of New York has added Italian Americans to its affirmative admissions programs.

The extension of affirmative action to women, who constitute 51 percent of the national population and 45 percent of the working population, and to persons with disabilities, who comprise 3-5 percent of working-age adults, made it applicable to at least two-thirds of the population. Each year, the minority population is augmented by hundreds of thousands of legal and illegal immigrants who have not suffered from prior discrimination here but who immediately benefit from affirmative action and increase the under-representation of minorities in high-income jobs and higher education.

Affirmative action is afflicted by gigantism. A single idea, discrimination, cannot adequately explain the greatly varied conditions and economic status of groups comprising a majority of the population. The persons operating thousands of affirmative action programs cannot effectively administer and police such massive activities. The statistics on which the entire structure rests are utterly inadequate to support the weight of decisions based upon them. Nonetheless, the political force of a large majority of the population has sustained, if not fully enforced, grandiose programs based upon inadequate ideas, information, and procedures.

If affirmative action is warranted for any group, that group is composed of African Americans. As Hamilton and Lipset point out, blacks were legally a group apart: first as slaves, then as a legally segregated caste. Yet how long is the past to govern us? "When," Hamilton asks, "do we put the memory of slavery and the experience of segregation behind us? . . . Does not this harping on the past create an impossible situation?" To base present policy on laws and conditions under which most of the nation never lived, which over a hundred thousand white men died to change, which southerners have long abandoned, is strange.

Lipset calls for replacing policy that helps all members of defined groups, rich or poor, by one that helps all poor or sick persons, regardless of the group into which they were born. The editors of this issue of *The Annals* agree. But affirmative action based on the rights of groups is now so widespread, so politically entrenched, that it will not soon disappear.

Each editor has been responsible for inviting and editing a separate set of articles: Harold Orlans, for articles by Hamilton, Graham, Lipset, LaNoue, Kellough, Orlans, Povall, Butler, and Williams; June O'Neill, for articles by Loury, Taylor and Liss, Reynolds, Chavez, O'Neill and O'Neill, Thernstrom, and Oi.

HAROLD ORLANS
JUNE O'NEILL

ANNALS, *AAPSS*, 523, September 1992

Affirmative Action and the Clash of Experiential Realities

By CHARLES V. HAMILTON

ABSTRACT: The different historical experiences of African Americans and other immigrants have engendered different approaches to the social and economic discrimination they encountered. Immigrating voluntarily to improve their status, other ethnic groups met de facto discrimination but not dehumanization. Glad to leave worse conditions, they expected little from the state and advanced by their own work. Blacks, free in Africa, entered in chains as de jure property. They had to struggle for de jure human status, for full legal equality as citizens. Demanding that the state restore rights it had deprived them of, they also demanded, in affirmative action programs dating to the mid-1930s, a fair proportion of jobs. Ghetto poverty, it is said, is an economic and social, not a racial, problem. Civil rights groups have long recognized that the welfare of blacks and the welfare of other citizens are united.

Charles V. Hamilton, Wallace S. Sayre Professor of Government at Columbia University, received a J.D. from Loyola University, Chicago, and a Ph.D. from the University of Chicago. His books include Adam Clayton Powell, Jr. *(1991),* American Government *(1981), and* Black Power *(with Stokely Carmichael, 1967). He has been vice president of the American Political Science Association and a board member of the Joint Center for Political and Economic Studies; he is a board member of the Twentieth Century Fund and the NAACP Legal Defense Fund.*

THE invitation to write on this subject generously suggested a paper discussing "in broad terms the basic principles and practical realities of affirmative action." Equally generous, the editors offered, "It is for you to decide which 'principles' and 'realities' you wish to emphasize."

My initial inclination was to discuss the several—sometimes overlapping—principles that have been prominent over recent years in the affirmative action debate. These principles have been enunciated in speeches, books, judicial opinions, and articles in professional and popular journals.[1] Most often they are stated in dichotomous form: individual rights versus group rights; equality of opportunity versus equality of results; individualism versus egalitarianism; color blindness versus color consciousness; compensatory action versus preferential treatment; universal programs versus racially targeted—or gender-targeted—programs.

The writings on this subject invariably incorporate some aspects of these principles as they contend for support for various public policies for or against affirmative action. Frequently, various sorts of empirical data—opinion polls, elite surveys, election trends—serve to describe the political realities involved—that is, exactly how much support one argu-

ment has over another at any given time. These realities cover such phenomena as white backlash, perceptions of inferiority, stigma, victimization, reverse discrimination, and the desirability of "diversity."

These discussions are relevant and useful, but also, I suspect, rather well known to a reasonably attentive audience.

I have chosen to focus on another aspect of the subject, one not so often discussed or appreciated: the differential historical experiences of various groups and how those experiences have shaped recent policy demands as well as the reaction to those demands. These experiences constitute an important set of realities not too often factored into the various analyses of the debate. The clear, but sometimes simplistic, principles stated earlier may in fact mask deeper feelings—or realities—not fully explored by the superimposed set of political philosophical principles. There may be something less lofty but no less profound at work in the affirmative action policy debate in this country.

THE CLASHING REALITIES
OF ETHNICS AND BLACKS

The evolution of the affirmative action debate demonstrates a fundamental clash of experiential realities. Americans have taken an understandable and deserved pride in an ideology of individualism, egalitarianism, equality before the law, constitutionalism, and political freedom. At the same time, they have admitted—more honestly at some times than at others—the discrepancy between these ideological pronounce-

1. See Nathan Glazer, *Affirmative Discrimination* (New York: Basic Books, 1975); Seymour Martin Lipset, *Equality and the American Creed* (Washington, DC: Progressive Policy Institute, 1991); Gertrude Ezorsky, *Racism and Justice* (Ithaca, NY: Cornell University Press, 1991); Gerald R. Gill, "Debate on Affirmative Action," *CAAS Newsletter* (UCLA Center for Afro-American Studies), 2(1) (1987).

ments and actual practices. They have always known of discrimination against racial and ethnic groups and, of course, women, and they have responded to this discrepancy in various ways.[2]

Especially since the Civil War, the law has been a major vehicle for dealing with these discrepancies. De jure segregation and discrimination could be most vulnerable to attack as repugnant to the written constitution. (To be sure, there were intense constitutional debates and disagreements—nullification, states' rights, interposition—but there was something particularly unacceptable morally about enshrining the discrepancy so overtly in the law.) De jure discrimination was what the government sanctioned; it was public. In the minds of many, this clearly created an uncomfortable "dilemma."[3]

De facto discrimination against immigrants

Notwithstanding this dilemma, over a 300-year period, various groups came to this country and faced both official and unofficial discrimination. The stories are told in countless research on the ethnic immigrant experiences.[4] Germans, Irish, Jews, Italians, Chinese, and

many others came seeking political, economic, and religious refuge and freedom. They certainly were discriminated against: "No Irish Need Apply," "No Jews or Dogs Allowed." American history is replete with such accounts.

In some instances, the groups sought redress through the courts and legislatures, but often as not, they simply accepted the conditions and endured. When Mike Masaoka of the Japanese American Citizens League told of his parents' response to land fraud deals against them in the early years of their arrival, he explained why they did not go to court: "You must understand what it was like to be a Japanese immigrant in those days. . . . They called America a democracy, but its benefits were not for those who were not white. . . . So we swallowed our anger and persevered."[5]

A politicization process was taking placed that was substantially influenced by the terms of understanding related to the group's entry. It involved expectations and implications for what constituted legitimate reciprocal behavior between the state and the people. The groups would be admitted under certain conditions as, for instance, with the 23 Jews coming to New Amsterdam in 1654. They came from Recife, Brazil, but were not permitted to engage in certain commercial activities and were made to understand that "the poor among them shall not become a burden on the [West India] Company or the pub-

2. An especially good account of the various responses is found in Samuel P. Huntington, *American Politics* (Cambridge, MA: Harvard University Press, 1981).

3. Gunnar Myrdal, *An American Dilemma* (New York: Harper & Bros., 1944).

4. See Lawrence H. Fuchs, *The American Kaleidoscope* (Hanover, NH: University Press of New England, 1990); Thomas Kessner, *The Golden Door* (New York: Oxford University Press, 1977); Mike Masaoka, *They Call Me Moses Masaoka* (New York: William Morrow, 1987); Stanley Lieberson, *A Piece of the Pie* (Berkeley: University of California Press, 1980).

5. Masaoka, *They Call Me Moses Masaoka*, p. 21.

lic, but shall be maintained at the expense of the Jewish Nation."[6] Other groups faced similar discrimination over the centuries.

Basically, most ethnic groups came to this land under three important circumstances: (1) they came voluntarily, by choice; (2) the immigration was perceived by the immigrants as a relative, or certainly potential, improvement of their status: economic, political, or religious; (3) while clearly oppressed and discriminated against, they were not dehumanized. In fact, they often could be and were welcomed as eventual contributors—through their "free" labor—to the economic development of the society. They did not expect the state to play a major, direct role in their development. They had to accept certain restrictions on their economic and cultural development as prerequisites to their entry.

Private sector gains

These three circumstances had enormous consequences for the politicization of the groups involved. Perhaps most important was—and remains—a sense of gratitude for being permitted to immigrate to a land that offered even the slightest hope for growth, advancement, and escape from personal persecution. Likewise, many immigrants could compare their new situation favorably to what they left behind. Finally, they were politicized to believe that if they worked hard, they could achieve and contribute to the overall vitality and growth of the society as productive human beings.

6. Milton Goldin, *Why They Give* (New York: Macmillan, 1976).

They had no expectation that the state had a responsibility to facilitate this contribution, and this laid the foundation for an almost unquestioned loyalty to the society despite its glaring imperfections. These imperfections could be tolerated because the immigrants did not naively believe they were coming into a paradise, the grand ideological language of the Declaration of Independence and the Constitution notwithstanding. There was a subtle, implicit trade-off.

The immigrants' expectations were related to their ability to function in the private economic sectors. Though they had to start at the bottom—in the sweatshops, on the exploitative railroads, as exploited domestics and low-paid factory laborers—at least they could start and in the process develop a faith that in time their children could experience upward mobility. They were intensely aware of discrimination against them in those sectors, but they could accommodate to this because of the very terms of their entry. Under the circumstances, it would not necessarily occur to them to turn to the state for legal redress of their economic problems. If the political realm was to be used, as the Irish so skillfully did, it was by the traditional mode of local group mobilization and electoral politics. Importantly, over time, the private economic sectors did yield economic gains both for the ethnic working class and for entrepreneurs.

Thus the initial test of social legitimacy for many European ethnics—and even present-day Southeast Asians and Cubans—was the availability of the private economic sector to improve their status. They had always experienced de facto economic discrimination, but not to the extent that their individual and group efforts would be extensively thwarted. The various de jure obstacles they faced were never so oppressive as ultimately to countermand their gratitude and their faith in the system or themselves.

De jure dehumanization of blacks

The African American experience is substantially different. Blacks came involuntarily, often from freedom to slavery; they came as dehumanized property.

In such circumstances, the first test of social legitimacy for blacks would be in the political—public—realm. Blacks had first to struggle to define themselves as humans, as citizens. This meant that, of necessity, their experience would be much more politicized than that of European ethnics. The blacks had first to engage in a distinctively political struggle; other immigrants could immediately engage in an economic struggle. Most European and Asian ethnics came to acquire property. Blacks came as property.

Thus the African American experience reversed the normal social struggle. Blacks had to cease being property before they could begin to acquire it. After the Civil War, the black talent that would normally have gone into the business, financial, and entrepreneurial sectors had to be channeled into the legal-political arenas. Well into the twentieth century, the system of de jure subordination had to be dismantled, whereas other ethnic groups faced

only de facto discrimination. This legal exclusion set the stage for the twentieth-century politicization of many African Americans and fueled the dynamic civil rights movement that continues to occupy the nation's attention.

This analysis does not overlook the legal restrictions many European ethnics and Asians suffered. But many factors—sheer numbers, geographical location, changing agricultural and industrial regional economies, the linkage of race to fears of political dominance—made the legal black apartheid exceptionally onerous.

DIFFERENT POLITICAL DEMANDS

The immense political implications and consequences of these clashing experiences produce different political demands and attitudes toward what is owed by the society. This brings us to affirmative action.

Many African Americans, aware of the long political struggle out of servitude, peonage, and segregation, cannot adopt an attitude of gratitude. More often, one finds in their political oratory and demands a sense of entitlement, of righteous indignation and resentment, a sharper edge of anger and contempt than in the usual pluralist bargaining politics of much American governance.

The language of rights

Accordingly, the language of rights is a prominent part of the black political struggle: first, a struggle for constitutional rights to be free from chattel slavery; then, to be a free citizen with civil and political rights. This protracted struggle has been the major politicizing feature of the African American political experience. It is reflected in overt language: a civil rights movement.

Many people remember Dr. Martin Luther King, Jr.'s "I Have a Dream" speech at the March on Washington, 28 August 1963. They remember and cite the passages of reconciliation, of white and black children someday living harmoniously together and being judged not by the color of their skin but by the content of their character. These parts of the stirring speech are repeatedly cited and made the titles of books and documentaries. But many overlook the part of the speech that spoke of "entitlement." King also said in that speech, "America has a due bill . . . a promissory note we now intend to cash"!

This is hardly political oratory that would emanate from the political leadership of other ethnic groups.

As the civil rights movement evolved from victories over de jure segregation and discrimination to increased concern with de facto conditions, it took the language of rights with it. And here, in the last two decades especially, experiential realities clash.

They clash when affirmative action remedies aim to overcome the past effects of de jure discrimination and present de facto discriminatory practices.

Imperfect realities

Most Americans have always understood and accepted de facto group discrimination. They winked. They accepted the imperfect system and sought privately—collectively and individually—either to accommodate or to overcome it. They heard the lofty language of the Declaration of Independence, the U.S. Constitution, and the Fourth of July speeches, but they winked.

They accepted the imperfections as long as they were not too blatant or abusive. And indeed they could gradually come to support a civil rights movement that was aimed at ending the most glaring de jure aspects of the dilemma, very likely because they saw that movement in some way related to the overthrow of the remaining vestiges of a thoroughly unacceptable system of human slavery.

Once this major victory was achieved in the 1964 Civil Rights Act and the 1965 Voting Rights Act, the arena essentially shifted to the non-legal—de facto—realm. Here political claims for special help to those who had been left behind or still suffered from disadvantages were not received the same way as earlier demands to end de jure segregation. When many Americans tell blacks to "pull yourself up by your bootstraps, as we did," they are really saying, "Resort to the same kinds of private group and individual efforts we did." Thus they are impatient with demands for official, formal government assistance that legally sets one group up for preferred treatment.

They object to this assistance not because they subscribe to the lofty ideology of individual rights over group rights. In fact, much of their experience and present-day reality is precisely the opposite. They continue to vote for their own ethnic candidates—but they do not make a loud public display of it. They give and expect employment favors based on family and kin—again, no noise. They quietly choose their schools and residents to fit their ethnic and cultural preferences—and resent being told they are bigots opposed to open occupancy. These are the accommodations they earlier experienced and that they now expect others to make, and they become furious when government steps in to impose a different set of rules and norms.

They know about slavery and legal segregation, but those conditions no longer exist. They see de facto discrimination as something that imperfect societies must live with. Even with this imperfection, America is a far better place than any other on the globe. The best way to minimize imperfections is to rely not on overt politics and laws but on covert, informal approaches. At times, this view gets translated into language of self-help and private group cohesion. And, of course, any official policies aimed at minimizing the effects of discrimination are seen as unfair reverse discrimination.

*Precise compliance
standards*

Advocates of affirmative action are not convinced that such privatized approaches are effective or, if they are, adequate. The society— public and private—is never so evenhanded in allocating resources. Groups with such a heritage of de jure exclusion can hardly overcome that disadvantage by the passage of

a few laws. Fairness requires diligent, official follow-up. The best way to monitor compliance is to set standards of measurement as precisely as possible. Thus, at times, southern voter registrars were ordered to register blacks in very exact terms.[7] The experience with implementing the *Brown* v. *Board of Education* decision is another example.

Affirmative action remedial quotas are a more exact way to guarantee against continued discrimination. This is the same reason Interior Secretary Harold Ickes utilized employment quotas from 1935 to 1937 in the Public Works Administration.

The Public Works Administration ordered contractors building low-income housing to show that skilled and unskilled black workers received a certain percentage of their payroll. The figure was one-half of the percentage of skilled black workers in the city's construction work force in the 1930 occupational census.[8] Hard numbers were the best indicators of performance—or nonperformance.

This emphasis on specificity, on spelling out exactly what is meant and intended, is an important part of the African American political experience. Too much of the current discussion of affirmative action begins with the executive decrees and court decisions of the 1960s and 1970s.[9] This misses the vital earlier history

7. See Charles V. Hamilton, *The Bench and the Ballot* (New York: Oxford University Press, 1973).

8. Mark W. Kruman, "Quotas for Blacks," *Labor History*, 16(1):37-51 (Winter 1975).

9. See William Julius Wilson, *The Truly Disadvantaged* (Chicago: University of Chicago Press, 1987); Lipset, *Equality and the American Creed*; William Raspberry, "Civil

that has contributed to the politicization process.

Some would argue that such historical explanations are of limited usefulness. When do we put the memory of slavery and the experience of segregation behind us? Does this not lead to an emphasis on white guilt, on the sins of the fathers, on the portrayal of blacks as perennial victims? Does not this harping on the past create an impossible situation?

Perhaps the "promissory note" can never be collected. After more than a century of struggle in one mode, however, it is not easy to adopt another.

RACIAL OR UNIVERSAL POLICIES?

Both liberals and conservatives now want to get beyond the emphasis on race. Racial discrimination, it is said, is not the primary cause of many socioeconomic problems of African Americans. These are problems of the "underclass" or "ghetto poor," which should be addressed by "deracialized" economic and social policies and programs.

This analysis places much less emphasis on remedies such as affirmative action and more on such universal policies as full employment, national health insurance, and changes in the total economy that would benefit all poor people. Racially targeted programs, many liberals believe, are clearly detrimental to the traditional civil rights coalition. Many whites who joined the struggle against de jure segregation simply do

not support race-specific affirmative action policies perceived as reversing discrimination and imposing undue burdens on white males who did not and do not oppose black advancement.

This important substantive and political debate requires a clearer historical perspective than has thus far been evidenced. Even in the days of de jure segregation, the major civil rights groups have always attempted to reconcile a race-specific and a universal agenda.[10] The National Urban League and National Association for the Advancement of Colored People grappled with this problem in dealing with the 1935 Social Security Act and the health, housing, and full-employment legislation of the 1940s.

These and other organizations have always recognized the necessity for both agendas: for black civil rights and for universal social policies. For years they sought to reconcile the two, at times even subordinating the former to the latter. A fuller understanding of this five-decade struggle would illuminate current efforts in the same direction. As one studies that history, it becomes clear that the political realities of the 1990s are old realities.

The so-called traditional liberal alliance was not solid. Conflicts and tension between the two agendas always arose, not because civil rights groups were unwilling to compromise but because they seldom had the requisite liberal allies to achieve a viable universal social policy agenda.

___

Rights Act of 1991 Targets the Wrong Problem," *Herald-Sun* (Durham, NC), 19 Mar. 1991.

10. See Charles V. Hamilton and Dona Cooper Hamilton, "The Dual Agenda" (Paper delivered at the annual meeting of the American Political Science Association, Washington, DC, 31 Aug. 1991).

Blacks have always understood the need for progressive policies: opinion data and electoral choices have consistently demonstrated this preference. Civil rights advocates have usually turned to race-specific remedies only when their efforts to achieve universal—deracialized—policies have failed.

However one approaches this vexing topic, it is difficult to escape the clash of experiential realities. If we cannot escape them, we should at least understand them.

ANNALS, *AAPSS*, 523, September 1992

Incentive Effects of Affirmative Action

By GLENN C. LOURY

ABSTRACT: This article illustrates with a formal economic model a concern often raised by critics of affirmative action—that the policy may discourage its beneficiaries from acquiring work skills. Ironically, this can happen for reasons analogous to those evoked to explain why discrimination may discourage its victims from investing in skills: when skilled workers are less likely to succeed, fewer find it worthwhile to become skilled. Similarly, when unskilled workers are more likely to succeed, fewer deem it necessary to become skilled. Discrimination can lead to the former situation; affirmative action can lead to the latter. The analysis shows how affirmative action can lead employers to patronize minority workers, that is, hold them to a different standard. This patronization can have the effect of making skill acquisition less beneficial for minority workers. The labor market conditions under which this counterproductive effect of affirmative action is most likely are identified.

Glenn C. Loury is professor of economics at Boston University. He holds a B.A. in mathematics from Northwestern University and a Ph.D. in economics from the Massachusetts Institute of Technology. He has published numerous scholarly articles in the area of applied microeconomic theory. He has also written extensively on the issues of racial inequality and social policy toward the poor. A former Guggenheim fellow, Dr. Loury has lectured on his ideas throughout Europe and North America.

NOTE: This article draws on ideas generated in collaboration with Stephen Coate of the Department of Economics, University of Pennsylvania. Our joint paper "Will Affirmative Action Eliminate Negative Stereotypes?" mimeographed (Cambridge, MA: Harvard University, May 1991) develops a more thorough analysis of the issues considered here. Professor Coate, of course, is not responsible for or implicated by any opinions expressed or errors committed in this article.

I have a dream that my four little children will one day live in a nation where they will not be judged by the color of their skin but by the content of their character.

Martin Luther King, Jr.
Washington, D.C.
August 1963

One often encounters the following argument against affirmative action: Ultimately, racial justice requires that people behave toward each other in their economic dealings without regard to skin color—that they obey the color-blind ideal so eloquently expounded by Martin Luther King, Jr. Affirmative action, by encouraging the use of color as a basis for allocating positions, directly violates this color-blind ideal and is thus inconsistent with the attainment of racial justice in the long run. How can we hope to achieve a discrimination-free society while engaging, through public policy, in racial discrimination?

Proponents of affirmative action dismiss this argument as naive and ahistorical. They argue as follows: To remedy the effects of past discrimination, one must direct benefits to those who, because of color, have had their opportunities reduced. Moreover, the ongoing use of color by employers in ways deleterious to minorities requires offsetting color-conscious government action to ensure equal opportunity today, regardless of the effects of past discrimination. The departure from the color-blind ideal that affirmative action represents is a necessary, temporary concession to the realities of race in our society, which will be abandoned in the future, once opportunities have become truly equal.

While this rebuttal makes several valid points,[1] I believe that the concern that affirmative action may be inconsistent with the ultimate achievement of a color-blind society deserves more serious consideration than it currently receives. The reason is that a policy of affirmative action may alter the terms on which employers and workers interact with each other so as to perpetuate, rather than eliminate, existing disparities in productivity between minority and majority populations. In particular, the use of color as a basis for distributing opportunities may have the unintended effect of dulling the incentive to acquire skills for those whom the policy is intended to benefit. The presence of such a counterproductive effect gives greater force to the seemingly naive objection to racial preferences stated previously. This is true even when affirmative action has been introduced in order to counteract the effects of ongoing discrimination by employers.

To illustrate, suppose employers believe that minority workers are, on average, less skillful than majority

1. For an extended discussion of problems with a pure color-blind approach to public policy in the face of racial inequality, see my essay "Why Should We Care about Group Inequality," *Social Philosophy and Policy*, 5(1):249-71 (Autumn 1987). I also provide there an informal discussion of some negative unintended effects of affirmative action other than the one analyzed in the present article. An important theme in that essay, having answered in the affirmative the question "Should 'color' ever be taken into account?" is that preferential treatment is often not the best method of doing so. I make the case that targeting social service benefits to disadvantaged minorities may be a superior means of taking into account the history of racial discrimination.

workers. As a result, they are less willing to assign them to high-level positions. Such discriminatory beliefs can be self-confirming because, knowing it is more difficult to get the higher positions, minority workers may rationally choose not to invest in the requisite skills, thereby confirming the employers' initial views. Now suppose an affirmative action policy is adopted, requiring employers to assign minority workers to the higher positions at the same rate as the majority. Believing they are on average less skillful, employers may calculate that to comply with this policy they must now make it easier for a minority worker to get a high-level position. But, seeing that they do not have to be as skilled as their majority counterparts in order to achieve the same success, minority workers may have less of an incentive to invest in those skills that enhance a worker's performance. If minorities choose to invest less than the majority, employers' beliefs that they are less skillful will once again be confirmed.

When discriminated against, minorities may invest less in skills than majority workers because it is more difficult for them to achieve high-level positions. When favored by affirmative action they may invest less because, given employers' response to the policy, it has become easier for them to achieve high-level positions. The point is that the incentive to acquire a skill can be lowered by either reducing the likelihood that a skilled worker will succeed or increasing the likelihood that an unskilled worker will succeed. Behavior by employers that is not color-blind can produce

the first effect; behavior by the government that is color-conscious—namely, affirmative action—can produce the second effect. In both cases, because minorities have lower incentives to invest than majority workers, there is a systematic difference in the acquisition of skills by workers in the two racial groups.

Under affirmative action, employers may think they have to patronize minorities—that is, not hold them to as high a standard—in order to meet the government hiring requirements. Yet because this patronization can lower incentives for the acquisition of skills by minorities, it can perpetuate the racial skill differential that made the affirmative action policy necessary in the first place. In this sense, the government's departure from the color-blind ideal, by generating the unintended consequence of reduced incentives for the acquisition of skills by minority workers, makes the ultimate attainment of a color-blind outcome impossible. In this article, I illustrate, with the aid of formal economic reasoning, just how and why such an outcome might come about.

A FORMAL MODEL
OF DISCRIMINATION

I first consider an idealized model of an employer interacting with a racially diverse population of workers. This model is not a complete or realistic description of any particular setting in which affirmative action is practiced. Rather, it is an abstraction, a thought experiment that, by focusing explicitly on a few key variables of the problem, allows one to gain insight into how these variables interact with each other. My basic concern is with the standards employers use to decide which workers get desirable positions, the effort workers expend to acquire skills useful in those positions, and the ways in which decisions about these two variables change in the presence of racial hiring standards. These are the factors that figure prominently in the following model.[2]

(1) There is an employer and a population of workers divided into two racial groups, blacks and whites. The employer can distinguish between workers by their color and thus has the option to treat black and white workers differently. The sole action of the employer is to assign each worker to one of two tasks, called task zero and task one. Think of task one as the more demanding and more desirable of these two positions.

(2) All workers can perform satisfactorily at task zero. Workers decide, before the employer assigns them to a task and without the employer's knowledge, whether to invest in the acquisition of a skill essential for effective performance at task one. The investment is costly for a worker to make. The size of this cost varies from worker to worker, though

2. The argument set out in the model is largely expressed verbally and is, therefore, less rigorous than the mathematical model that it approximates. Due to space limitations, mathematical proofs of the propositions have been omitted. They are available from the author on request, or, for a more complete treatment, see Stephen Coate and Glenn C. Loury, "Will Affirmative Action Eliminate Negative Stereotypes?" mimeographed (Cambridge, MA: Harvard University, May 1991).

in a manner that is statistically the same for each racial group; imagine, for example, that more able workers find it easier to acquire the skill needed for task one, and that the distribution of ability is the same within each group. The employer cannot observe a particular worker's cost. What he can observe is the group identity of each worker and the outcome of a skills test, to be described momentarily. Although the two groups are characterized by the same distribution of ability, they need not exhibit the same pattern of investment. Workers with the same investment cost but belonging to different groups might make different investment decisions, as will be explained further.

(3) Since task one is more desirable, a worker is assumed to obtain a premium whenever he gains the assignment, whether he has acquired the needed skill or not. But, because an unskilled worker performs inadequately, the employer wants a worker in task one only if he has acquired the requisite skill. Otherwise he wants that worker to go to task zero. The employer maximizes profits when skilled workers are assigned to task one, and unskilled workers to task zero. The size of his gain need not be the same in these two cases. The employer may care more about avoiding the error of putting an unskilled worker in task one than about avoiding the mistake of putting an overqualified, skilled worker in task zero, or he may have the reverse priority.

(4) The employer wants to match workers to their most productive tasks. Lacking any prior information, the employer tests a worker's qualifi-

cation for doing task one. That is, he gathers what information he can— from an interview, analysis of previous work history, written exam, and so on—in order to assess the worker's capabilities. I assume that this test has three possible outcomes: (1) it shows clearly that the worker can do task one; (2) it shows clearly he cannot; and (3) its outcome is ambiguous, so the employer remains uncertain of the worker's skill. The worker passes the test in case (1); in case (2) he fails it; and in case (3) his result is unclear. Only investors pass the test and only noninvestors fail it, but each has some chance of getting an unclear result. I assume the test is better at revealing noninvestors than investors in this sense: an investor has a lower chance of passing the test than does a noninvestor of failing it.[3]

(5) The behavior of workers and the employer in this model may be described as follows. Each worker, knowing his color and his investment cost, decides whether to acquire the skill needed for task one. The employer then encounters the worker, gives him the test, and, on the basis of the test result and a worker's color, assigns the worker to a task. I assume that all of these decisions are made in a way that maximizes the decision maker's anticipated net reward, given the available information. An equilibrium for this model is defined as a joint specification of behavior for the employer and the workers in each racial group that is optimal for all parties, given the behavior specified for the others. I will show in the following that, despite the absence of any racially invidious motive on the part of the employer, discrimination against blacks can arise in an equilibrium of this model.

(6) To find the equilibria, I begin by considering the employer's decision in each contingency. Clearly, he assigns anyone passing the test to task one, and anyone failing it to task zero, regardless of color. If the test result is unclear, however, he needs to estimate the likelihood that the worker has invested to determine which assignment is best. If that likelihood is great enough, he puts the worker in task one; otherwise he puts the worker in task zero. Given an unclear test result, the odds that the worker producing it has invested depend on the relative number of investors in the population from which the worker comes and on the respective probabilities that investors and noninvestors get unclear results. For a given worker population, if the employer believes the fraction of investors is large, he will think that anyone with an unclear result is probably an investor. Conversely, if he thinks the fraction of investors is small, he will take an unclear result as a probable indicator of a noninvestor. So his assignment decision for a worker whose test is unclear ultimately rests on his belief about the fraction of investors in the subpopulation from which that worker has been drawn. If he thinks the fraction of investors is large enough, he will give the benefit of the doubt to a worker with an unclear test and assign him to task one; otherwise he will assign that worker to task zero.

3. Specifically, let p_1 (p_0) be the probability that an investing (noninvesting) worker gets an unclear test result. Then $1 - p_1$ is the probability that an investing worker passes the test, and $1 - p_0$ is the probability that a noninvesting worker fails it. I assume $p_0 < p_1$.

(7) I call the employer optimistic about a group of workers if he believes enough of them to have invested that when he sees one with an unclear result he nevertheless assigns him to task one. Otherwise I say he is pessimistic. I can express this by using the symbol π to denote the employer's belief about the fraction of investors in a group and by saying there is a critical belief π^* such that if $\pi \geq \pi^*$, then he is optimistic about the group, while if $\pi < \pi^*$ then he is pessimistic. I call the employer liberal toward a group if he gives them the benefit of the doubt, and conservative if he does not. So the employer is liberal toward groups about which he is optimistic, and conservative toward groups about which he is pessimistic. Because the employer observes a worker's color, he can distinguish between those drawn from the subpopulations of blacks and whites. Therefore, if his beliefs about the fractions of investors in these groups are not the same, it is possible that he treats black and white workers with unclear tests differently, based on this difference of belief. I say that the employer discriminates against blacks—and in favor of whites—if he is pessimistic about and conservative toward blacks while being optimistic about and liberal toward whites. To see how the employer might end up discriminating in an equilibrium of this model, we must consider the workers' behavior.

(8) A worker decides to invest only if he expects to gain more by doing so than it costs him. His gain from investing is the difference between the reward he expects if he invests and the reward he expects if he does not. Investing is beneficial because it raises the chance that a worker will be assigned to task one and thus enjoy the reward associated with that assignment. But the amount by which investing raises a worker's chance of getting this reward depends on whether the employer is liberal or conservative toward members of his group. If the employer is liberal, an investor is guaranteed to get task one, while a noninvestor gets it only if he does not fail the test. Thus investing raises the chance of getting the reward by an amount just equal to the probability that a noninvestor fails. On the other hand, if the employer is conservative, an investor gets task one only if he passes the test, and a noninvestor has no chance to get it. So in this case investing raises the chance of getting the reward by an amount just equal to the probability that an investor passes. Since I assumed the test is better at revealing noninvestors than investors, it follows that the gain from investing is greater if the employer is liberal than if he is conservative. Hence the fraction of a group of workers who would choose to invest is greater if they expect the employer to be liberal than if they think he will be conservative.

(9) I now identify the equilibria in this model. Denote by π_l (π_c) the fraction of workers in a group who would invest if they expected the employer to be liberal (conservative). If $\pi_l \geq \pi^*$, then, when a group of workers expects the employer to be liberal, sufficiently many invest as to make him optimistic. If $\pi_c < \pi^*$, then, when a group of workers expects the em-

ployer to be conservative, sufficiently few invest as to make him pessimistic. But an optimistic employer wants to be liberal and a pessimistic one wants to be conservative. So when $\pi_l \geq \pi^*$, it can be an equilibrium for the employer to be optimistic about and liberal toward any group and for that group to invest at rate π_l. And if $\pi_c < \pi^*$, it can be an equilibrium for the employer to be pessimistic about and conservative toward any group and for that group to invest at rate π_c. At least one of these conditions always holds. I will assume the parameters of the model to be such that they both hold, that is, $\pi_c < \pi^* \leq \pi_l$. Then there can be equilibria in which the employer is either optimistic or pessimistic about any group of workers, and in every case his belief turns out to be self-confirming.

(10) When the parameters of this model are such that $\pi_c < \pi^* \leq \pi_l$, it is possible for a discriminatory equilibrium to exist. In such an equilibrium the employer is, at the same time, pessimistic about one group—blacks, say—and optimistic about the other. Being pessimistic about blacks, he is conservative toward them when their test result is unclear. Being optimistic about whites, he is liberal toward them in the same situation. By behaving in this discriminatory way, he creates different incentives for workers in the two groups to become skilled at doing task one. But this difference in incentives is precisely what induces black and white workers to invest at different rates in the first place. That is, in a discriminatory equilibrium, the belief that blacks are on average less skillful than whites is a self-fulfilling prophecy. Given such beliefs, blacks do not enjoy equality of opportunity.

THE PROBLEM WITH AFFIRMATIVE ACTION AS A REMEDY IN THIS SITUATION

Of course, the foregoing model is highly stylized. It does not reflect many considerations that are important in real-world employment relationships. Nevertheless, it captures the essence of the problem I described in the introduction. It shows how an employer can come to rely on color as an indicator of the character of a worker, when other means of assessing the worker's merit—the test—fail. Moreover, it illustrates that the racial generalizations on which the employer relies need have nothing to do with the intrinsic qualities of the groups but instead may be the result of the fact that discrimination reduces the incentives of workers in the disadvantaged group to acquire skills.

In this discriminatory equilibrium, the employer is obviously not color-blind. A natural way for a policymaker to try to correct this discrimination would be to force the employer to assign workers from each group to each task at the same rate.[4]

4. A more direct way to eliminate discrimination would be to forbid the employer to treat whites and blacks with unclear tests any differently. That is, the government could merely insist on color-blind behavior from the employer, without regard to results. This would be difficult to enforce in practice. The government would have to observe all information upon which an employer might base his assignment—interviews, work history, and so on—to determine if he is really treating blacks and whites the same. In most employment situations this is not possible. The analysis offered

This policy, which I refer to as "affirmative action," is itself a departure from color-blind practice. It involves the government in monitoring the racial composition of the employer's work force in each task, insisting on equal proportionate representation. I will now examine in the context of the model set out previously whether this intervention eliminates the black-white difference in investment incentives that prevails in the discriminatory equilibrium. Imagine then that the employer, when faced with a worker whose test is unclear, assigns that worker to task one if he is white and to task zero if he is black. The fractions π_l of whites and π_c of blacks acquire the skill needed to do task one ($\pi_c < \pi^* \le \pi_l$). Let the government enact a policy requiring that each racial group be assigned to each task at the same rate. Initially the employer is violating this policy. All whites who invest plus those who do not but whose test is unclear end up in task one, while only those blacks who invest and who pass the test do so. Since proportionately more whites than blacks are investing in this initial situation, a larger fraction of whites is being assigned to task one.

Therefore, in order to comply with the affirmative action mandate, the employer must either assign more blacks or fewer whites to task one. Since he is maximizing his profits in the initial equilibrium, both alternatives lower his net payoff. Which course is least undesirable to him,

however, depends on the relative numbers of black and white workers in the population. In general the employer will try to minimize the number of instances where, in order to comply with the affirmative action policy, he has to assign a worker of either race to a task that he believes will not be most profitable for him. If blacks are comparatively few, then, by assigning more of them than he might desire to task one, he could meet the affirmative action mandate with a relatively small number of unprofitable assignments. On the other hand, if blacks are numerous in comparison to whites, then, by reassigning a relatively small number of whites to task zero instead of task one, he could meet the government's hiring requirement at least cost to himself.

I will assume here that blacks are a relatively small proportion of the total work force. If whites are sufficiently numerous relative to blacks, then the employer's best response to the government's mandate is to increase the number of blacks assigned to task one, while continuing to be liberal toward whites. Notice, however, that initially he will not think it adequate simply to engage in equal treatment of black and white workers in order to achieve this goal. Because a smaller fraction of blacks than of whites are investing initially, the employer anticipates that even if he becomes liberal toward blacks, he still will be assigning them to task one less frequently than whites. To achieve equal racial representation in the face of unequal racial investment rates, the employer will need to assign some of the blacks who fail the

---

here applies to those situations where affirmative action takes mainly a results-oriented rather than a process-oriented form, with the government's focus being on the numbers hired, not the hiring procedures.

test, and who he therefore knows have not invested, to task one as well. When he does this, I say that he is patronizing these black workers. The probability that a black worker who fails the test will nevertheless be assigned to task one is what I call the employer's degree of patronization. The precise degree of patronization the employer thinks he will need depends on his beliefs about the rates of investment by members of the two racial groups. The less skilled he thinks blacks are relative to whites, the more he anticipates a need to patronize them so as to comply with the government's mandate.

On the other hand, if blacks anticipate that they will be patronized, then they will want to reassess their decisions about skill acquisition. Any positive degree of patronization makes a worker's expected gain from investing less than it would have been if his group were merely treated liberally, but not patronized. Compared with liberal treatment, a positive degree of patronization raises the chance for a noninvestor to get into task one without affecting the fact that an investor is guaranteed to gain that assignment. Hence, compared with merely liberal treatment, a positive degree of patronization reduces the amount by which investing improves a worker's chances to get task one, and so lowers the fraction of workers who calculate that the benefit of investing exceeds its cost.

Consider now what happens when, starting from a discriminatory equilibrium, an affirmative action mandate is imposed. Because blacks are a relatively small fraction of the worker population, the employer's best response to the government's policy is to continue being liberal toward whites. Initially, he thinks the fractions π_c of blacks and π_l of whites are investing. He therefore anticipates the need for some patronization. By patronizing blacks, however, he alters their investment incentives and hence changes the rate at which they acquire the skill needed for task one. This change in black workers' behavior in turn implies that the employer must alter the degree of patronization required for compliance. Define an "equilibrium under affirmative action" to be a degree of patronization toward blacks together with a fraction of black investors such that (1) if the employer expects this fraction of blacks to invest, he would select the indicated degree of patronization in order to comply with the government's mandate; and (2) if the workers expect this degree of patronization, they would choose to invest at the indicated rate.

One equilibrium under affirmative action is obvious: if the employer should come to believe that blacks are investing at rate π_l, the same as whites, he would want to be liberal but not patronizing toward them and would comply with the government's mandate by doing so. If blacks expect liberal but not patronizing treatment they, like whites, would invest at rate π_l. When this equilibrium arises, the employer's initial discriminatory beliefs have been eliminated by the use of affirmative action. This is the ideal outcome predicted by proponents of the policy. The government's insistence on equal representation for each racial group creates a situation in which the opportunities, and so the distribution of skills, for each group of workers are equalized. Having achieved this result, the policy of affirmative action can wither away, because the employer's discriminatory beliefs that warranted the initial unequal treatment of blacks have been dispelled.

Another equilibrium under affirmative action is less obvious: the employer continues to think blacks invest less frequently than whites. He therefore persists in patronizing them to some degree; but because blacks, when patronized, have less of an incentive to invest than whites, the employer's belief that patronization is needed becomes a self-fulfilling prophecy. This is not the outcome forecast by proponents of affirmative action. Rather than creating equality of opportunity, the policy in this case leads to a situation in which, in order to meet the government's requirement of equal representation, the employer favors unskilled blacks. Because noninvesting blacks have superior opportunities, the return from acquiring a skill is lower for blacks than whites, and relatively fewer blacks invest. The employer, therefore, has to continually favor black workers in order to comply with the government's mandate. In this equilibrium, affirmative action, far from withering away, sets in motion a sequence of events that guarantee that it will have to be maintained indefinitely. The incentives for the employer, and hence for black and white workers, are altered by the government's use of color-conscious strategy in such a way that a racial difference in workers' acquisition of skills is sustained. This is precisely the unintended negative consequence of racial preferences to which I alluded in the introduction.

It is therefore of some interest to determine which of these two equilibria under affirmative action will actually obtain. At the initial discriminatory equilibrium, the employer thinks he needs some patronization, but his use of it alters blacks' investment incentives. As black workers change their behavior, the degree of patronization that the employer thinks he needs also changes. Imagine a process in which the employer and black workers alternately adjust their behavior over a sequence of stages, each party reacting to the behavior observed from the other at the previous stage of adjustment. It is plausible to postulate that the equilibrium reached under affirmative action is the one that eventually emerges from this iterative process.

Using simple mathematics one can show that when $\pi_l < \frac{1}{2}$, this process culminates at the first—obvious—equilibrium described previously, and when $\pi_l > \frac{1}{2}$, it culminates at the second—less obvious—one. Another way of saying this is that the undesirable outcome obtains under affirmative action if, when facing a liberal employer, the average worker would strictly prefer to invest in the skill needed for task one. Recall that the average worker will want to invest when facing a liberal employer only if the expected return from doing so exceeds his investment cost. This expected return is greater, the greater the gain is to a worker from being assigned to task one and the lower the probability is that a worker who does not invest gets an unclear test result. Thus the higher the value of assignment to task one is, relative to the average worker's investment cost, and the more powerful the test at identifying noninvestors is, the more likely it is that a patronizing equilibrium will arise under affirmative action. The patronizing outcome is also more likely when the disadvantaged group is a relatively small fraction of the total population.

CONCLUSION

The point of this exercise has been to illustrate, with the aid of formal economic reasoning, that the concerns expressed by some critics of affirmative action should be taken seriously. I have shown, in the context of a simple, stylized model of worker-employer interaction under racial hiring guidelines, that requiring equal representation of minority and majority groups in high-level positions may produce a situation in which the incentives provided minorities to acquire the skills needed to perform adequately in such positions are maintained permanently below the incentives provided majority workers. Whether this outcome occurs depends upon such factors as the proportion of the total work force belonging to the minority group, the advantage to a worker of obtaining a high-level position relative to the average cost in the population of acquiring the skill needed to perform in that position, the relative importance to the employer of assigning skilled and unskilled workers to their most productive positions, and the extent to which the employer can accurately gauge a worker's productivity in a given task before actually employing him there.

This article is not an attack on the practice of using preferential treatment as a tool to enhance opportunity for minority workers. Indeed, I have shown that sometimes the use of racial preference can have the desired results that its advocates predict. Departure from color-blind practice by the government, however, need not have these desirable consequences. It is important that we try to understand, in the many concrete circumstances in which preferences are now employed, just when the risks of generating negative unintended consequences of the sort I identify here are worth taking. Thus I am urging that more empirical research be done on the actual effects of affirmative action. Too often, both advocates and critics are content to base their arguments entirely on first principles, without reference to the direct or indirect consequences of this contentious policy. The analysis offered here is meant to graphically illustrate a possibility. Further study is required to identify practically significant cases exemplifying the effects uncovered here.

ANNALS, *AAPSS*, 523, September 1992

Affirmative Action in the 1990s: Staying the Course

By WILLIAM L. TAYLOR and SUSAN M. LISS

ABSTRACT: The phrase "affirmative action," while capable of fairly narrow definition, also serves as the line that divides people who have starkly different views on the nation's most enduring problem—how American society should treat people of color. A critical question is whether affirmative action policies have been effective, that is, whether they have worked in conjunction with other policies to provide opportunities for education and economic advancement that had previously been unavailable. Data demonstrate the effectiveness of these policies in enhancing the economic status of minorities. The legal standards governing affirmative action demonstrate an effort to balance competing interests in order to meet a test of practical fairness to all parties. With the changes on the Supreme Court, however, it seems likely that the legal standards for assessing the validity of affirmative action will be guided increasingly by ideology rather than pragmatism. \Affirmative action is under siege in the 1990s. Nonetheless, a recommitment to the national promise of racial justice may yield tangible opportunity for all.

William L. Taylor (B.A., Brooklyn College; LL.B., Yale Law School) is vice chair of the Citizens' Commission on Civil Rights and a former staff director of the U.S. Commission on Civil Rights. His law practice specializes in issues affecting the rights of children. He teaches at the Georgetown University Law Center.

Susan M. Liss (B.A., University of Michigan; J.D., Georgetown University Law Center) is the director and counsel of the Citizens' Commission on Civil Rights. She is coeditor of Lost Opportunities: The Civil Rights Record of the Bush Administration Mid-Term *(1991).*

THE phrase "affirmative action," while capable of fairly narrow definition,[1] also serves as the line that divides people who have starkly different views on the nation's most enduring problem—how American society should treat people of color. On one side of that line are the messengers of the last 12 years who argue that discrimination is no longer to be viewed as a serious problem in this nation; what occurred in the past does not have any impact on the present. Their claim is that it is time to wipe the slate clean, to assume, in an extension of Lyndon Johnson's vivid imagery, that everyone who is now at the starting line is unburdened by any chains and has an equal chance. Government may have a continuing duty to see to it that no flagrant fouls are committed against minority competitors in the running of the race, but that is the limit of its responsibility.

On the other side of the line are those who believe that the vestiges of past discrimination are continuing barriers to the opportunities of the present generation of black people, that discrimination is still an active problem, and that substantial progress will not be made without affirmative government.

Defined in these terms, affirmative action is a touchstone for defining the role of government. Will government, acting affirmatively, extend a helping hand to those who need special assistance in order to achieve their potential, or will government, in the posture of neutrality, leave to the vagaries of the marketplace those who continue to be affected by the legacy of discrimination?

This article will assess the efficacy and fairness of affirmative action policies, review the legal standards that have guided our policymakers and courts in crafting affirmative remedies for discrimination, and conclude with a few observations about future directions for affirmative action policies.

THE LINK BETWEEN AFFIRMATIVE ACTION AND BLACK PROGRESS

A critical question about affirmative action policies is whether they have been effective, that is, whether they have worked in conjunction with other policies to provide opportunities for education and economic advancement that had previously been unavailable.

Affirmative action policies

Beginning with the passage of the Civil Rights Act of 1964, rules barring racial discrimination in the private sector began to be enforced, and affirmative remedies were developed to prevent or redress violations of the law. Particularly after the 1971 Supreme Court decision in *Griggs* v. *Duke Power*,[2] which prohibited practices that deny opportunities to minorities even when the practices are not intentionally discriminatory,

---

1. One definition is that affirmative action encompasses "any measure, beyond simple termination of a discriminatory practice, adopted to correct or compensate for past or present discrimination or to prevent discrimination from recurring in the future." U.S., Commission on Civil Rights, *Statement on Affirmative Action*, Oct. 1977, p. 2.

2. 401 U.S. 424 (1971).

courts finding the existence of pervasive patterns or practices of discrimination ordered strong affirmative remedies.[3]

Toward the end of the decade, the Supreme Court ratified lower-court interpretations of Title VII to permit employers and unions to enter into voluntary agreements that made conscious use of race to eliminate "old patterns of racial segregation and hierarchy."[4]

Similar regulatory policies governed the employment practices of government contractors who do business with the federal government. The requirements of goals and timetables, first applied to the construction trades and later to all contractors, called upon employers to compare their utilization of minorities and women to the available labor pool and, where a significant gap existed, to develop concrete plans for tapping the market of minorities and women who possess the needed skills or who could readily acquire them through training programs.[5] Goals and timetables survived a frontal attack by Reagan administration Attorney General Edwin Meese and Assistant Attorney General Brad Reynolds, but the period of active enforcement ended in the 1980s, and the continued vitality of the pol-

icy now depends on voluntary observance by employers and private enforcement efforts.[6]

Affirmative action policies in education were enforced by the Department of Health, Education, and Welfare (later the Department of Education). Those policies strongly encouraged colleges and universities to engage in affirmative recruiting of minority students and to support counseling and training programs that would bolster chances of success. The enforcement of these policies, too, ended during the Reagan administration.[7] Indeed, the Bush administration has proposed invalidating programs at institutions of higher education that target scholarships for minority students.[8]

Progress

As evidence that affirmative action policies have not been effective in addressing the needs of black Americans, critics of affirmative action like to point to the fact that in overall terms the economic progress of blacks relative to whites peaked in the early 1970s and since has stag-

3. In particularly blatant cases of discrimination, courts restrained employers from hiring new white employees until proportionate numbers of qualified minority employees were hired. See, for example, *Boston Chapter, NAACP* v. *Beecher*, 504 F.2d 1017 (1st Cir. 1974), *cert. denied*, 421 U.S. 910 (1975).

4. *United Steelworkers of America* v. *Weber*, 443 U.S. 193 (1979).

5. See Executive Order 11246, § 203, in U.S., *Federal Register*, 24 Sept. 1965, p. 12319.

6. For an extensive review of the Reagan administration's civil rights record, including documentation of its failures to enforce the civil rights laws, see Reginald C. Govan and William L. Taylor, eds., *One Nation, Indivisible: The Civil Rights Challenge for the 1990s* (Washington, DC: Citizens' Commission on Civil Rights, 1989).

7. Ibid., pp. 88-168, assesses the Reagan record on equal educational opportunity.

8. The proposed policy guidance by the Department of Education would prohibit student financial aid based on race or national origin. See U.S., *Federal Register*, 10 Dec. 1991, pp. 64548-49.

nated or deteriorated. But no proponent of affirmative action has claimed that economic advancement for minorities can be divorced from the economic health of the nation. The issue is not whether affirmative action policies are sufficient conditions for progress but rather whether they are necessary and important conditions.

In fact, there have been a number of studies that demonstrate the effectiveness of affirmative action policies, particularly during the period of the 1970s when civil rights and affirmative action policies were being vigorously implemented.[9] Studies of the contract compliance program have indicated that companies subject to goals and timetable requirements had greater success during the 1970s in increasing minority employment in several job categories than did companies not subject to such requirements.[10] Other evidence can be gathered from examining changes in the employment patterns of companies subject to civil rights litigation. For example, studies of the huge Bell Telephone system conducted after the company entered into a Title VII consent decree in 1973 calling for the use of numerical goals and timetables showed that black workers had made substantial gains in entering managerial and skilled-craft positions.[11]

Similarly, the rapid growth in the enrollment and completion rates of black students in colleges and universities in the 1970s must be attributed in part to the application of affirmative action policies encouraging institutions of higher education to seek out minorities, as well as to the improved preparation of black students that came about through school desegregation and other improvements in educational opportunity.[12] In addition, affirmative action had an impact on the growth in minority business development that took place in skill-intensive areas of business services, finance, insurance, and real estate, areas outside the traditional realm of entrepreneurship.[13]

Mobility

Some critics of affirmative action argue that even if there are some benefits from the policy, those benefits flow largely to minorities who are already advantaged or middle class. Thus, they say, the policy is at best selective and at worst unneeded since middle-class people might advance without the aid of affirmative action.

9. See Gerald David Jaynes and Robin M. Williams, Jr., eds., *A Common Destiny: Blacks and American Society* (Washington, DC: National Academy Press, 1989), pp. 269-329. See also *Affirmative Action to Open the Doors of Job Opportunity* (Washington, DC: Citizens' Commission on Civil Rights, 1984), 121-47.

10. See, for example, J. Leonard, *The Effectiveness of Equal Employment Law and Affirmative Action Regulation* (Berkeley: University of California, School of Business Administration, 1985).

11. See statement of economist Bernard Anderson in U.S., Congress, House, Committee on Education and Labor, Subcommittee on Employment Opportunities, *Oversight Hearings on Equal Employment Opportunity*, 97th Cong., 1st sess., 1981, pt. 1, pp. 219, 221. For a report on similar progress following a consent decree in the steel industry, see statement of Phyllis Wallace, in ibid., pp. 528-29.

12. See studies summarized in W. Taylor, *Brown, Equal Protection and the Isolation of the Poor, Yale Law Journal*, 95:1709-10 (1986).

13. See Jaynes and Williams, eds., *Common Destiny*, p. 314.

This view is contradicted by studies showing, for example, that, of the increased enrollment of minority students in medical schools in the 1970s, significant numbers were from families of low income and job status, indicating that affirmative action policies have resulted in increased mobility, not simply in changing occupational preferences among middle-class minority families.[14] Moreover, many of the gains have come in occupations and trades not usually associated with advantaged status, such as law enforcement, fire fighting, and skilled construction work.[15]

For those seeking to achieve professional status, affirmative action has been applied at the gateway points, namely, at college and professional school admissions. Admissions policies designed to encourage minority participation in the professions may offer those who are otherwise qualified an equal chance at success in occupations with a more advantaged status. But affirmative action does not guarantee success for those who would not otherwise succeed as professionals; it merely provides the opportunity to compete.

Other critics of affirmative action have argued that there is a "creaming

process" in which those most likely to seize the opportunities provided by affirmative action are apt to be the most motivated in the less advantaged group.[16] This may well be the case. Affirmative action is unlikely to be sufficient for those who are truly bereft of educational, social, and material resources. Other initiatives are called for to address the urgent needs of this group.

THE LEGAL STANDARDS GOVERNING AFFIRMATIVE ACTION

In assessing the legality of affirmative action under both the Constitution and statutes, the courts have struggled conscientiously to balance competing interests in order to meet a test of practical fairness to all parties. Cases such as *University of California Regents* v. *Bakke*, which invalidated an affirmative action plan for minority admissions to the medical school at the University of California,[17] and *United Steelworkers* v. *Weber*, which upheld a voluntary plan to remedy past discrimination in occupations traditionally closed to minorities,[18] reflect a pragmatic approach by the courts to the difficult legal and policy questions posed by affirmative action.

Using a pragmatic approach, the Supreme Court has ruled that black workers may be denied positions they would have held "but for" the discriminatory practices of an employer if awarding the positions would re-

14. See M. Alexis, "The Effect of Admission Procedures on Minority Enrollment in Graduate and Professional Schools," in *Working Papers: Bakke, Weber and Affirmative Action* (New York: Rockefeller Foundation, 1979), pp. 52-71.

15. In law enforcement, the numbers of black police officers nearly doubled from 1970 to 1980. In Philadelphia, after the initiation of the goals and timetables program for federal contractors, the percentage of skilled minority construction workers rose from less than 1 percent to more than 12 percent of the total.

16. See William Julius Wilson, *The Truly Disadvantaged* (Chicago: University of Chicago Press, 1989), pp. 114-15.

17. 438 U.S. 265 (1978).

18. 443 U.S. 193 (1979).

quire the displacement of an incumbent white worker.[19] The test, as articulated in *Weber*, is whether race-conscious remedies "unnecessarily trammel the interest of the white employees." In employing this test, courts have drawn lines between actions that disappoint the expectations of whites and those that uproot them from a status that already has been vested.[20]

This practical approach to balancing competing rights may have been ushered out by a 1989 decision invalidating a minority business set-aside program adopted by the city of Richmond, *City of Richmond* v. *Croson*.[21] In that case, the Supreme Court, having grown more conservative and increasingly hostile to affirmative action as justices appointed by President Reagan joined the Court, applied new constitutional ground rules for state and local affirmative action programs, requiring that localities demonstrate an evidentiary predicate for affirmative action that may be nearly impossible for most state and local governments to meet.[22] During the term following the *Croson*

decision, a majority of the Court in *Metro Broadcasting* v. *FCC*[23] rejected the applicability of the *Croson* standards to affirmative action programs mandated by Congress. Nevertheless, with the subsequent retirements of Justices Brennan and Marshall, the legal standards for assessing the validity of affirmative action are likely to be guided increasingly by ideology rather than the pragmatism of the last decade.

THE FUTURE OF
AFFIRMATIVE ACTION

Affirmative action is under siege in the 1990s. The courts are no longer a friendly forum for deprived and powerless citizens who in the past were often able to find redress when it was denied in the more political arenas. The pragmatic efforts of the Supreme Court in *Bakke*, *Weber*, and other cases to strike a balance between the legitimate needs and expectations of white and minority workers may soon be replaced by an ideological commitment to color blindness, a cruel irony when it results in the courts' turning a blind eye to the legacy of past and continuing discrimination.

The situation also is bleak in the more explicitly political arenas. During the debate over the Civil Rights Act of 1991, the Bush administration found political gold in labeling civil rights requirements of the legislation as "quota" provisions, seeking in a flagging economy to channel the dis-

19. See, for example, the statement of Justice White that even a person adversely affected by discrimination "is not automatically entitled to have a non-minority employee laid off to make room for him." *Firefighters Local Union No. 1784* v. *Stotts*, 104 S.Ct. 2576, 2588 (1984). The Court in *Stotts* decided that the benefits of an affirmative action plan would have to be negated by laying off recently hired black firefighters rather than displacing more senior white workers.

20. See 443 U.S. at 208 (1979).

21. 488 U.S. 469 (1989).

22. For a comprehensive analysis of the Court's standards in the *Croson* case, see Michael Small, "The New Legal Regime: Affirmative Action after *Croson* and *Metro*," in *Lost*

Opportunities: The Civil Rights Record of the Bush Administration Mid-Term, ed. S. M. Liss and W. L. Taylor (Washington, DC: Citizens' Commission on Civil Rights, 1991).

23. 110 S.Ct. 2997 (1990).

content of many white workers toward the scapegoating of minority workers and Democratic advocates of affirmative action. The administration was pulled back from the brink only through the efforts of moderate and conservative Republican senators concerned about the long-range consequences of their party's being seen as having made common cause with David Duke and his fellow racists. But the administration has not taken any pledge of moral sobriety, threatening even on the eve of the signing ceremony for the Civil Rights Act to dismantle long-standing federal affirmative action programs. The difficulties of defenders of affirmative action are compounded by the fact that their ability to persuade depends on reasoned explication, not easily reducible to the 30-second sound bites used effectively by their opponents.[24]

In these circumstances, some observers have suggested that goals and timetables and other effective

24. The problem may be illustrated by the television ad used by Senator Jesse Helms in his successful 1990 reelection campaign. The ad depicted a white worker denied a job because the employer used a quota system to hire black applicants. Of course, an alternative explanation in many situations is that the white applicant lacked the requisite qualifications. Indeed, critics of civil rights enforcement have charged that minority workers are being encouraged to think of themselves as victims rather than to examine the need to upgrade their skills and develop self-discipline. Yet, without any conscious irony, Senator Helms and other affirmative action bashers do precisely the same thing by encouraging whites to view themselves as victims. For understandable reasons, however, few politicians would seek to counter a Helms attack by suggesting that some white applicants may lack the qualifications.

affirmative action measures be abandoned in favor of other ameliorative approaches. Paul Starr has proposed, for example, that the response to a Supreme Court reversal of the *Weber* decision should not be a legislative struggle for restoration but a dual effort "toward the reconstruction of civil society in minority communities and toward the promotion of broad policies for economic opportunity and security that benefit low- and middle-income Americans, black and white alike."[25] However well-intentioned the proposal to view civil rights and economic and social programs as alternatives may be, several questions need to be asked.

One is whether legislative efforts to secure such "economic opportunit[ies]" through greater public investments in education, job training, and national health and welfare reform have been stymied by continued adherence to affirmative action policies and whether affirmative action will be an impediment in the future. While there have been facile suggestions that this is the case, the evidence does not support it. Legislation to fully fund Head Start, to provide family and medical leave, and to accomplish other economic and social goals has been threatened by the same kinds of attitudinal barriers founded on race and class as undergird the resistance to affirmative action.

A second question is whether sufficient progress has been made in eliminating racial discrimination to warrant a conclusion that the forms of affirmative action that have occa-

25. Paul Starr, "Civil Reconstruction: What to Do without Affirmative Action," *American Prospect*, Winter 1992, p. 7.

sioned the greatest controversy are no longer necessary. If indeed discrimination is a sporadic phenomenon that is no longer the norm, a case can be made for changing course. But here again, despite the progress that has been made, the evidence points in another direction. Studies by the Urban Institute of the treatment of black and white job seekers, by the Department of Housing and Urban Development of the treatment of black and white home seekers, by the Federal Reserve and several newspapers of the persistence of redlining by financial institutions all strongly suggest that discrimination remains a pervasive and institutional problem.[26] Given these facts, individual lawsuits

26. Regarding the Urban Institute study, see the working papers prepared for "Testing for Discrimination in America," a conference sponsored by the Rockefeller Foundation and the Urban Institute, Washington, DC, 26 Sept. 1991. See also Margery Austin Turner, Raymond Struyk, and John Yinger, *Housing Discrimination Study (Synthesis)* (Washington, DC: Department of Housing and Urban Development, Aug. 1991); Glenn B. Canner and Dolores S. Smith, "Home Mortgage Disclosure Act: Expanded Data in Residential Lending," *Federal Reserve Bulletin*, Nov. 1991, pp. 859-81.

are simply inadequate; the rationale for affirmative action policy—that it is necessary to counter the effects of past, as well as ongoing, discrimination—continues to have vitality.

Ultimately, the question is whether it is possible to develop effective measures to assure that all people will have the opportunity to develop to their full potential without confronting the nation's most entrenched social problem—racial oppression and inequality. Again, those who propose that racial issues be finessed have little evidence to suggest that such evasions will be productive.

Interestingly, the current debate over affirmative action is taking place at a time when the antigovernment binge of the Reagan era appears to be losing force. There appears to be a growing recognition that if the productivity of the private sector of the U.S. economy is to be restored, government must play an affirmative role in investing in human resources. That recognition, if coupled with a recommitment to the unredeemed national promise of racial justice, may yet yield tangible opportunity for all. Now is not the time to lose our nerve.

ANNALS, *AAPSS*, 523, September 1992

Affirmative Action and
Its Negative Repercussions

By WM. BRADFORD REYNOLDS

ABSTRACT: Whether preferential treatment comes packaged as a quota, a goal-and-timetable, a set-aside, or affirmative action, the consequence is the same. Favoring certain individuals because of race, gender, religion, or national origin inescapably means that individuals not similarly endowed are disfavored for the most offensive of reasons. To pretend such action is affirmative—or that such discrimination is benign—mocks the valiant struggle for an equal opportunity society that has defined America's domestic agenda for the last four decades. The nation lost sight of this fundamental truth during the decade of the 1970s and permitted governments to fashion affirmative action policies that made race, gender, and nationality the final arbiter of employment, student admissions, and contract decisions. It took a series of Supreme Court rulings in the late 1980s to right that wrong and restore the equality ideal that the Court had earlier resurrected in *Brown* v. *Board of Education*.

Wm. Bradford Reynolds is a 1967 graduate of Vanderbilt University School of Law and a partner in the Washington, D.C., firm of Dickstein, Shapiro & Morin. He served in the Department of Justice from 1981 to 1988 as the Assistant Attorney General of the Civil Rights Division and also, from 1987 to 1988, as Counselor to the Attorney General of the United States.

NOTE: This article is adapted in part from the author's "Tending the Civil Rights Garden," *Wake Forest Law Review*, 25:197-221 (1990).

THE phrase "affirmative action" has been so much a part of civil rights policy over the past three decades that it rarely is defined or explained by those who use it. For the most part, the omission is calculated. Few dare to quarrel with a program offered to promote civil rights objectives and described simply as "affirmative action."

Yet it is just such programs that have energized much of the debate in the field of civil rights since the early 1960s. First introduced by President John F. Kennedy in Executive Order No. 10925,[1] "affirmative action" was originally defined in terms of active recruitment and outreach measures aimed at enhancing employment opportunities for all Americans. Its race-neutral character could not have been more clearly expressed: employers contracting with the federal government were directed to "take affirmative action to ensure that the applicants are employed, and that employees are treated during employment, without regard to race, creed, color or national origin."[2]

It should come as no surprise that in the early 1960s, measures devised to tear down racial barriers and affirmatively promote equal opportunity were required to be themselves indifferent to racial distinctions. Discrimination on account of skin color was, after all, the evil identified as constitutionally intolerable in the Supreme Court's landmark decision in *Brown* v. *Board of Education*.[3] "At stake," wrote Chief Justice Earl Warren for the full Court in *Brown II*, "is

the personal interest of plaintiffs' admission to public schools . . . on a [racially] nondiscriminatory basis."[4] What the school children were seeking, their counsel Thurgood Marshall argued, was the assignment of students to the public schools "without regard to race or color."[5]

The Supreme Court's dramatic reversal of its half-century precedent of *Plessy* v. *Ferguson*[6] precipitated an outpouring of condemnation directed at all forms of racial segregation. During the next decade, the color line

1. 3 CFR 1959-63, pp. 448-54.
2. Ibid.
3. 347 U.S. 483 (1954).

4. *Brown* v. *Board of Education*, 349 U.S. 296, 300 (1955).
5. Reprinted in *O. Brown, Argument: The Oral Argument before the Supreme Court in Brown v. Board of Education of Topeka, 1952-55*, ed. L. Friedman (New York: Walker, 1969), p. 47.
6. 163 U.S. 537 (1894). The case involved a suit by Plessy, petitioner, a "resident of the State of Louisiana, of mixed descent, in the proportion of seven-eighths Caucasian and one-eighth African blood," against the Honorable John H. Ferguson, judge of the Parish of Orleans. Ibid., p. 538. While seated in the "white race" section of an East Louisiana railway passenger train, Plessy was required by the conductor to vacate the seat and find another in a section of the train "for persons not of the white race." Ibid. Upon his refusal to move, Plessy was ejected, arrested, and charged with a criminal violation. Ibid. He was convicted and thereafter appealed the constitutionality of the Louisiana law "providing for separate railway carriage for white and colored races." Ibid., p. 539. In its now roundly criticized opinion, delivered by Justice Brown, the Court affirmed the conviction, ruling the law within the bounds of the Fourteenth Amendment. Ibid., p. 540. Laws providing for "separate but equal" public accommodations were thereby given the stamp of constitutionality. Ibid., p. 550. But see ibid., p. 559 (Harlan, J., dissenting) ("Our constitution is color-blind, and neither knows nor tolerates classes among citizens . . . . The law regards man as man, and takes no account of his surroundings or of his color").

that had officially divided Americans came under stinging attack from all quarters. Racial distinctions, declared the High Court, were by their very nature "odious to a free people whose institutions are founded upon the doctrine of equality."[7]

Thus the visible barriers of everyday life that had for so long kept blacks out began to tumble, one by one. Water fountains, restrooms, hotels, restaurants, trolley cars, lunch counters, movie theaters, and department stores all were finally opened to blacks and whites alike throughout the 1960s and into the 1970s.

The congressional response to *Brown* was no less emphatic. With enactment of the Civil Rights Acts of 1957, 1960, and 1964,[8] the Voting Rights Act of 1965,[9] and the Fair Housing Act of 1968,[10] Congress demanded removal of the race factor in the work force, the classroom, places of public accommodation, the voting booth, and the housing market. The message was that public and private decision makers in the areas covered were to be wholly blind to color differences.

The legislative debates of that era underscored the wholesale nature of this neutrality mandate. Significantly, much of the discussion leading up to the 1964 act centered on the issue of preferential treatment, that is, whether the measure under consideration, while condemning racial discrimination, would countenance race-conscious hiring and promotion practices. Proponents of the bill's employment provisions—Title VII of the act—uniformly and unequivocally denied that the legislation should or could be so interpreted. Favoring black employees in the selection process would violate Title VII "just as much as a 'white only' employment policy," declared Senator Harrison Williams.[11] "How can the language of equality," he asked, "favor one race or one religion over another? Equality can have only one meaning, and that meaning is self-evident to reasonable men. Those who say that equality means favoritism do violence to common sense."[12]

Senator Edmund Muskie, another key supporter of the 1964 act, expressed a similar understanding of the legislation. "Every American citizen," said Muskie, "has the right to equal treatment—not favored treatment, not complete individual equality—just equal treatment."[13] Senator Hubert Humphrey agreed. The principal force behind the passage of the 1964 Civil Rights Act in the Senate, Humphrey repeatedly stated that Title VII would prohibit any consideration of race in employment matters. On one occasion he used these words:

The title does not provide that any preferential treatment in employment shall be given to Negroes or to any other per-

---

7. See *Loving* v. *Virginia*, 388 U.S. 1, 11 (1966) (quoting *Hirabayashi* v. *United States*, 320 U.S. 81, 100 (1943)).

8. Civil Rights Act of 1957, Pub. L. 85-315, 71 Stat. 634 (codified as amended in scattered sections of 42 U.S.C.).

9. Pub. L. 89-110, 79 Stat. 437 (codified as amended at 42 U.S.C. §§ 1971, 1973 to 1973 bb-1 (1982)).

10. Pub. L. 90-284, 82 Stat. 81 (codified as amended at 42 U.S.C. §§ 3601-19 (1982)).

11. 110 Cong. Rec. 8921 (1964).

12. Ibid.

13. Ibid., p. 12,614.

sons or groups. It does not provide that any quota system may be established to maintain racial balance in employment. In fact, the title would prohibit preferential treatment for any particular group, and any person, whether or not a member of any minority group, would be permitted to file a complaint of discriminatory employment practices.[14]

The leadership of the civil rights movement echoed the same view. Appearing at congressional hearings during consideration of the 1964 civil rights laws, Roy Wilkins, executive director of the National Association for the Advancement of Colored People (NAACP), stated unabashedly, "Our association has never been in favor of a quota system."[15] "We believe the quota system is unfair whether it is used for Negroes or against Negroes," he testified.[16] "We feel people ought to be hired because of their ability, irrespective of their color. . . . We want equality, equality of opportunity and employment on the basis of ability."[17]

The same theme was sounded by Jack Greenberg, then director counsel of the NAACP Legal Defense Fund, in his successful 1964 argument to the Supreme Court in *Anderson* v. *Martin*,[18] urging that a state statute requiring the ballot designation of a candidate's race be invalidated. "The fact that this statute might operate to benefit a Negro candidate and against a white candidate . . . is not relevant," he insisted, "for . . . the state has a duty under the fifteenth amendment and the fourteenth amendment to be 'color-blind' and not to act so as to encourage racial discrimination . . . against any racial group."[19]

Color blindness was, in fact, the banner under which the civil rights movement marched, largely in unison, through most of the 1960s. Those who joined in—both black and white—drew legal strength from the Supreme Court's landmark decision in *Brown*, policy support from the recent acts of Congress, and moral inspiration from the words and deeds of Dr. Martin Luther King, Jr. His dream became America's dream on that summer afternoon in 1963, as he stood at the foot of the Washington Monument and, with millions of

14. Ibid., p. 11,848. At another point, Senator Humphrey's exasperation with the opposition's preference argument prompted him to make the following offer: "If . . . in the title VII . . . any language [can be found] which provides that an employer will have to hire on the basis of percentage or quota related to color . . . I will start eating the pages [of the bill] one after another . . . ." Ibid., p. 7,420.

15. Statement of Roy Wilkins, in U.S., Congress, House, Committee on the Judiciary, Subcommittee no. 5, *Miscellaneous Proposals Regarding the Civil Rights of Persons within the Jurisdiction of the United States, 1963: Hearings on H.R. 7152.* 88th Cong., 1st sess., 1963, p. 2144.

16. Ibid.

17. Ibid.

18. *See Anderson* v. *Martin*, 375 U.S. 399 (1964), a case involving a state statute requiring that the race of each candidate for public office be accurately designated on each ballot. Noting that any governmental endorsement of racial bloc voting would tend to favor the race having a numerical majority, the Court held that the state could not constitutionally encourage racial discrimination of any kind, whether it worked to the disadvantage of blacks or whites. The state's designation of candidate's race was, according to a unanimous Court, of "no relevance" in the electoral process. Ibid., pp. 401-3.

19. Jurisdictional Statement of Appellants at 11-12, *Anderson* v. *Martin*, 375 U.S. 399 (1964) (No. 51).

Americans watching, challenged a country to bring about the day when his children would at last be judged "by the content of their character" and measure of their abilities, not "the color of their skin."[20]

As we moved through the decade of the 1960s, there were innumerable signs of progress as the "whites only" signs were removed. The outlawing of racial discrimination in employment, coupled with the government impetus behind affirmative action recruitment and outreach efforts, introduced blacks into a significant number of workplaces previously having white employees only. With increasing regularity, the courts began issuing orders that white public schools open their doors to black students. The message of equal opportunity had broken through.

There was, however, a growing undercurrent of discontent. Many in the civil rights movement began to express dissatisfaction over the pace of desegregation initiatives. By the early 1970s, a perception had set in that the momentum had peaked and was even slipping backward. The policymakers could have pointed out that educational and economic disparities between blacks and whites due to the long history of segregation made inevitable the sort of slowdown that followed the dramatic first-wave breakthrough. It is painfully obvious that many blacks forced into segregated classrooms in the South had been denied a quality education—some had received almost no educa-

tion at all; they could hardly have been expected to compete effectively with better-educated whites for employment.

Yet, to focus on this systemwide failing and face it forthrightly was seen by many as too prolonged an effort to satisfy the political demands of the time. Instead, the policymakers sought a quick fix, without giving serious thought to its long-term repercussions or implications. The concept of racial neutrality gave way to a concept of racial balance, on the representation that the former could not be fully realized unless the latter was achieved.

In the employment arena, the principal tool used was affirmative action, not in its original race-neutral sense but now endorsing racial preference. The claim was that regulation and allocation by race were not wrong per se; rather, their validity depended upon who was being regulated, on what was being allocated, and on the purpose of the arrangement. If a racial preference would produce the desired statistical result, it was argued, its discriminatory feature could be tolerated as an unfortunate but necessary consequence of remedying the effects of past discrimination. Using race "to get beyond racism" was the way one Supreme Court Justice explained it.[21]

Once again, the use of race as a criterion for governmental classifica-

20. M. King, Jr., "I've Got a Dream," in Martin Luther King, Jr., A Documentary . . . Montgomery to Memphis, ed. F. Schulte (New York: Norton, 1976), p. 218.

21. Board of Regents of Univ. of Cal. v. Bakke, 438 U.S. 265, 407 (1978) (Blackmun, J., concurring). But see DeFunis v. Odegaard, 416 U.S. 312, 343 (1974) (Douglas, J., dissenting) ("The Equal Protection Clause commands elimination of racial barriers, not their creation in order to satisfy our theory as to how society ought to be organized").

tion became acceptable during the decade of the 1970s. Having been rescued in *Brown* from the insidious policy of separate but equal, the country found itself only two short decades later drifting steadily toward the policy of separate but proportional: separate avenues to school, separate employment lines, separate contract-bid procedures, all inspired by the objective of achieving proportional representation by race in the classroom, in the work force, and on the job site.

Proponents of preferential affirmative action soon discarded the precept that a race-based employment preference was constitutionally permissible only when necessary to place an individual victim of proven discrimination in a position he or she would have attained but for the discrimination. Instead they focused on entire groups of individuals said to be disadvantaged because of race.[22] Quotas, goals and timetables, and other race-conscious techniques gained increasing acceptance among federal bureaucrats and judges, and by the decade's end, racial considerations influenced public employment decisions of every kind, from hirings to layoffs.

It did not seem to matter that those favored solely because of race frequently had never been wronged by the employer or that the preferential treatment afforded them was at the expense of other employees who were themselves admittedly innocent of any discrimination or other wrongdoing. The preoccupation was on removing from the work force any racial imbalance between employees in a discrete job unit, no matter how large or small. Lost in the scramble for strictly numerical solutions was the fundamental truth that "no discrimination based on race is benign, . . . no action disadvantaging a person because of color is affirmative."[23]

By the early 1980s, the use of race in the distribution of the country's limited economic and educational resources had sadly led to the creation of a kind of racial spoils system in America, fostering competition not only between individual members of contending groups, but between the groups themselves. The color-blind ideal had largely given way to a color-conscious mentality, one that encouraged stereotyping and that invited people to view others as possessors of racial characteristics, not as unique individuals. Thus the policy of preferential affirmative action had effectively submerged the vitality of personality under the deadening prejudgments of race. The very purpose intended to be served was being defeated, for race-based preferences cut against the grain of equal opportunity. In the broadest sense, color consciousness and racial polarization pose the greatest threat to members of minority groups because it is they who are, by definition, outnumbered. As individuals, members of all racial groups suffer, because an individual's energy, ability, and dedication can

22. Cf. *Board of Regents of Univ. of Cal.* v. *Bakke*, 438 U.S. at 299 (Powell, J. concurring) ("It is the individual who is entitled to judicial protection against classifications based upon racial or ethnic background because such distinctions impinge upon personal rights, rather than the individual only because of his membership in a particular group").

23. See *United Steelworkers of America* v. *Weber*, 443 U.S. 193, 254 (1979) (Rehnquist, J., dissenting).

take him or her no further than permitted by the group's allotment or quota.

What began as a pursuit for equality of opportunity became, therefore, through preferential affirmative action, a forfeiture of opportunity in absolute terms. Individual opportunity was diminished in order to achieve group equality, measured solely in terms of proportional representation and numerically balanced results. Yet, as Justice Powell stated in his *Bakke* concurrence, "Nothing in the Constitution supports the notion that individuals may be asked to suffer otherwise impermissible burdens in order to enhance the societal standing of their ethnic groups."[24]

Justice Powell's view was not shared by all of his colleagues on the High Court, however. Indeed, in many respects, the public debate in the late 1970s over whether use of racial preferences was affirmative or negative action was mirrored in the Supreme Court's opinions. Alan Bakke won admission to the University of California Medical School on the ground that a minority preference program designed to benefit all but Caucasian applicants excluded him unconstitutionally because of race. But the Court was sharply divided, and no single opinion could command a majority.[25]

The heart of the judicial controversy did not appear to be a differ-

ence of view as to the fundamental commitment to eradicate all forms of racial discrimination. As Justice Marshall made clear in his opinion for the Court in *McDonald* v. *Sante Fe Trail Transportation Co.*, color-conscious bias was condemned by law with equal force whether it operated in forward gear or reverse.[26] Rather, the break point came over whether and to what extent the antidiscrimination principle should be compromised on the strength of a promise that its equal protection guarantee would be thereby more likely to be achieved.

The signals sent by the Court were at best mixed and invariably muddled.[27] At one end of the compendium, there was the view expressed by Jus-

24. See *Board of Regents of Univ. of Cal.* v. *Bakke*, 438 U.S. at 298 (Powell, J., concurring).

25. There were four separate opinions. Chief Justice Burger, joined by Justices White, Stewart, and Rehnquist, wrote the plurality opinion, as to which Justices Blackmun, Stevens, and Powell concurred separately. Justice Brennan dissented, joined by Justice Marshall.

26. 427 U.S. 273 (1976). In *McDonald*, petitioners, two white employees of respondent company, were discharged for cause while a black employee charged with the same offense was not discharged. Petitioners filed suit alleging racial discrimination in violation of Title VII. The district court dismissed petitioners' claims on the ground that Title VII was unavailable to white people. 427 U.S. at 275. The Supreme Court reversed. Ibid., p. 296. Justice Marshall, writing for the Court, stated, "We therefore hold today that Title VII prohibits racial discrimination against white petitioners in this case upon the same standards as would be applicable were they Negroes and Jackson white." Ibid., p. 280.

27. The Court was sharply divided on the preference issue in the 1970s and for most of the 1980s, often speaking through multiple opinions without a clear majority (see *Board of Regents of Univ. of Cal.* v. *Bakke*; *Fullilove* v. *Klutznick*; *United Steelworkers of America* v. *Weber*; *Wygant* v. *Jackson Bd. of Educ.*, 467 U.S. 267 (1986) or with an exceedingly narrow (5-4) margin (see *United States* v. *Paradise*, 480 U.S. 149 (1987); *Local 28, Sheet Metal Workers* v. *EEOC*, 478 U.S. 421 (1986); *Firefighters Local Union No. 1784* v. *Stotts*, 467 U.S. 561 (1984); *Wards Cove Packing Co.* v. *Antonio*, 490 U.S. 642 (1989).

tice Blackmun in *Bakke* that the use of race was necessary "to get beyond racism."[28] On the other end, then Associate Justice Rehnquist argued no less forcefully that to compromise the principle of nondiscrimination, no matter how slightly, was to lose it forever to the emerging compromise.[29] Between the two was the rationale commanding the most support in *United Steelworkers* v. *Weber*.[30] In upholding the minority training program favoring in-plant black employees over their white counterparts for 50 percent of the openings, Justice Brennan stressed the restricted nature of the affirmative action preference that was allowed to stand: its adoption was intended to correct persistent racial exclusion from the work force; it was of limited duration; and it was tailored to remedy the identified exclusionary practices, not to maintain racial balance or skin-color proportionality.[31]

When the affirmative action issue came again to the Court two years later in a constitutional setting, the split between the justices was no less pronounced. The case was *Fullilove* v. *Klutznick*,[32] and, again, enough votes were pulled together to uphold a minority set-aside provision enacted by Congress. The 10 percent contracting preference survived judicial scrutiny, however, only because a majority of the justices regarded it to be (1) re-

medially "compelled" in order to counter persistent, industrywide discrimination and (2) "narrowly tailored" as to duration, scope, and application.[33]

If such program constraints had been endorsed by the full Court, they undoubtedly would have been taken more seriously by the lower federal courts. But, precisely because the Supreme Court spoke with many voices, a number of appellate court judges took it upon themselves to read both *Fullilove* and *Weber* expansively and assign undeserved weight to dictum in *Bakke*.[34] As a consequence, the racial preference acquired a respectability it did not justifiably deserve.[35]

---

28. See fn. 21.

29. See fn. 23.

30. 443 U.S. 193 (1979).

31. Ibid., p. 208. The Court did not elaborate on how the persistent racial exclusion was to be proven or on how the tailoring and duration of the remedy must be fashioned in relation to the proof of prior exclusion.

32. 448 U.S. 448 (1980) (plurality).

33. Ibid., p. 478. In upholding a minority set-aside provision enacted by Congress, the Court's plurality—Burger, C. J., joined by Justices White and Powell—found that "Congress had abundant historical basis from which it could conclude that traditional procurement practices, when applied to minority businesses, could perpetuate the fact of past discrimination."

34. Justice Powell suggested in his separate concurrence that "in light of the countervailing constitutional interest . . . of the First Amendment," 438 U.S. at 313, a university could permissibly exercise its academic freedom to consider race as one factor in promoting a diverse student body. Ibid., pp. 311-15. Whatever force such a reading of the Fourteenth Amendment may have to accommodate First Amendment freedoms where the two come into direct conflict, there is no countervailing First Amendment interest implicated in the usual employer-employee relationship. See generally Wm. Bradford Reynolds, "The Justice Department's Enforcement of Title VII," *Labor Law Journal*, 34:259-65 (1983).

35. See, for example, *H. K. Porter Co., Inc.* v. *Metropolitan Dade County*, 825 F.2d 324 (11th Cir. 1987), vacated and remanded, 489 U.S. 1062 (1989); *Higgins* v. *City of Vallejo*, 823 F.2d 351 (9th Cir. 1987) (rejecting constitutional and Title VII challenges to award of firefighter-engineer position to third-ranked black candidate over first-ranked white candidate); *Smith* v.

Such programs, however, have been unable to sustain lasting support—a consequence that, in the final analysis, is as much a tribute to the Supreme Court as the flirtation with a racial-quota policy was one of the Court's more noticeable embarrassments. The issue of preference revisited the High Court repeatedly in the 1980s, and by the end of the decade there emerged a far clearer understanding of its acceptable use. Wholesale return to the days in the early 1960s—when "affirmative action" was a neutral phrase that demanded outreach efforts aimed at all Americans without regard to race—has not occurred.[36] But neither is it any longer the case that a racial so-

lution can be fashioned to correct a statistical imbalance in the workplace that is attributed to discrimination in the past, not the present.[37]

Rather, in a series of decisions authored by justices on both sides of the philosophical spectrum, affirmative action preferences have been assigned a modest, albeit not unimportant, role in the fight against discrimination. They are available not as a first-resort measure but as a remedy of last resort, to be used when—and only when—compelled by racially exclusionary practices that persist notwithstanding concerted efforts, nonracial in character, to bring them to a halt.[38] Even then, the race-conscious

---

Hennesy, 831 F.2d 1068 (llth Cir. 1987), *aff'g*, 648 F.Supp 1103 (M.D. Fla. 1986) (upholding a one-for-one policy adopted by city's firefighter department over constitutional and Title VII challenges); *Kromnick v. School Dist.*, 939 F.2d 894 (3d Cir. 1984) (upholding teacher assignment program); *South Florida Chapter, Associated General Contractors of America, Inc. v. Metropolitan Dade County*, 723 F.2d 846 (11th Cir.), *cert. denied*, 469 U.S. 871 (1984) (upholding local set-aside program); *Bratton v. City of Detroit*, 704 F.2d 878 (6th Cir. 1983), *cert. denied*, 464 U.S. 1040 (1984) (upholding voluntary police quota); *Ohio Contractors Association v. Keip*, 713 F.2d 167 (6th Cir. 1983) (upholding state set-aside); *Schmidt v. Oakland Unified School Dist.*, 662 F.2d 550 (9th Cir.) (upholding local set-aside), *vacated on other grounds*, 457 U.S. 594 (1982); *Geier v. Alexander*, 593 F.Supp 1263 (M.D. Tenn. 1984), *aff'd*, 801 F.2d 799 (6th Cir. 1986) (approving special tracking of 75 black sophomores to state professional schools); *M.C. West, Inc. v. Lewis*, 522 F.Supp 338 (M.D. Tenn. 1981) (upholding U.S. Department of Transportation set-aside regulations on the basis of *Fullilove*).

36. Only Justice Scalia has insisted that the Fourteenth Amendment is truly color-blind and tolerates no racial preferences for nonvictims of discrimination, even if the stated purpose is remedial. See *City of Richmond* v.

Croson, 488 U.S. 469, 520-28 (Scalia, J., concurring separately).

37. A plurality of the Court in *Wygant* v. *Jackson Bd. of Educ.* rejected outright the proposition that racial preferences could be constitutionally justified or remedially necessary to correct "historical" or "societal" discrimination. 476 U.S. at 274-75. See also ibid., pp. 288-89 (O'Connor, J., concurring). This conclusion was adopted by five justices in *Croson*, 488 U.S. at 496-97 (O'Connor, J., joined by the Chief Justice and Justices White and Kennedy, with Scalia, J., concurring separately).

38. See, for example, *Local 28, Sheet Metal Workers* v. *EEOC*, 478 U.S. at 449 ("Where an employer or union has engaged in particularly long-standing or egregious discrimination . . . requiring recalcitrant employers or unions to hire and to admit qualified minorities roughly in proportion to the number of qualified minorities in the work force may be the only effective way to ensure the full enjoyment of the rights protected by Title VII"); *United States* v. *Paradise*, 480 U.S. at 171-72 (a promotions quota was justified by a compelling governmental interest in remedying " 'long-term, open and pervasive' discrimination, including absolute exclusion of blacks from . . . upper ranks [of the Alabama State Troopers]"). And see *City of Richmond* v. *Croson*, 488 U.S. at 509 (It is only "in the extreme case [that] some form of narrowly tailored racial preference might be nec-

alternative must be narrowly tailored to the remedial purpose it is intended to serve, so as not to intrude needlessly on the rights of others who have done no wrong or last longer than necessary to correct the discrimination.[39]

Accordingly, there is good reason to believe that we are entering an era when government will no longer feel the need to rely so heavily on racial classifications. To be sure, there are those who still insist that minorities are bound to remain on the sidelines without some racial-preference measure to get them into the game. Rather than demanding rigid quotas, however, they claim to be content with goals and timetables.

But racial goals, tied to short- or long-term timetables, offer no solution to the real problems at hand. Whether racial preference is enforced by the raw racism of a quota program or guided by the more subtle hand of a flexible goal, it still confers benefits on some while denying them to others for the worst of reasons: because of skin color or ethnic origin. The unfortunate reality is that under either regime, the specter of racial inferiority is kept alive; behind every goal and timetable lurks the message that minorities cannot make it under the same rules, that they need a special set of privileges that come with being members of a particular race.

The recently concluded debates over the Civil Rights Act of 1991 reverberated around that theme. The advocates of racial preference lobbied hard for codification of a legal standard that would effectively define discrimination in terms of proportional representation—not just in terms of race and ethnicity, but also with respect to gender and religion. Any work force imbalance as to one or more of the designated groupings was, under their proposal, presumptively unlawful, and the traditional defense of merit selection would be unacceptable against any claimant minimally qualified for the job in question.

Those who opposed and ultimately defeated this measure were not far off the mark to call it a quota bill. Unless companies hired and promoted by race, gender, ethnic background, and religion, work force proportionality would simply not be achievable and therefore litigation would be a virtual certainty.[40] The most cost-effective corporate response would thus be to maintain separate lists of applicants and select new hires or promotees proportionately according to skin color, sex, ethnicity, and religious beliefs. Self-imposition of employee quotas to avoid presumptive liability was the unstated, but fully understood, objective of the offered legislation.

40. The irony is that, under the new act, the employer is put in a catch-22 position. If the hiring is done along racial, gender, ethnic, and religious lines—so as to avoid work force disparity in any or all of the designated categories—the employer faces the prospect of a Title VII lawsuit alleging intentional discrimination on account of race, sex, national origin, or religion. Conversely, if the hiring is done without regard to race, gender, or ethnic or religious affiliation—which will invariably produce disparity on one or another basis—the employer similarly faces the prospect of a Title VII lawsuit alleging impermissible disparity.

essary to break down patterns of deliberate exclusion").

39. See *City of Richmond* v. *Croson*, 408 U.S. at 497-98; and see *Wygant* v. *Jackson Bd. of Educ.*, 476 U.S. at 282-84.

What finally was passed by Congress and signed by President Bush was the product of compromise and, in candor, probably eases the quota pressure on corporate America to some degree, even if it does not eliminate it altogether. The presumption of discriminatory selection procedures on a showing of work force disproportionately remained in the final bill.[41] But the employer—who, under the 1991 act, inherits the burden of proof once a *prima facie* showing of racial, gender, ethnic, or religious disparity has been made[42]—can rebut the presumption on a showing that its alleged discriminatory procedure is related to the job in question and necessary to the business.[43] In other words, proof that the selection process was designed to, and did in fact, produce the best-qualified candidates for the particular job is an acceptable defense.

To be sure, the new statute lacks definition in a number of important respects,[44] but that has become an expected character flaw in virtually all congressional legislation that is the product of extended debate and compromise. In this instance, the shortcoming probably bodes well for the forces whose understanding of civil rights continues to rest, at bottom, on the color-blind ideal of equal opportunity for all Americans and not just a preferred group or groups. For it is they who now seem to have the ear of a majority of the Supreme Court justices as well as many lower federal court judges who will be called upon to resolve definitional disputes and matters of statutory interpretation.[45]

That is the more gratifying news. An immediate legislative threat to an eventual return to race neutrality has been diverted. The new civil rights legislation at least pays symbolic deference to a principled assault on the evils of discrimination, and nothing it says provides a basis for any more expansive use of the remedy of racial—or ethnic or gender or religious—preference than has been permitted by the Supreme Court. Affirmative action measures thus are readily available as a remedial tool to respond to acts of bias and prejudice, but they must remain unconscious to color differences except as a "narrowly tailored," last-resort effort to rid a work force of persistent discrimination.[46]

41. Despite much debate over whether the new act was or was not a quota bill—and assurances from both proponents and opponents of the legislation that quota hiring was not permitted by the language ultimately adopted—the reality is that the Civil Rights Act of 1991 makes suspect a numerical disparity in the work force based on race, gender, national origin, or religion. Pub L. 102-166, sec. 105, 42 U.S.C. § 2000e-2 (k) (1) (A) (1991).

42. The new act shifts the burden of proof to the employer upon a showing by the complainant of a racial—or other—disparity among employee hires attributable to a particular selection practice or practices utilized by the employer. Pub. L. 102-166, sec. 105 (a), 42 U.S.C. § 2000-2 (k) (1) (B) (1991).

43. See Pub. L. 102-166, sec. 105 (a), 42 U.S.C. § 2000e-2(k) (1) (A) (i) (1991). In order to pass statutory muster, the challenged employment practice must be "job related for the position in question and consistent with business necessity."

44. For example, the term "business necessity" is not defined. Nor does the statute explain the appropriate comparative analysis for determining that a particular statistical imbalance creates a presumption of "disparate impact."

45. See fnn. 36-39 and accompanying text.

46. See fnn. 38-39 and accompanying text.

This is not to suggest that the 1991 act deserves no criticism. Its new provisions on punitive damages,[47] standing,[48] limitation periods,[49] attorney and witness fees,[50] and retroactivity each raise questions that are already subject to litigation or soon will be. As a consequence, the real beneficiaries of the compromise that emerged from the prolonged legislative battle are, for now, likely to be the lawyers who will, predictably, further clog the courts' crowded dockets with numerous new lawsuits seeking to exploit the damages and fee-recovery provisions—the beneficiaries will not be the ever-expanding minority population, which is still waiting, largely in vain, for the employment opportunities promised in the Civil Rights Act of 1964. That promise has, for most, too long been thwarted by the policy of racial preference. The real disappointment is that its prospects under the new act are only marginally brighter, even on the best of assumptions that preferential affirmative action has been caged and will henceforth be available only for tailored, last-resort, remedial use.

47. See Pub. L. 102-166, sec. 102, 42 U.S.C. § 1981 A(b) (1991).

48. See Pub. L. 102-166, secs. 108, 112, 42 U.S.C. §§ 2000e-2(n) (1) (A) and (B) (1991), 2000e-5(a) (1991).

49. See Pub. L. 102-166, sec. 112, 42 U.S.C. § 2000e-5(e) (1991).

50. See Pub. L. 102-166, sec. 103, 113, 42 U.S.C. § 1988 (1991).

ANNALS, *AAPSS*, 523, September 1992

The Origins of Affirmative Action: Civil Rights and the Regulatory State

By HUGH DAVIS GRAHAM

ABSTRACT: Affirmative action policy developed during the 1960s and 1970s in two phases that embodied conflicting traditions of government regulation. The first phase, culminating in the Civil Rights Act of 1964 and the Voting Rights Act of 1965, was shaped by the presidency and Congress and emphasized nondiscrimination under a "race-blind Constitution." The second phase, shaped primarily by federal agencies and courts, witnessed a shift toward minority preferences during the Nixon administration. The development of two new agencies created to enforce the Civil Rights Act, the Equal Employment Opportunity Commission under Title VII and the Office of Federal Contract Compliance under Title VI, demonstrates the tensions between the two regulatory traditions and the evolution of federal policy from nondiscrimination to minority preferences under the rubric of affirmative action. The result has strengthened the economic and political base of the civil rights coalition while weakening its moral claims in public opinion.

Hugh Davis Graham is Holland N. McTyeire Professor of History at Vanderbilt University. He received the B.A. in history from Yale University in 1958 and the Ph.D. from Stanford University in 1964 and has taught at Johns Hopkins and the University of Maryland, Baltimore County. His recent books include Civil Rights and the Presidency *(1992),* The Civil Rights Era *(1990), and* The Uncertain Triumph: Federal Education Policy in the Kennedy and Johnson Years *(1984).*

IN 1978, in *Regents of the University of California* v. *Bakke*, Supreme Court Justice Harry Blackmun voted to uphold the exclusion of white applicants from affirmative action programs like the minority set-aside at the Davis medical school. Blackmun was apologetic about supporting a government policy of racial exclusion: "I yield to no one in my earnest hope that the time will come when an 'affirmative action' program is unnecessary and is, in truth, only a relic of the past."[1] Defending the Davis program as a stage of "transitional inequality," he expressed the hope that "within a decade at the most," American society "must and will reach a stage of maturity where acting along this line is no longer necessary." "Then persons will be regarded as persons and discrimination of the type we address today will be an ugly feature of history that is instructive but that is behind us."

Blackmun misjudged the period of transition. A generation after the Civil Rights Act of 1964, which prohibited "discrimination because of race, color, religion, or national origin," minority preferences have become standard policy, and their supporters seldom defend them as temporary. Yet public controversy over affirmative action has increased, not faded. Most other major government initiatives of the 1960s had worked their way into the public consensus: Medicare, federal aid to education, protection of the environment, regulation of consumer products, requirements for transporta-

tion and workplace safety. But the public remained profoundly divided over affirmative action programs keyed to minority preferences. The history of affirmative action helps to explain the way the policy evolved and its consequences.

Much of the polarization, confusion, and resentment shared by both sides in the affirmative action dispute can be traced to a crucial but poorly understood moment of transition in the late 1960s. Between 1964 and 1972, the federal government apparatus was committed to a pervasive new structure of social regulation.

The shift was largely unplanned and unforeseen. A breakthrough in civil rights policy, codified in the Civil Rights Act of 1964, marked the beginning of the transition. Yet the Civil Rights Act also represented the culmination of an older tradition of regulation whose mainstream assumptions and methods differed sharply from the norms of the new social regulation. Thus in 1964 two traditions of government regulation were combined in a major regulatory initiative that rested on contradictory assumptions.

The main intended results were dramatic: the destruction of legal segregation in the South and a sharp acceleration in the drive for equal rights for women. The unanticipated result, however, was a social cleavage that fractured the American consensus on the meaning of justice itself.[2]

---

1. *Regents of the University of California* v. *Bakke*, 438 U.S. 265, 403 (1978).

2. Hugh Davis Graham, *The Civil Rights Era: Origins and Development of National Policy, 1960-1972* (New York: Oxford University Press, 1990), pp. 450-76.

THE FAIR-EMPLOYMENT COMMISSIONS

During the spring of 1964, debate over the civil rights bill concentrated on Title VII, which would create the Equal Employment Opportunity Commission (EEOC) to police job discrimination in commerce and industry. This was the "FEPC" title under a less controversial name. To conservatives it summoned memories of Franklin Roosevelt's wartime Committee on Fair Employment Practices (FEPC) of government bureaucrats telling businesses whom they must hire. To liberals, it offered the nationwide extension of an enlightened and effective model of employment fairness: the independent state commissions against discrimination.

Patterned after the Progressive and New Deal tradition of national regulatory commissions like the Federal Trade Commission (1915) and the National Labor Relations Board (NLRB) (1935), the state commissions had been pioneered in New York, where the legislature in 1945 established the State Commission against Discrimination (SCAD). Based on the NLRB model sponsored by Senator Robert Wagner, Democrat of New York, SCAD was a regulatory commission that received complaints, screened them for probable cause, negotiated conciliations, and, when persuasion failed, held formal hearings. SCAD had subpoena power and could issue desist orders enforceable in the courts.

By 1960, the New York model had spread across the northern urban-industrial states from Massachusetts to the Midwest and then to the West Coast. The FEPC states included a majority of the U.S. population, although most blacks still lived in the segregated South.[3]

Even among employers, the state and municipal fair-employment commissions earned a reputation for efficiency and fairness. One study found that, in 12 major industrial states between 1945 and 1961, only 62 of 19,394 job discrimination complaints required public hearings and, of these, only 26 led to desist orders.[4] Most studies found that the threat and expense of the full hearing process was enough to persuade employers to satisfy commission officials "voluntarily."[5] Racial discrimination by employers appeared to be minimized under such a system. If extended nationwide through Title VII, this system promised to destroy the segregated political economy of the South and enforce nondiscrimination throughout the nation.

CONTRACT COMPLIANCE

During the debates of 1963-64, little attention was paid in Congress or the media to the civil rights bill's Title VI, which prohibited discrimination in programs receiving funds from federal grants, loans, or contracts. Unlike the long and compli-

3. Jay Anders Higbee, *Development and Administration of the New York Law against Discrimination* (Tuscaloosa: University of Alabama Press, 1966): Paul H. Norgren and Samuel E. Hill, *Toward Fair Employment* (New York: Columbia University Press, 1964).

4. The most comprehensive study of state and municipal fair-employment commissions is Morroe Berger, *Equality by Statute: The Revolution in Civil Rights* (New York: Farrar, Straus & Giroux, 1978).

5. Graham, *Civil Rights Era*, pp. 129-32.

cated Title VII, to establish a controversial new enforcement agency, Title VI was brief and general. Its vague provisions for enforcement by federal funding agency regulations were hedged with requirements for judicial review and congressional oversight. Yet Title VI turned out to be the sleeper provision of 1964.

Title VI drew its authority from the law of contract compliance, which flows from the responsibility of public executives—kings, presidents, governors—to stipulate and enforce the terms of government contracts. Since the founding of the Republic, executive departments have contracted for goods and services:. warships for the navy, rifles for the army, dams for the rivers, funds for highway and hospital construction. The contracts detailed the technical specifications, performance standards, work schedule, time of completion or delivery, costs, and so forth. Contract compliance was backed by the authority to cancel the contracts of failed performers and ban the contractors from future contract work.

President Roosevelt's FEPC (1941-46) was an advisory committee created by executive order under contract compliance authority, not an independent regulatory commission created by statute. The difference is fundamental, though "FEPC" became a generic term that muddied the distinction between contract enforcement by executives and regulation by statutory commissions. Roosevelt's fair-employment committee added to defense contracts a new social provision that required contractors to protect the civil rights of minorities. The Roosevelt and Tru-

man administrations justified FEPC on the grounds that the national defense and economy were strengthened by bringing minorities into the skilled work force.

During the five stormy years that the tiny, courageous FEPC tried to enforce nondiscrimination in defense contracts, employers, the American Federation of Labor unions, the armed forces, Congress, and public opinion were inhospitable. When attempts to legislate a national fair-employment commission were blocked by a coalition of southern Democrats and conservative Republicans, President Truman appointed his own advisory committee to police job discrimination by government agencies and contractors. President Eisenhower established a similar committee, also by executive order.[6]

President Kennedy's 1961 fair-employment Executive Order 10925 differed from its predecessors in two respects. First, to compensate for his unwillingness to ask Congress for significant civil rights legislation, Kennedy signed the order at a highly publicized White House ceremony at which he emphasized his administration's executive initiatives on behalf of civil rights.[7] Second, Kennedy's order for the first time

6. William C. Berman, *The Politics of Civil Rights in the Truman Administration* (Columbus: Ohio State University Press, 1970); Donald R. McCoy and Richard Reutten, *Quest and Response: Minority Rights in the Truman Administration* (Lawrence: University of Kansas Press, 1973); Robert Fredrick Burk, *The Eisenhower Administration and Black Civil Rights* (Knoxville: University of Tennessee Press, 1984).

7. Carl M. Brauer, *John F. Kennedy and the Second Reconstruction* (New York: Columbia University Press, 1977).

linked the phrase "affirmative action" to civil rights enforcement policy. The phrase had been used in the Wagner Act of 1935, which had authorized the NLRB to redress unfair labor practices by ordering offending parties "to cease and desist from such . . . practice, and to take such affirmative action, including reinstatement of employees with or without back pay, as will effectuate the policies of this act."

In the administrations of Presidents Kennedy and Johnson, affirmative action meant that government employers and contractors had to recruit aggressively to bring minorities into the applicant pool. Decisions on hiring, promotions, and appointments, however, would continue to be governed by traditional criteria of merit selection.

Kennedy's order directed federal contractors to "take affirmative action to ensure that applicants are employed, and that employees are treated during employment, without regard to their race, creed, color, or national origin." The governing principle was classical liberalism's command not to discriminate. In the memorable phrase of Justice John Marshall Harlan, dissenting with lonely passion in the *Plessy* decision of 1896, the goal of federal policy must be a "color-blind Constitution."

BANNING
RACIAL PREFERENCES

By 1963, the civil rights movement, through the accumulated pressure of the sit-ins, freedom rides, and especially the televised demonstrations in Birmingham led by Martin Luther King, had created a national demand for change that threatened to overwhelm conservative defenses in Congress. In June 1963, President Kennedy sent Congress a bill to prohibit segregation in public accommodations (Title II). By November, on the eve of Kennedy's assassination, the administration and congressional leaders of both parties had agreed to add a job-discrimination provision—Title VII—to be administered by a fair-employment commission called the EEOC.

During the spring 1964 Senate showdown, minority leader Everett Dirksen, armed with decisive bargaining leverage because Republican votes were essential to break the southern filibuster, demanded and won the addition of provisions to prohibit minority preferences. Conservatives had been alarmed when, in March 1964, a black hearing examiner for the Illinois fair-employment commission ordered the Motorola Corporation to hire a rejected black applicant who had flunked its general ability test. Finding that such tests were unfair to "culturally deprived and disadvantaged groups" because they did not take into account "inequalities and differences in environment," the examiner also ordered Motorola to stop using them.[8]

Alarmed by this incident, which raised anew the specter of bureaucrats telling businesses whom to hire, Dirksen assailed the prospect of racial quotas. Democratic leaders agreed to amend the civil rights bill to address his concerns. The bill's Democratic floor manager explained

8. Graham, *Civil Rights Era*, pp. 145-52.

that "any deliberate attempt to maintain a racial balance . . . would involve a violation of Title VII because maintaining such a balance would require an employer to hire or refuse to hire on the basis of race. It must be emphasized that discrimination is prohibited to any individual."[9]

Majority Whip Hubert Humphrey denied that the bill would permit "preferential treatment to any individual or group." He explained that Title VII barred intentional discrimination and "inadvertent or accidental discrimination will not violate the title or result in entry of court orders."[10] Humphrey promised to eat his hat if the civil rights bill ever led to racial preferences.

With Dirksen's support, the southern filibuster was broken. The House accepted the Senate language on 2 July, and on the same day President Lyndon Johnson signed the Civil Rights Act of 1964 into law.[11]

TITLE VII AND THE EEOC

Dirksen's compromise had concentrated on amending Title VII in order to confine the Civil Rights Act to nondiscrimination. No congressman defended the Motorola hearing examiner's order. To Republicans, the bureaucratic regulatory commission model posed a threat to free-market business enterprise. Virtually all of

Dirksen's negotiations focused on the coverage and exceptions in Title VII and on the proposed EEOC. The Republican minority stripped the new agency of both cease-and-desist power and prosecuting authority.

What remained was essentially a defanged enforcement agency. The EEOC could receive and process individual complaints of discrimination due to race, color, religion, sex, or national origin and could seek conciliation by negotiating with the employers or unions named in the complaints. It could hold hearings, conduct studies, issue reports, make recommendations. Unlike state FEPCs, however, it could not issue desist orders or sue offending employers in court.[12]

The EEOC got off to a poor start in 1965. The agency was reasonably effective, working with the Justice and Labor departments, in dismantling the structure of segregated jobs and unions in the South. But it was attacked by black civil rights leaders for weakness and timidity in a period of violent racial crisis. Feminist leaders, who in 1966 formed the National Organization of Women, attacked the EEOC for halfhearted action against sex discrimination. Michael Sovern's 1966 study of equal employment called the EEOC a "poor enfeebled thing."[13]

During the long debate over the Civil Rights Act, most attention was devoted to the complex Title VII provisions on nondiscrimination and

9. Ibid., pp. 150-51.

10. Humphrey, quoted in U.S., Congress, Senate, *Congressional Record*, 88th Cong., 2d sess., 4 June 1964, pt. 10, pp. 12723-24.

11. Charles Whalen and Barbara Whalen, *The Longest Debate: Legislative History of the Civil Rights Act of 1964* (Cabin John, MD: Seven Locks Press, 1985).

12. *The Civil Rights Act of 1964* (Washington, DC: Bureau of National Affairs, 1964).

13. Michael I. Sovern, *Legal Restraints on Racial Discrimination in Employment* (New York: Twentieth Century Fund, 1966), p. 88.

their enforcement by the EEOC. Little time was spent on the brief Title VI on nondiscrimination in federally assisted programs, which gave statutory approval to the President's contract compliance authority.

Title VI began with an unambiguous ban on discrimination: "No person in the United States shall, on the ground of race, color, or national origin, be excluded from participation in, be denied the benefits of, or be subject to discrimination under any program or activity receiving Federal financial assistance."[14] Congress then directed federal agencies to enforce this ban by issuing rules and regulations. The main goal was to use the power of the federal purse to stop, rather than subsidize, segregated programs in the South.

TITLE VI AND THE PHILADELPHIA PLAN

While public attention during 1964-68 was focused on the hobbled EEOC, the Labor Department launched an initiative based on the government's multi-billion-dollar budget for contracts and grants. In June 1965, President Johnson told the graduates at Howard University's commencement:

You do not wipe away the scars of centuries by saying: Now you are free to go where you want, and do as you desire. . . . You do not take a person who, for years, has been hobbled by chains and liberate him, bring him to the starting line of a race and then say, "You are free to compete with all the others," and still justly believe that you have been completely

fair. . . . We seek . . . not just equality as a right and a theory but equality as a fact and equality as a result.[15]

In September, Johnson issued Executive Order 11246, abolishing the tangled arrangements for contract compliance and directing the Labor Department to create new enforcement machinery. Despite the Howard speech, affirmative action played no role in the planning for this order. Johnson's overarching concerns were interagency coordination and the avoidance of politically damaging battles between enforcement officials in Washington and Democratic organizations in the major cities, like Mayor Richard Daley's Chicago. His order repeated the boilerplate language of Kennedy's 1961 order tying affirmative action to nondiscrimination.[16]

To implement the order, Labor Secretary Willard Wirtz established the Office of Federal Contract Compliance (OFCC) and appointed as its director a black administrator with a degree in engineering, Edward Sylvester. Working closely with federal officials in metropolitan areas, Sylvester concentrated on the construction industry, where organized labor's hiring-hall contracts with builders gave job-assignment control to skilled craft unions. Father-son traditions and guildlike patterns in the American Federation of Labor had largely excluded minorities from apprenticeships and union membership, and, hence, from high-wage construction jobs.

14. Title VI, Nondiscrimination in Federally Assisted Programs, § 601.

15. *Public Papers of the Presidents: Lyndon B. Johnson, 1965* (Washington, DC: Government Printing Office, 1965), 2:636.

16. Graham, *Civil Rights Era*, pp. 180-89.

The OFCC designed a model of contract compliance based on a metropolitan Philadelphia plan. Assuming that nondiscrimination was inadequate to uproot white job entrenchment, building contractors were required to submit "pre-award" hiring schedules listing the number of minorities to be hired. The ultimate goal was to make the proportion of blacks in each trade equal to their proportion of metropolitan Philadelphia's work force: 30 percent.[17]

Both builders and unions attacked the minority preferences. The American Federation of Labor and Congress of Industrial Organizations (AFL-CIO) brought pressure on Wirtz, and Pennsylvania construction contractors sued the Labor Department in federal court, charging that the Philadelphia Plan violated the nondiscrimination provision of the Civil Rights Act. The builders also appealed to the General Accounting Office, which enforced low-bid protocols in federal contracting. In November 1968, Comptroller General Elmer Staats ruled that the plan violated federal contract law. The lame-duck Johnson administration did not resist; the Philadelphia Plan appeared to be dead.[18]

By fall 1968, federal civil rights policy still seemed anchored in the nondiscrimination doctrine of the 1964-65 statutes. Richard Nixon, avowed opponent of racial quotas, had won election to the presidency. Yet by 1972, when Nixon was reelected by landslide margins in a campaign that included his call for a constitutional amendment to ban school busing for racial balance, federal policy had shifted away from the equal-treatment standard toward proportional results that required minority preferences.

How can we explain this shift? Four reasons can be given: (1) a new etiology of social disadvantage that implied more radical remedies; (2) clientele control of civil rights agencies; (3) the Nixon administration's commitment to affirmative action preferences; and (4) the federal courts' intervention in social policy.

INSTITUTIONAL RACISM

During the 1960s, a significant shift occurred in the theory of social disadvantage. The Kennedy-Johnson war on poverty had emphasized the stunting effects of deprivation: the "culture of poverty" trapped its victims in a chain of disadvantage. Antipoverty planners therefore concentrated on compensatory programs, like Head Start interventions in early childhood education.

In civil rights, black disadvantage was explained not only as a legacy of slavery and segregation but as a consequence of institutionalized racism woven into the fabric of American life. Discrimination was thus seen to persist even in the absence of conscious prejudice and specific acts of discrimination.[19] This was held to explain the fact that, in the late 1960s, the unemployment rate of blacks was double that of whites, even in the

17. William B. Gould, *Black Workers in White Unions* (Ithaca, NY: Cornell University Press, 1972), pp. 172-88.

18. Graham, *Civil Rights Era*, pp. 278-97.

19. Julie Roy Jeffrey, *Education for the Children of the Poor* (Columbus: Ohio State University Press, 1977).

industrial North, where fair-employment commissions had policed discrimination for a generation.

The urban riots of 1965-68, following the triumph of nondiscrimination in 1964-65, seemed to confirm these explanations. The "long, hot summers" of racial violence burned through northern and western cities, leaving little mark on the South. The 1968 Kerner Report, blaming the black rioting on "white racism," reinforced an apocalyptic vision. Alarmed by social chaos and racial warfare, liberal theorists found nondiscrimination inadequate to overcome institutional racism. Liberals concluded that a temporary, results-driven recourse to minority preferences was necessary.[20]

CLIENTELE CAPTURE

The pressures for change converged upon an expanding network of civil rights agencies receptive to more aggressive, results-centered methods. After 1965, the EEOC quickly became the national coordinating center and personnel networking hub for state and local fair-employment agencies.

By 1968, the OFCC was mirrored by contract-compliance offices in 27 federal agencies. These included the Department of Health, Education, and Welfare's Office of Civil Rights, which in 1965 had threatened a fund

cutoff to speed school desegregation, and the Department of Justice Civil Rights Division, which after 1964 coordinated Title VI enforcement. In 1969, President Nixon added the Office of Minority Business Enterprise in the Department of Commerce. Like the OFCC, the Office of Minority Business Enterprise had no statutory basis but leveraged federal contract funds toward minority-owned businesses.

During the 1970s, affirmative action personnel and administrative units became standard in state, municipal, and county governments; in private industry and commerce; in educational systems and nonprofit organizations; and in all but the smallest enterprises and institutions.[21]

The groups allied in the civil rights coalition, politically coordinated by the Leadership Conference on Civil Rights, gravitated toward the network of program and enforcement agencies. Following the traditional practice of clientele capture, whereby interest groups seek a dominant voice in programs and agencies that enter their turf—veterans in the Veterans Administration, farmers in the Department of Agriculture, unions in Labor, small businesses in Commerce—the minority constituencies—especially African Americans and, in the bilingual programs, Hispanics—rapidly dominated the new civil rights bureaucracies.[22]

20. James W. Button, *Black Violence: Political Impact of the 1960s* (Princeton, NJ: Princeton University Press, 1978); *Report of the National Advisory Commission on Civil Disorders* (Washington, DC: Government Printing Office, 1968); Hugh Davis Graham, "Riots and Riot Commissions," *Public Historian* 2:7-27 (Summer 1980).

21. Alfred W. Blumrosen, *Black Employment and the Law* (New Brunswick: Rutgers University Press, 1971), pp. 9-20; Jeremy Rabkin, *Judicial Compulsions* (New York: Basic Books, 1989), pp. 147-81.

22. Paul Sabatier, "Social Movements and Regulatory Decay: Toward a More Adequate—and Less Pessimistic—Theory of Clientele

THE REVIVED
PHILADELPHIA PLAN

This kind of political leverage, however, was insufficient to overcome the Civil Rights Act ban on minority preferences. The urban riots and Nixon's 1968 victory led observers to expect weakened enforcement by federal agencies. Nixon's "southern strategy" was seen as a cynical appeal to racial backlash, and his early nomination of conservative southern jurists to Supreme Court vacancies drew sharp attacks from the civil rights coalition. Nonetheless, Nixon institutionalized numerical hiring goals and timetables.

The Nixon administration during its first year joined with liberal congressmen to rescue the Philadelphia Plan from conservative attack. This strange turn of events pitted the Nixon White House and the Leadership Conference against an equally expedient alliance of organized labor and southern conservatives. In 1969, Nixon's Secretary of Labor, George P. Shultz, a labor economist and former dean of the University of Chicago business school, revived the Philadelphia Plan in order to free the construction industry from the guildlike grip of craft unions. Nixon hoped to expand the black middle class and to split the Democrats' black-labor alliance.

In the autumn of 1969, congressional conservatives led by Senator Sam Ervin of North Carolina sought to prohibit the plan's proportional minority hiring requirements. The AFL-CIO agreed and rallied to defend labor contracts and the seniority principle. In a December 1969 showdown, Nixon's ad hoc coalition of loyalist Republicans and liberal Democrats defeated Ervin's conservative coalition and saved the Philadelphia Plan.[23]

COURT APPROVAL
OF PREFERENCE

The tide of affirmative action thereby turned sharply toward minority preferences. In February 1970, Labor Department Order No. 4 required all federal contractors to submit written affirmative action plans modeled on the Philadelphia Plan. Numerical goals and timetables were required to achieve approximate proportional representation for minorities in the area work force.

In a parallel development in 1968, impatience with the glacial pace of school integration prompted the Warren Supreme Court, in *Green* v. *New Kent County School Board*, to direct desegregating school systems to "take race into account." The Court charged school boards with an "affirmative duty" to produce racial integration in classrooms and in teaching and administrative staffs.[24] In 1971, the Supreme Court affirmed lower court rulings that the minority preferences of the Philadelphia Plan did not violate the Civil Rights Act.[25]

Capture," *Policy Sciences* 6:301-42 (1975); Nathan Glazer, *Affirmative Discrimination* (New York: Basic Books, 1975); Abigail Thernstrom, *Whose Votes Count?* (Cambridge, MA: Harvard University Press, 1987).

23. Graham, *Civil Rights Era*, pp. 322-45.
24. J. Harvie Wilkinson III, *From Brown to Bakke: The Supreme Court and School Integration* (New York: Oxford University Press, 1979), pp. 115-18.
25. The OFCC's Philadelphia Plan was upheld in federal appeals court in *Contractors*

The EEOC, which was more tightly circumscribed by Title VII's elaborate codicils than was the OFCC by Title VI, pursued a similar strategy. The EEOC attempted to circumvent the Title VII equal-treatment requirement by applying an equal-results standard of statistical proportionality to employee testing. In 1970, the commission issued testing guidelines based on a disparate-impact standard that challenged tests whose results led to hiring proportionally fewer minorities than whites.

The disparate-impact standard, like the Philadelphia Plan's proportional hiring requirements, sought to correct institutional racism rather than identifiable discriminatory acts. In disparate impact, intentional discrimination, which was difficult to prove, was irrelevant. In the landmark 1971 case *Griggs* v. *Duke Power Co.*, the Supreme Court, deferring to EEOC regulations as expressing the intent of Congress, adopted the agency's disparate-impact theory of discrimination.[26]

In 1972, Congress extended the EEOC's jurisdiction to state and local governments and educational institutions, exempted in 1964 for political reasons. Thereafter, Congress expanded the model of affirmative action incrementally, adding rights and benefits for specific constituencies—

Association of Eastern Pennsylvania v. Secretary of Labor, 442 F.2d 1959 (3rd Cir. 1971); the Supreme Court denied certiorari in the autumn of 1971.

26. Derrick A. Bell, Jr., *Race, Racism and American Law*, rev. ed. (Boston: Little, Brown, 1980), pp. 619-23; Gary Bryner, "Congress, Courts, and Agencies," *Political Science Quarterly*, 96:411-30 (Fall 1981).

Hispanics, Asians, American Indians, the physically and mentally disabled. But Congress did not change the core language of nondiscrimination in the Civil Rights Act of 1964. Thus, over the years, Congress implicitly accepted, without explicitly endorsing, the model of minority preferences fashioned by agency officials and affirmed by federal courts.

THE STRANGE CAREER OF AFFIRMATIVE ACTION

In the decade following Kennedy's 1961 Executive Order, affirmative action policy evolved in two phases. The first phase, culminating in the Civil Rights Act of 1964 and the Voting Rights Act of 1965, emphasized familiar ingredients of the liberal reform tradition: grass-roots mobilization by social movements, presidential sponsorship, a congressional coalition, a constitutional grounding in individual rights, compromise in coverage, and due process constraints in enforcement. The second phase, which peaked during 1969-71, was characterized by agency implementation and court approval of a regulatory process that was technically complex, obscure to the public, and based on a model of group rights and proportional representation. This peculiar, dual origin has had dual coalition policy consequences: it has strengthened the economic and political base of the minority while weakening its moral claims and public support.

Numerical goals and timetables resemble the compliance standards that environmentalists and consumer-protection regulators have set for clean air or product safety. Such wholesale no-fault rule making is faster and more efficient than investigating charges of discrimination against individuals case by case.

The economic impact of compensatory preferences is still debated. Most economic gains by African Americans came during 1964-1975, when nondiscrimination policy destroyed segregation in the South. The slowing of relative black economic progress since 1975 has coincided with increased enforcement in affirmative action. The chief beneficiaries have been the black middle class, which has expanded from some 10 to 30 percent of black families in the generation since 1964.[27]

The "iron triangles" formed by the civil rights coalition have greatly strengthened the political power of previously excluded minorities. The umbrella Leadership Conference on Civil Rights, which represented 20 organizations at its founding in 1949 —and lost most congressional battles during the 1950s—represented more than 150 organizations by 1980 and was rarely denied its policy preferences by Congress.

These regulatory, economic, and political gains, however, have not led to the public acceptance characteristic of such other social programs of the 1960s as Medicare and Medicaid, federal aid to education, food stamps, Head Start, and environmental and consumer protection. On the con-

trary, affirmative action has evoked growing controversy.

Minority preferences conflict with the historical commitment of liberals to nondiscrimination.[28] During the late 1960s, when black and Hispanic organizations were shifting from the latter policy toward the former, organized labor was attacking the Philadelphia Plan. Feminist groups, moreover, were moving in an opposite direction, away from special protection for women and toward a sex-blind Constitution. Led by highly educated, middle-class white women under the open-competition banner of the Equal Rights Amendment, the feminist movement neither concentrated on nor greatly benefited from affirmative action preferences.[29] Neither did Asian-Americans, whose numbers were swollen by immigration and whose culture stressed traditional notions of competition and merit.

Though affirmative action was introduced as a weapon in the war on poverty, middle-class groups appear to have been its major beneficiaries. This is not surprising. Well-orga-

27. John J. Donohue III and James Heckman, "Continuous Versus Episodic Change: The Impact of Civil Rights Policy on the Economic Status of Blacks," *Journal of Economic Literature*, 29:1603-43 (Dec. 1991).

28. Edward G. Carmines and James A. Stimson, *Issue Evolution: Race and the Transformation of American Politics* (Princeton, NJ: Princeton University Press, 1990).

29. Feminist leaders of the 1960s and 1970s routinely supported affirmative action but not gender preferences. The Equal Rights Amendment drive was rooted in nondiscrimination. Affirmative action for feminists, for example, meant aggressive enforcement of Title IX of the education amendments of 1972, where contract compliance required equal opportunity for women in graduate and professional school admissions and in intercollegiate athletics. See Hugh Davis Graham, *Civil Rights and the Presidency* (New York: Oxford University Press, 1992), pp. 232-34.

nized, affluent groups have often benefited more from government programs than poorer groups the programs have sought to serve—by mortgage deductions, farm subsidies, college loans, veterans' hospitals. The tendency of minority preferences to assist the middle classes in college and professional school admissions, civil service appointments, corporate promotions, and government contracts has fueled criticism and embarrassed supporters of affirmative action.[30]

The original rationale for affirmative action stressed its temporary nature. But minority constituencies have followed the standard script for successful interest groups. To protect their programs and benefits, they have entrenched themselves deeply in networks of clientele groups, legislative committees, and program agencies.[31]

In summary, the regulatory, economic, and political consequences of the strange career of affirmative action have strengthened the policy's institutional base while weakening its claims to public legitimacy. The constitutional command that the rights of all citizens be equally protected has been compatible with the expansion of social regulation to protect citizens from harmful water, workshops, highways, and toys. But the equal-results model of social regulation, when applied to civil rights policy, has clashed with the vision of a color-blind Constitution. As a consequence, American society is polarized, with both blocs—the supporters of equal individual opportunity and of equal group results—claiming moral grievance and social injustice.

30. William Julius Wilson, *The Truly Disadvantaged* (Chicago: University of Chicago Press, 1987).

31. Jeremy Rabkin, "Office for Civil Rights," in *The Politics of Regulation*, ed. James Q. Wilson (New York: Basic Books, 1980), pp. 304-53.

ANNALS, *AAPSS*, **523**, September 1992

Equal Chances versus Equal Results

By SEYMOUR MARTIN LIPSET

ABSTRACT: Affirmative action has two meanings: to affirm equal individual opportunity and to ensure equal group representation. The former meaning predominated until 1969, when the Nixon administration introduced numerical quotas or goals in hiring. Subsequently, Republicans opposed and Democrats endorsed group goals. As polls show that most Americans, including blacks, oppose such policies, the Democratic Party has been hurt by supporting them. Despite the strength of American egalitarianism, blacks have been an oppressed caste for most of the nation's history of statutory slavery and segregation. How best to resolve this contradiction between our egalitarian creed and the legacy of slavery remains the American dilemma.

Seymour Martin Lipset is the Hazel Professor of Public Policy at George Mason University and Senior Fellow of the Hoover Institution at Stanford. His most recent book is Continental Divide: The Values and Institutions of the United States and Canada *(1990).*

NOTE: An earlier version of this article was written for the Progressive Policy Institute.

A FFIRMATIVE action policies, perceived as special preferences or numerical goals for women, blacks, and other defined minorities, have become a major political issue, a subject for congressional debate and action in new civil rights legislation. These policies have introduced a new approach to the concern for equality in American life initially voiced in the Declaration of Independence. That early concern stressed equal opportunity for individuals. The new one focuses on equality of results for groups.

TWO PEOPLES, TWO STRATIFICATION SYSTEMS

From its beginning as a string of colonies, this country has been composed of two peoples in two different stratification systems. One system emphasized egalitarianism, respect across class lines, equal opportunity, meritocracy. For most of our history, the other has been a system of explicit hierarchy, caste, and hereditary inequality.

The treatment of blacks has been the foremost deviation from the American creed. Blacks have been here since the early 1600s. Until 1865, however, most were slaves; during the next 100 years, most worked as a lower caste under Jim Crow policies, with little chance to gain much education or money. The caste system of slavery and segregation was far more hierarchical and hereditary than European feudalism. Only since the 1950s and 1960s have blacks had a true claim to political equality and economic opportunity.

Thomas Jefferson and George Washington voiced their concern over how the treatment of blacks would affect the nation's future. Jefferson wrote, "I tremble for my country when I reflect that God is just."[1] Anticipating that the nation might break up because it could not resolve the problem, Washington told a friend that, if this happened, "he had made up his mind to move and be of the northern."[2]

GROUP SOLUTIONS

Growing attention to the caste situation of blacks from the 1950s on resulted in efforts to find a group solution. These have been called "affirmative action." The term has had two meanings. The first, emerging in the 1960s, involved attempts to incorporate blacks into the general race for success. Lyndon Johnson explained this policy at Howard University in 1965. He said that, as a society, we want all Americans to engage in the race, but some have shackles on their legs; hence programs are needed to remove the chains so that all can compete equally. These programs became the war on poverty, including Head Start, Aid to Families with Dependent Children, and other programs to help poor, predominantly black, families gain a better education and better skills.

These programs were backed by strong Fair Employment and Fair Housing acts designed to end discrimination against blacks in the

1. Thomas Jefferson, *Notes on the State of Virginia* (New York: Harper & Row Torchbooks, 1964), p. 156.
2. James T. Flexner, *Washington: The Indispensable Man* (New York: New American Library, 1984), pp. 389-90.

workplace, education, housing, and clubs. The assumption was that, with equal education and the full political citizenship ensured by Voting Rights acts, blacks could win their legal rights as individuals in the courts and administrative tribunals.

Concern that these policies were not working as quickly as was hoped and that racial barriers still operated in various arenas led to the second type of affirmative action. It emphasizes group solutions: not equal opportunity for individuals but equal results for groups. It assumes that the best way to improve the situation of blacks is by numerical goals and preferences in education and jobs.

Such goals and preferences, advocated by the black leader Martin Delany as early as 1871,[3] were introduced in 1969 by the Nixon administration. George Shultz, Nixon's first Secretary of Labor, concluded that antidiscrimination judgments by courts and administrative agencies would do little and take too long to open discriminatory parts of the labor market to blacks. He issued an order setting quotas for black apprentices in the Philadelphia construction trades, where both employers and unions excluded blacks. The policy was soon extended to other cities and industries. Similar programs for faculty and students in higher education were pressed by other officials with Nixon's approval.[4]

These policies were strongly opposed by a Johnson appointee, Comp-troller General Elmer Staats, trade union leaders, and most congressional Democrats, who argued that the 1964 Civil Rights Act outlawed numerical hiring. Congress, however, rejected a rider to bar the so-called Philadelphia Plan. Republicans opposed the rider 124 to 41, while Democrats supported it 115 to 84.[5] George Bush, then a Texas congressman and planning a campaign against liberal Democratic Senator Ralph Yarborough, who opposed employment quotas, emphasized his vote for a fair-housing bill and racial job preferences. The leaders and the parties were soon to reverse their positions.

The government has applied the principle of group rights to other minorities and women, though opinion polls show that overwhelming majorities of white men and women and often a majority of blacks believe that only individuals, not groups, should be treated equally. Nonetheless, major segments of American elites believe in group remedies for blacks and other groups perceived to lack equal rights: Hispanics, Native Americans, Asians, women, and the handicapped.

THE CASE FOR
GROUP PREFERENCE

Blacks are the quintessential distinctive American minority group, better able than any other ethnic or social group but Native Americans to justify a claim for preferential treatment. Some even argue for reparations as follows: whites profited greatly from the labor of slaves and the Jim Crow years when blacks, as

---

3. Martin Delany, *Homes for the Freedman* (Charleston, SC, 1871).

4. Hugh D. Graham, *The Civil Rights Era* (New York: Oxford University Press, 1990), pp. 326-31.

5. Ibid., pp. 339-40.

outcasts under the law, did the hard, low-paid work of unskilled laborers, field hands, servants, and maids. Thereby whites acquired the leisure, education, and wealth of which they deprived blacks and for which blacks deserve compensation.

Parallel cases are the compensation of Indian tribes for removal from their lands; the acknowledgment by Congress of an obligation to recompense Japanese Americans for their detention during World War II; and the German government's reparations to Jews and Israel. Veterans receive preference for civil service jobs, special educational benefits, and cheap home mortgages.

Individualistic values handicap the socially depressed in all societies. People tend to hire and favor members of their own social and ethnic groups. Few institutions acknowledge such preferences. Many or most private universities, including Harvard, Chicago, and Stanford, have given preference to the children of alumni, faculty, and athletes, however. Many scholarships have been limited to persons from special regional, gender, ethnic, or religious groups; some but not all of these are now illegal.

In 1963, I noted, "Perhaps the most important fact to recognize about the current situation of the Negro is that *equality is not enough to assure his movement into the larger society*."[6] Other minorities and women have required only genuine equal opportunity, not special help. In any case, immigrants have no claim to preferential treatment, since any handicaps they may have are clearly not the fault of American society. Immigrants, including Hispanics and West Indians, generally do better economically the longer they are in this country.

Lawrence Fuchs has argued that preferential employment should be confined to jobs requiring adequacy or competence. Jobs requiring higher standards—for example, medicine, scholarship, sports, management, airline pilots—should not be subject to preferential policies. Thus affirmative programs for Navy pilots or ballet dancers should be "limited to special recruitment and training efforts," whereas numerical goals can serve to increase the number of minority "fire fighters, machinists, computer operators, and candidates for dental school."[7]

Whatever the merits of the distinction between mere competence and high ability, fire fighters, police officers, or assembly-line workers do not accept this disparaging assessment of their worth and skills. In many opinion polls, such workers favor meritocratic standards for their jobs. In fact, white elites, whose economic and social status is more secure, are more likely than workers to endorse preferences for minorities.

PUBLIC OPINION

Mass opinion remains opposed to preferential treatment. Thus the Gallup poll has repeated one question five times between 1977 and

6. Seymour M. Lipset, *The First New Nation* (New York: Basic Books, 1963), p. 331; italics in original.

7. Lawrence H. Fuchs, *The American Kaleidoscope* (Middletown, CT: Wesleyan University Press, 1990), pp. 451-52.

1989: "Some people say that to make up for past discrimination, women and minorities should be given preferential treatment in getting jobs and places in college. Others say that ability, as determined by test scores, should be the main consideration. Which point of view comes close to how you feel on the subject?" In each survey, 81-84 percent replied "ability" and 10-11 percent, "preferential treatment." In 1989, 56 percent of blacks favored "ability, as determined in test scores"; only 14 percent, compared to 7 percent of whites, supported preferential treatment. Women and men responded alike: 85 percent favored ability and 10 percent, preferential treatment.[8]

Gallup presented the issue somewhat differently in 1987 and 1990: "We should make every effort to improve the position of blacks and other minorities even if it means giving them preferential treatment." In this formulation, with no mention of ability or test scores, 71-72 percent opposed and 24 percent supported preferential treatment in both years. Over two-thirds of blacks rejected preference, while 32 percent—and 18 percent of whites—favored it. Over four-fifths of Republicans and two-thirds of Democrats opposed preference.[9]

In 1991, when Gallup posed the issue in terms of equal qualifications, whites were still opposed, but blacks were more favorable. The question was this: "Do you believe that because of past discrimination against black people, qualified blacks should receive preference over equally qual-

8. *Gallup Poll Monthly*, p. 18 (Dec. 1989).
9. In the 1987 survey; the 1990 results were similar.

ified whites in such matters as getting into college or getting jobs?" Only 19 percent of whites but 48 percent of blacks said "yes," while 72 percent of whites and 42 percent of blacks opposed such preference.

Americans will, however, support affirmative action programs that do not involve quotas. In an ABC News-*Washington Post* poll in July 1990, 66 percent of whites and 84 percent of blacks responded favorably to the question, "All in all, do you favor or oppose affirmative action programs in business for blacks, provided there are no rigid quotas?" The Harris poll reported similar responses to comparable questions several times in the 1980s.

Many inconsistencies in racial attitudes point to a deep contradiction between two core values in the American creed—individualism and egalitarianism. Political debate often takes the form of one value opposing the other. Liberals and conservatives typically do not take opposing positions on issues of equality and freedom; instead, they appeal to one or the other value. Liberals stress egalitarianism and the social injustice that flows from unfettered individualism. Conservatives enshrine individual freedom and the social need for mobility and achievement as values endangered by the collectivism inherent in liberal nostrums. Both sides treat the entire American public as their natural constituency. In this sense, liberals and conservatives are less opponents than competitors, like two department stores on the same block trying to draw the same customers by offering different versions of what everyone wants.

The egalitarian element in the American creed created the consensus behind the civil rights revolution of the past thirty years. The more recent focus on group equality and preference, conflicting with the individualistic, achievement-oriented element, has broken the consensus.

Poll data reveal a pro-civil-rights consensus when only egalitarian questions are raised, but an anti-civil-rights consensus when an issue also challenges basic notions of individualism. Public opinion, even in the white South, is powerfully against racial discrimination. Many whites, however, deeply resent compulsory integration and quotas, believing that they violate their rights. Liberals note the inegalitarian consequences of de facto segregation, but most whites prefer individual freedom to compulsory social egalitarianism.

Most whites and many blacks feel it is better for disadvantaged groups to resolve their problems by individual effort and advancement than to demand benefits for all group members. Most oppose special treatment for blacks even when it does not involve preferences, because it violates the idea of racial equality. Thus, in a 1989 poll, 64 percent of whites and 44 percent of blacks disagreed with the statement "Because of past discrimination, blacks who need it should get some help from the federal government that white people in similar economic circumstances don't get."

The claims of women and of blacks and other minorities to full equality are now widely accepted. The General Social Survey, conducted by the National Opinion Research Center every two years, indicates steady improvement in attitudes toward racial equality in many spheres from 1972 through 1990. A large majority of white Americans believes that discrimination is wrong and that government should guarantee the application of competitive merit principles to all, blacks and whites. In a 1991 Gallup poll, 47 percent of whites and 63 percent of blacks said they "socialize regularly with members of another race." Only 6 percent of whites said they would be "uncomfortable working with members of another race" or "for a boss of another race."[10] But every national survey shows that a sizable majority of whites opposes giving special consideration in hiring or school admission to less formally qualified persons.

Americans distinguish compensatory action from preferential treatment. Few object to the former, which helps disadvantaged people improve their qualifications by special training and community development.[11] But most object to the latter, in which standards of admission or employment are lowered for disadvantaged people.

The major support for preferential policies seems to come from the liberal intelligentsia, the well-educated, and those who have studied liberal arts in college or have gone to graduate school. It is strong among the political elite, particularly Democrats but many Republicans as well. Congressional Democrats increasingly support such policies; the proportion of these Democrats with a liberal vot-

10. *Newsweek*, 6 May 1991, pp. 30-31.
11. S. M. Lipset and William Schneider, "The Bakke Case," *Public Opinion*, 1:38-44 (Mar.-Apr. 1978).

ing record has grown steadily since the 1960s. Universities, more liberal than other institutions, also support them. Their most extensive use of numerical goals occurs in the humanities and soft social sciences, whose faculty and students are more liberal than those in other academic fields.

POLITICAL IMPLICATIONS

The affirmative action debate shows no sign of moderating. Quotas were a major issue in several 1990 elections. HR 1, the first bill introduced by Democratic leaders of the House of Representatives in the 1991 session, was a civil rights measure called a quota bill by its opponents. A revised, but essentially similar bill was eventually passed and signed by George Bush.

The arguments over quotas or preferences appear increasingly to strengthen Republicans, who now vigorously emphasize meritocratic standards. Their earlier support for quotas has been forgotten. Most Democrats face a dilemma: how to respond to pressure from civil rights groups and the intelligentsia without alienating the party's traditional white working-class support. In 1965, in a private discussion of civil rights, Lyndon Johnson said, "We have to press for them as a matter of right, but . . . by doing so we will destroy the Democratic party." He anticipated that much of the white South and northern white workers would defect.[12] This has happened, particularly in presidential elections since 1968.

12. Nicholas Lemann, *The Promised Land* (New York: Knopf, 1991), p. 183.

In 1990, North Carolina Senator Jesse Helms won reelection by exploiting the issue of affirmative hiring. Ex-Klansman David Duke did the same in Louisiana and received a majority of white votes in the senatorial primary. Democrat Dianne Feinstein's espousal of quotas in state government employment contributed to her losing the California gubernatorial race. Two studies commissioned by the Michigan Democratic Party in 1985 and 1987 showed that affirmative action played a major role in the party's loss of support. "Quotas and minority preferences were a primary source of anti-government, anti-Democrat anger among white blue-collar voters. Democratic campaign themes such as 'fairness,' 'equity,' and 'justice' had been perceived . . . as code words for quotas."[13]

National polls report similar findings. In 1986 and 1990, 70 percent or more of whites agreed that it was "very likely" or "somewhat likely" that "a white person won't get a job or promotion while an equally or less qualified black person gets one instead." A 1991 poll sponsored by the Leadership Conference on Civil Rights reported that "many white voters believe there is pervasive reverse discrimination in the work place and that civil rights leaders are more interested in special preference than in equal opportunity."[14] Commenting on this study, black columnist William Raspberry wrote,

13. Study report by Stanley Greenberg of the Analysis Group, cited in Frederick R. Lynch, *Invisible Victims* (Westport, CT: Greenwood Press, 1989), p. 3.

14. Thomas B. Edsall, "Rights Drive Said to Lose Underpinnings," *Washington Post*, 9 Mar. 1991.

"White Americans . . . do not see themselves as racists, or as opponents of equal opportunity. . . . they oppose . . . preferential benefits for minorities."[15]

BLACK PROGRESS— A CONTENTIOUS ISSUE

Blacks remain considerably behind whites in income and employment levels but are much better off than they were before the civil rights movement and the adoption of various remedial programs. Awareness of such gains is not widespread, however, in part because black, Hispanic, and women leaders do not admit to significant progress. In the mid-1980s, three-fifths of black leaders told pollsters the situation of blacks was "going backwards." Contrariwise, two-thirds of a national black sample said they were "making progress," though support for this view declined somewhat in the latter years of the Reagan era.[16] In July 1990, an NBC News-*Wall Street Journal* poll reported that 60 percent of blacks felt that blacks were "better off" than ten years before.

The refusal of black leaders to acknowledge improvement is understandable. The worse things seem, the more the leaders can demand. Yet their emphasis on how little progress has been made sustains the argument that programs to help blacks do not work, that some factors inherent in the black situation prevent prog-

ress. Most whites and many blacks have absorbed such negative images. In an ABC News-*Washington Post* survey in 1989, over half of whites and blacks agreed that "discrimination has unfairly held down blacks, but many of the problems blacks in this country have today are brought on by blacks themselves."

Black youths are often told that society is racist, that there is, therefore, no point in trying to work hard or study. Many develop the same invidious stereotypes about blacks as do whites. These images are sustained by the great social morbidity of poor blacks in the ghettos that is so very visible to the media and the public. Reports pour out about the high rate of black crime, homelessness, drug addiction, infant mortality, youth homicide and unemployment, and adult illness.

But the underclass, both black and white, is small. Paul Peterson reports that the metropolitan census tracts in which 40 percent or more of the people are poor—William J. Wilson's definition of the ghetto poor—contained "little more than one percent of the U.S. population in 1980."[17] An Urban Institute study estimates the size of the underclass, both white and black, as 2 or 3 million in 1980.[18]

The status of a major proportion of blacks has improved dramatically. From 1970 to 1988, the proportion

15. William Raspberry, "Why Civil Rights Isn't Selling," *Washington Post*, 13 Mar. 1991.

16. Linda S. Lichter, "Who Speaks for Black America?" *Public Opinion*, 8:41-44, 58 (Aug.-Sept. 1985).

17. Paul E. Peterson, "The Urban Underclass and the Poverty Paradox," in *The Urban Underclass*, ed. Christopher Jencks and Paul Peterson (Washington, DC: Brookings Institution, 1991), p. 22.

18. Ronald B. Mincy et al., "The Underclass: Definition and Measurement," *Science*, 27 Apr. 1990, p. 451.

comprising high school dropouts fell from 31 to 18 percent, compared to 14 percent of whites in both years.[19] The proportion of blacks living in poverty fell from 55 percent in 1959 to 31 percent in 1989.[20] The black middle class outnumbers the black poor.[21] The proportion of blacks living in urban ghettos has declined. Most blacks have steady jobs, are members of the middle or working class, and are married or in stable relationships. Middle-class black fertility is below that of middle-class whites.[22] The sharp rise in the proportion of black births in female-headed households—from 23 percent in 1960 to 62 percent in 1990—reflects not a big increase in the number of illegitimate births but a drastic fall in the birth rate of married black women.[23]

It is doubtful that racial preference has done or can do much for socially fatherless black ghetto youths who lack marketable skills. The federal contract compliance program has "raised demand for black males more in highly skilled white-collar and craft jobs than in the blue-collar operative, laborer, and service occupations." Antidiscrimination litigation has led to gains in white-collar, professional, and managerial positions.[24] Similar class differences have been reported in the effects of affirmative action on women's employment.[25]

As William J. Wilson observes, "affirmative action programs are not designed to deal with the unique problems of the black poor"[26] but with "minority individuals from the most advantaged families . . . [who are] most qualified for preferred positions —such as higher-paying jobs, college admissions, promotions and so forth."[27] One study showed that, from 1974 to 1981, young black college graduates "obtain[ed] more prestigious posts than their white counterparts," a result attributed to "employer sensitivity to affirmative action requirements" and the "concentration of educated blacks in the public sector."[28] This pattern declined with the early 1980s recession and the halt in the growth of government employment, however. By the late 1980s, the "earning gap between blacks and

19. Ben J. Wattenberg, *The First Universal Nation* (New York: Free Press, 1991), p. 67.

20. U.S., Department of Commerce, Bureau of the Census, *Money Income and Poverty Status in the United States 1989*, Current Population Reports, Consumer Income, series P-60, 1990, no. 168, pp. 57-58.

21. James P. Smith and Finis R. Welch, *Closing the Gap* (Santa Monica, CA: RAND, 1986), p. ix.

22. Lemann, *Promised Land*, p. 283; Ben J. Wattenberg, *The Birth Dearth* (New York: Pharows Books, 1987), p. 7.

23. Christopher Jencks, "Is the American Underclass Growing?" in *Urban Underclass*, ed. Jencks and Peterson, pp. 86-89.

24. Jonathan S. Leonard, "The Impact of Affirmative Action Regulation and Equal Employment Law on Black Employment," *Journal of Economic Perspectives*, 4:53, 60 (Fall 1990).

25. James P. Smith and Michael Wood, "Women in the Labor Market and the Family," *Journal of Economic Perspectives*, 3:15 (Winter 1989).

26. William J. Wilson, "Race, Class, and Public Policy," *American Sociologist*, 16:126-27 (May 1981).

27. William J. Wilson, *The Truly Disadvantaged* (Chicago: University of Chicago Press, 1978), pp. 18-19.

28. In Soo Son et al., "Polarization and Progress in the Black Community," *Sociological Forum*, 4:323 (Sept. 1989).

whites with college education [had] widened sharply."[29]

CONCLUSION

White opposition to various forms of special government assistance for blacks and other minorities is in part a function of a general antagonism to statism and a preference for personal freedom.

Although Americans are less willing than Europeans to use government as an instrument of income distribution, their egalitarianism leads them to approve certain programs to provide more opportunities for blacks—for example, expenditures on education, special schools, and Head Start. But Americans are much less prone to endorse general measures to help the underprivileged. Thus in 1987 only 21 percent agreed that "the government should provide everyone with a guaranteed basic income," compared to 50 percent or more of Germans, Austrians, Italians, Dutch, and Britons. Only 29 percent of Americans but 60 percent or more of Europeans agreed that "it is the responsibility of the government to reduce the differences in income between people with high incomes and those with low incomes."[30]

The greater American opposition to state intervention is not limited to such economic measures. For instance, only 49 percent of Americans but 80 percent or more of Europeans and Australians feel that "the wearing of seat belts should be required by law."[31]

The vast majority of Americans, including most blacks, believe this is still a land of opportunity where merit and ambition are rewarded. In 1988, 71 percent—compared to 23-43 percent of Dutch, Germans, Britons, and Italians—said they had a good chance to improve their standard of living. More Americans than Europeans believe "ambition is [essential or very important] for getting ahead in life."[32]

Most Americans still think their children will do well. Though still concerned about the economy in 1992, large majorities say their personal economic situation is good. The rates of social mobility into professional and other privileged positions, measured in elaborate detail by sociologists, remain high. Changes in the occupational structure accompanying the shift to a postindustrial economy have led to increased upward movement, as measured by comparing the occupations of respondents to those of their parents. Most Americans believe that ambition and hard work, not "lucky breaks," "help from other people," or "a wealthy family," is what enables people to move up.

Success in postindustrial society requires a good education. While the education of blacks has improved significantly, it is often well behind that of whites, in real knowledge, at the same grade level. The black under-

29. Henry Aaron, "Symposium on the Economic Status of African Americans," *Journal of Economic Perspectives*, 4:5 (Fall 1990).

30. Tom Smith, "Social Inequality in Cross-National Perspective," in *Attitudes to Inequality and the Role of Government*, ed. J. E. Becker et al. (The Hague: CIP Gegevens Koninklije Bibliotheek, 1990), p. 24.

31. "America's Unique Outlook," *American Enterprise*, 1:116 (Mar.-Apr. 1990).

32. Tom Smith, "Social Inequality," p. 24; "America's Unique Outlook," p. 116.

class is proportionally much larger than the white. Preferences will not help poorly educated persons to secure good jobs. Extending and vastly improving education and training programs is the way to help poor people regardless of their race or ethnicity.

We can learn from the success of the integrated armed forces in offering stable employment, effective career training, and real economic opportunity to young black and white adults. If all youths were able to take part in a voluntary national service program for two or more years, those with inadequate education and skills could be trained for needed positions while helping to rebuild the national infrastructure.

Post-feudal European society was structured into a fixed hierarchy in which each lower class deferred to superior classes. Consequently, the emerging European working class responded to the political world in class terms marked by the development of socialist parties. Conversely, white America, the purest bourgeois and classically liberal society in the world, has treated class as an economic construct; its social class hierarchy was less visible and more open than the European. Hence class-conscious politics and socialist demands for measures of economic equalization have been limited. As Walter Dean Burnham put it, "No feudalism, no socialism."[33]

The situation of American blacks is analytically comparable to that of European peasants and workers. Their post-caste situation has limited their economic and social prospects more than the post-feudal situation restricted those of their European counterparts. It is not surprising, therefore, if blacks are more group conscious than European workers or if many support a version of the old socialist emphasis on equality of results. Ninety percent vote Democratic, much more than any other ethnic group or union members. Blacks back Jesse Jackson's Rainbow Coalition, which supports stronger income redistribution policies and greater state involvement in the economy than socialists in other countries. At least three black congressmen are openly socialist.

Poll data show blacks divided about how much to favor policies of group uplift or of individual opportunity. This debate goes back at least to the Reconstruction period, when Frederick Douglass ridiculed the idea of racial quotas as "absurd," as they implied, to him, that blacks "should constitute one-eighth of the poets, statesmen, scholars, authors and philosophers." Douglass opposed "special efforts" for the freedmen because "promoting an image of blacks as privileged wards of the state" might sustain prejudices that should be banished.[34] Like Douglass, Shelby Steele, once a Rainbow Coalition activist, now argues that blacks "stand to lose more from . . . [affirmative action] than they gain." He rejects the idea of leaping "over the hard business of developing a formerly op-

33. Walter D. Burnham, "The United States: The Politics of Heterogeneity," in Electoral Behavior, ed. Richard Rose (New York: Free Press, 1974), p. 718.

34. Philip S. Foner, ed., The Life and Writings of Frederick Douglass (New York: International, 1955), 4:280-81, 67-68.

pressed people to the point where they can achieve proportionate representation on their own" and suggests that preferences undermine morale, implying that successful blacks have not earned their positions but are inferior to whites.[35]

Civil rights leaders, liberals, and Democrats need to combat their identification with preferential policies and reverse discrimination. The American Left from Jefferson to Hubert Humphrey stood for equal opportunity. By a supreme irony, Richard Nixon, the man most hated by Democrats, initiated the policy that has placed them on the wrong side of this issue politically. The leaders of

strong Democratic factions—of minorities, feminists, liberals, and the intelligentsia—strongly endorse numerical goals and preferential policies, but a substantial majority of Americans, including most Democrats, oppose them. Americans basically agree with an emphasis on equal rights for individuals and social programs that serve everyone or all those in a given condition such as poverty or illness, not people with fixed hereditary characteristics.

White Americans have emphasized individual rights more than any other people. Yet the situation of blacks has contradicted the principles on which the nation was established. The American dilemma persists. Until blacks are absorbed into our economy and society, we must, in Jefferson's words, be fearful of a just God.

---

35. Shelby Steele, *The Content of Our Character* (New York: St. Martin's Press, 1990), p. 13.

ANNALS, *AAPSS*, **523**, September 1992

Hispanics, Affirmative Action, and Voting

By LINDA CHAVEZ

ABSTRACT: The Voting Rights Act of 1965 was originally intended to protect the rights of blacks living in the Deep South, who had been prevented from voting for nearly a century. In 1975, the act was amended to include jurisdictions where large numbers of Mexican Americans live, despite little evidence that Mexican Americans had been systematically excluded from voting as blacks in the South had been. In 1982, the act was again amended, this time to broaden the definition of voting discrimination to apply an effects standard similar to that used in employment discrimination. As a result of the 1982 amendments, Hispanics are now guaranteed the right to vote in safe districts in which they make up a majority of voters. The effect of this provision, coupled with large-scale immigration over the last decade, has been the creation of gerrymandered districts comprising large numbers of persons who are ineligible to vote because they are not yet citizens.

Linda Chavez is a senior fellow at the Manhattan Institute and author of Out of the Barrio: Toward a New Politics of Hispanic Assimilation *(1991). During the Reagan administration, she was director of the U.S. Commission on Civil Rights.*

NOTE: This article was adapted from the author's *Out of the Barrio: Toward a New Politics of Hispanic Assimilation* (New York: Basic Books, 1991).

THE Voting Rights Act of 1965 has frequently been called the most effective civil rights law ever enacted. Unlike the Civil Rights Act of 1964, whose provisions were broad and applied to all areas of the country, the Voting Rights Act was devised to correct a specific and regional problem of discrimination. For nearly one hundred years, in open defiance of the Constitution and federal civil rights laws, some southern states had denied blacks the right to vote. Civil rights proponents believed that a law was needed that would severely punish those jurisdictions and prevent them from enacting new measures to deny black voting rights. The result was a truly radical piece of legislation, which conferred unprecedented authority on the federal government to regulate voting in all elections in certain southern states. The effect was immediate. Within two years, black voter registration in Mississippi, for example, went from about 6 percent to 60 percent.[1] The number of black elected officials in the South increased rapidly as well, from only 100 in 1965 to nearly 5000 by 1990.[2]

By the early 1970s it had become clear to Hispanic leaders that the Voting Rights Act was a particularly effective tool to increase black political power. Not only did the act provide federal protection to individual blacks to register and vote, but it also provided a legal basis to challenge the rules governing elections so that newly enfranchised black voters would not see their voting strength diluted by gerrymandering or at-large elections intended to minimize black electoral power.

Hispanic civil rights activists were anxious to find a way to provide the same kinds of protections to Hispanic voters. There were two problems. The first was a technical one: the law's triggering mechanism was written originally to include only jurisdictions in the Deep South. The second problem was more fundamental; Hispanics had never been subject to the same denial of their basic right to vote as blacks, and it was unclear that legislators could be persuaded that Hispanics needed the kind of drastic protections that the Voting Rights Act authorized. Within 10 years of passage of the original act, however, Hispanics had overcome both obstacles. By 1975, Hispanics had won their right to be included in the act when it was expanded to cover more than 375 jurisdictions outside the South; in the process, Hispanics also secured the right to cast ballots printed in Spanish. Today, Hispanics are entitled to even more. Along with blacks, Hispanic voters are guaranteed the right to vote in districts in which they constitute a majority of the eligible voters; voting in such districts ensures that they can elect members of their own group to represent them. In the long run, however, these victories may cost Hispanics political influence and power.

1. Abigail Thernstrom, *Whose Votes Count? Affirmative Action and Minority Voting Rights* (Cambridge, MA: Harvard University Press, 1987), p. 2.

2. Joint Center for Political Studies, *Black Elected Officials: A National Roster* (Washington, DC: Joint Center for Political Studies, 1990).

EXPANDING COVERAGE

Unlike other civil rights laws, which were meant to protect the rights of any group that faced discrimination, the Voting Rights Act was originally intended to protect primarily one group, blacks, and only those blacks who lived in the Deep South. The reason was simple; no other group had so systematically been denied the right to vote. Every time any effort was made to help blacks exercise their basic right to vote, southern politicians devised new means to keep them from the polls. Clearly, both a new federal voting rights law and a drastic enforcement mechanism were needed to keep recalcitrant southerners from enacting new laws or rules to prevent blacks from voting. The Voting Rights Act established such a mechanism by requiring all covered jurisdictions to submit any changes in voting, no matter how insignificant—even switching a polling site from one side of the street to the other—to the U.S. Justice Department or the District Court of the District of Columbia for approval. This preclearance provision applied only to those states or political subdivisions that used a literacy test to determine voting eligibility and in which less than 50 percent of the voting-age population had voted in the previous presidential election. By design, these criteria captured nearly all offending southern jurisdictions and exempted jurisdictions outside the Deep South, which had no history of denying blacks the right to vote even though some employed literacy tests for all voters.

The preclearance provision became a powerful tool in the hands of civil rights groups. Originally intended to inhibit southern jurisdictions from erecting new barriers to black registration, it quickly became a way for civil rights groups to influence redistricting decisions. The transformation came about when the Supreme Court ruled that

the right to vote can be affected by a dilution of voting power as well as by an absolute prohibition on casting a ballot. Voters who are members of a racial minority might well be in the majority in one district, but in a decided minority in the county as a whole. This type of change could therefore nullify their ability to elect the candidate of their choice just as would prohibiting some of them from voting.[3]

The Court's ruling enlarged the meaning of the "right to vote," interpreting it to mean that blacks were entitled to vote in majority black districts. The decision handed civil rights groups the means to increase black voting strength by challenging redistricting plans and by eliminating multimember districts in areas with sizable black populations. Civil rights groups opposed at-large voting and multimember districts because such districts made it more difficult to elect blacks. If candidates for city offices were elected by wards rather than at large, for example, political lines could be drawn in such a way that smaller, concentrated pockets of black voters would have the opportunity to elect their own candidates.

It was this power to challenge districting plans, at-large elections, and

3. *Allen* v. *State Board of Elections*, 393 U.S. 569 (1969).

multimember districts that appealed to the Mexican American Legal Defense and Education Fund (MALDEF) and other Hispanic organizations that in 1975 sought to amend the Voting Rights Act to bring jurisdictions with large numbers of Hispanics under federal oversight. They knew they would be called on to demonstrate that Hispanics faced the same kind of discrimination that blacks had faced in 1965 in the South, and they knew that it would be a difficult case to make. As Abigail Thernstrom notes, Mexican Americans in the Southwest had a notoriously low voter turnout, but more than low voter participation was required to force inclusion under the special provisions of the act: "Some segments of the white population, after all, rarely voted. In the absence of a literacy test, a device that was unquestionably manipulated to screen registrants by race, black or Hispanic disfranchisement could not be inferred."[4]

After several attempts to draft amendments to the Voting Rights Act that would include Hispanics, MALDEF hit upon the idea of adapting its arguments to the act's original triggering device: the literacy test. Although Texas and most other states with large Mexican American populations did not use literacy tests, they did print their ballots and other voting materials in English. MALDEF asserted that English ballots were, in effect, literacy tests, used as a means to exclude otherwise qualified voters. This argument had already been made successfully in a suit brought by Puerto Ricans in New York, who alleged that printing ballots and election materials in English in a city with a large Puerto Rican population constituted a discriminatory form of a literacy test.[5] Hispanics had finally found their hook.

The final amendments added new criteria to trigger the special provisions of the act. The formula called for a jurisdiction to be covered whenever so-called language minorities comprised 5 percent of the population of a political jurisdiction and voter turnout in the previous presidential election was less than 50 percent of the voting-age population of that jurisdiction. In addition to triggering the preclearance provisions, the amendment required that bilingual ballots be made available for certain named "language minorities"— Spanish-speaking persons, Asians, American Indians, and Alaskan natives—in jurisdictions that met the preceding criteria or in which the literacy rate of these groups fell below that of the general population.

Initially, most mainstream civil rights organizations opposed amending the Voting Rights Act to include Mexican Americans. They feared that broadening the act would invite opposition in the Congress and that tampering with the trigger mechanism for the act's preclearance provision would attract unwanted attention to the very sections of the act that had proved most useful to their cause. According to Thernstrom, black opposition finally disappeared when veteran civil rights lawyer Joseph Rauh, Jr., urged the Leadership Conference on Civil Rights to accept

4. Thernstrom, *Whose Votes Count?* p. 51.

5. *Torres* v. *Sachs*, 381 F. Supp. 309 (S.D.N.Y. 1984).

changes that would permit Mexican American coverage.

With black opposition removed, the amendments won overwhelming approval by both houses of Congress—despite the almost complete failure of Hispanic organizations to establish that Hispanics faced discrimination in voting in any way comparable to that faced by blacks in the South before 1965. Both the Justice Department and the U.S. Commission on Civil Rights questioned whether Mexican Americans deserved coverage. Assistant Attorney General for Civil Rights J. Stanley Pottinger, Jr., testified, "The Department of Justice has concluded that the evidence does not require expansion based on the record currently before us. In other words, that record is not compelling."[6] The Civil Rights Commission noted that statistics on Hispanic voting " 'do not paint the shocking picture that, for example, 1965 statistics on Mississippi did.' "[7] Nevertheless, members of the House and Senate Judiciary committees, which heard testimony on the Voting Rights Act amendments, accepted uncritically the testimony of MALDEF and other Hispanic witnesses.

Contrary to MALDEF's claim that Mexican Americans had been systematically excluded from participating in politics, the facts told a different story. From at least 1960 on, presidential candidates had aggressively courted Hispanic voters. In Texas, where voting discrimination against Mexican Americans was alleged to have been greatest, Mexican Americans had never been barred from casting their votes in Democratic primaries as blacks had been in the Deep South. Thernstrom maintains that "[Mexican American] votes had become an important source of Democratic power by the late 19th Century."[8] Indeed, the New Mexico state legislature, in which scores of Hispanics had served since New Mexico had become a state in 1912, petitioned Congress to be exempted from inclusion, noting that "in the counties of New Mexico where most of the people of Spanish descent live, the voter registration and the number of those citizens voting at primary and general election are the largest in the state."[9] Moreover, Mexican American candidates had run for statewide office—with varying degrees of success—in California, Texas, New Mexico, and Arizona. At the time the Voting Rights Act amendments were passed, two Mexican Americans served as governors in the United States, Jerry Apodaca in New Mexico and Raul Castro in Arizona, a state in which Mexican Americans constituted slightly more than 10 percent of the population; one Mexican American was a U.S. Senator, Joseph Montoya of New Mexico; and five Hispanics were members of Congress: Henry B. Gonzales and Kika de la

---

6. U.S., Congress, Senate, Committee on the Judiciary, Subcommittee on Constitutional Rights, *Extension of the Voting Rights Act of 1965 Hearings*, 94th Cong., 1st sess., 1975, p. 544.

7. U.S., Commission on Civil Rights, "Expansion of the Coverage of the Voting Rights Act," staff memorandum, 5 June 1975, as cited in Thernstrom, *Whose Votes Count?* p. 55.

8. Thernstrom, *Whose Votes Count?* p. 56.

9. Joint Memorial 17, passed by the New Mexico state Senate 35-0 and the state House of Representatives 39-2.

Garza of Texas, Edward Roybal of California, Manuel Lujan of New Mexico, and Herman Badillo of New York. Ironically, most of these men represented jurisdictions that were added to those subject to the Voting Rights Act in 1975—ostensibly because these jurisdictions had limited the opportunities to elect Hispanics.

Hundreds of Mexican Americans held local office as well. One study cites 700 Mexican American local officials in 1971 in Texas alone; and in 12 of the 13 Texas counties with the largest Mexican American concentrations, the county commissions were controlled by Mexican Americans.[10] Says Thernstrom, "This situation was in glaring contrast with the Deep South prior to the Voting Rights Act, where the existence of large black population had not forced white racists to share power with blacks. In fact, it was precisely in the areas of greatest black concentration that white supremacy thrived most."[11] No mention of these facts was made during the hearings.

Mexican Americans in Texas did face some harassment in voting, but those problems were not universal or even nearly so. As one lobbyist admitted to Thernstrom in a confidential interview, " 'What we found, we portrayed . . . as a giant, statewide pattern, which it really wasn't.' "[12] Witnesses cited incidents of abuse from a handful of Texas counties out of more than 254 in the state, most notably Frio, Uvalde, and La Salle. Witnesses charged that Mexican

Americans did not receive bilingual assistance at the polls; that Mexican American voters were given misinformation on polling places and voting procedures; that Mexican American voters were harassed at the polls and that Mexican American poll watchers received similar treatment.[13] These abuses, while serious, did not constitute the same kind of denial of the right to vote that had provoked Congress in 1965 to usurp the right of southern states to make and enforce their own election laws. Nonetheless, Congress went ahead to extend the burdensome strictures of the Voting Rights Act to jurisdictions in which Mexican Americans and other Hispanics lived. More than 375 jurisdictions were added to those already covered under the special provisions of the act.

THE NEW ENTITLEMENTS

The decision to grant Hispanics the same extraordinary protections that southern black voters had been given did not occur in a public policy vacuum. Between the mid-1960s and the mid-1970s a dramatic shift took place on the meaning of discrimination. Indeed, this shift in definitions made it possible for MALDEF and other Hispanic organizations to claim—on the basis of quite shallow evidence—that Mexican Americans and other Hispanics were systematically being denied the right to vote. The civil rights legislation of the 1960s was based on the principle that

10. Cited in Thernstrom, *Whose Votes Count?* p. 56.
11. Thernstrom, *Whose Votes Count?* p. 57.
12. Ibid., p. 56.

13. U.S., Congress, House, Committee on the Judiciary, Subcommittee on Civil and Constitutional Rights, *Hearings on the Extension of the Voting Rights Act of 1965*, 94th Cong., 1st sess., 1975, pp. 880-83.

race, color, sex, national origin, or religion should not be an impediment to the enjoyment of rights entitled to all persons in this society. The principle underlying all of the laws passed during the 1960s to protect civil rights was that the rules that applied to one group—namely, whites—should apply to all other groups, whether in employment, education, housing, or voting.

By 1975, the civil rights movement had changed its goals. It was no longer sufficient that the same rules apply to whites and blacks, men and women. In fact, the civil rights movement now urged that the rules themselves be changed so that minorities and women could compete under separate standards, so long as the results sought would improve the status of these groups. In the mid-1960s, the byword was equal opportunity; by 1975, it had become equal results. Everything was viewed in terms of the group's right to its share of the pie. A "fair share" came to mean a share equal to the group's proportion of the population. This definition applied whether one was talking about the distribution of jobs, the racial composition of schools and neighborhoods, or the voting rates of minorities. If minorities did not vote in the same proportion as nonminorities, discrimination was presumed to be the cause. Moreover, by 1975 the right to vote was being equated with the right to elect minority candidates. The voting process was no longer the focus; the voting outcome was.

In this context, it is not surprising that Congress declared Hispanics the victims of voting discrimination. It was not essential to show that Mexi-

can Americans were being kept from casting their votes because of their ethnicity. All that was really necessary was for Hispanic organizations to demonstrate that proportionally fewer Hispanics voted and that fewer Hispanic candidates were elected than non-Hispanic whites. The fact that fewer Mexican Americans were eligible to vote because far fewer of them were citizens apparently made no difference. MALDEF argued that Mexican Americans were underrepresented, and that was sufficient rationale for Congress to fundamentally change the way elections could be conducted in more than 375 jurisdictions in the nation. MALDEF's victory extended the extraordinary protections of the Voting Rights Act to non-Hispanic groups as well: to Asians, American Indians, and Alaskan natives. Because of MALDEF's efforts, these specific groups became entitled to ballots in their own languages (though other non-English-speaking groups were not given this same right). In addition, the jurisdictions in which members of these groups lived became subject to extensive monitoring of their electoral processes.

NATIONWIDE APPLICATION

The 1975 Voting Rights Act amendments extended the special provisions of the act for an additional seven years. The 1982 amendments, however, went beyond a simple extension as they expanded the special protection of the act to cover minorities in all political jurisdictions, not just those with literacy tests and low voter turnout.

As noted earlier, the "right to vote" had been interpreted by court decisions to mean the right to elect members of one's own racial or ethnic group, although this principle had been applied only to jurisdictions covered by the preclearance provision. Under the 1982 amendments, this standard became part of the act that applied to all states and political jurisdictions. The only way for a political jurisdiction to prove that its voting procedures were nondiscriminatory would be to show "the extent to which members of a protected class have been elected to office in the state or political subdivision."[14] The practical effect of the 1982 amendments was to make it possible for minority groups to challenge virtually any practice that might result in fewer minorities being elected to office, especially in at-large voting and in multimember districts. Black and Hispanic civil rights groups—long critical of at-large voting and multimember districts—would now be able to challenge these practices everywhere in the country.

THE SEARCH FOR
SAFE HISPANIC SEATS

Hispanic organizations cite the changes in the Voting Rights Act as a major factor in the growth of Hispanic political power, but the real winners may be Hispanic political operatives, not Hispanics themselves. In its twenty-year anniversary report, issued in 1988, MALDEF credits the Voting Rights Act with its victory in a series of suits it filed to end at-large voting and multimember districts in

Texas, New Mexico, and elsewhere. MALDEF claims it was "actively involved in redrawing election districts at the local level based on the 1980 Census," citing a major victory in a Chicago redistricting case that led to the court-ordered creation of four Hispanic wards "which changed the political future of Chicago."[15] In 1985, the U.S. Department of Justice filed suit concerning a redistricting plan for the Los Angeles City Council, which forced the city to create a heavily Hispanic district from which a Mexican American ultimately was elected. A similar suit in 1988 against Los Angeles County also charged that Hispanics were being denied the right to elect a Hispanic member of the L.A. County Board of Supervisors.

Indeed, more Hispanic seats have been created because of the Voting Rights Act and more Hispanics have been elected to office from such districts. The effort currently under way to create new, safe districts as a result of reapportionment from the 1990 census is likely to add dozens of Hispanic elected officials in California, Texas, New York, Illinois, and elsewhere. But the growing number of Hispanic electoral districts is not necessarily an indication of greater Hispanic political participation—at least not as measured in actual voting. At the national level, the Hispanic voting rate was lower in 1990 than in 1976. Of course, a smaller percentage of all Hispanics were eligible to vote in 1990 because a

14. 42 U.S.C. 1973, § 2(a).

15. Mexican American Legal Defense and Education Fund, "MALDEF: The First Twenty Years, 1968-1988" (Report, Mexican American Legal Defense and Education Fund, 1989), p. 9.

smaller proportion were citizens, due to rising immigration levels and low naturalization rates. Yet Hispanic leaders cite low voting rates as proof of discrimination, even though such figures are based on population numbers that include a huge percentage of noncitizens ineligible to vote. This perceived discrimination in turn justifies creating safe Hispanic seats.

The manipulation of immigration data to create Hispanic electoral seats continues to provoke controversy, especially when it involves illegal aliens. Legislative seats are apportioned on the basis of population figures determined by the Census Bureau, which counts citizens and noncitizens alike. States with large numbers of immigrants and illegal aliens, like California, benefit from this practice at the expense of states with few immigrants. The number of seats in the U.S. House of Representatives, for example, is fixed at 435, which are apportioned among the states according to population. Those states that have experienced population growth from immigration will gain congressional seats through reapportionment. Recently, some states that will lose seats in the current reapportionment sued, charging that illegal aliens should not be counted to apportion legislative districts, but the Supreme Court upheld the practice.[16] Nonetheless, many people find it objectionable that growing Hispanic political clout is based at least partially on granting political representation to people who have no legal right to be here.

The practice has other consequences as well. Political scientist Peter Skerry warns that using illegal aliens to create safe minority voting districts will result in "rotten boroughs, with large and growing numbers of 'constituents' unable to vote." Politicians who represent these districts can act with impunity even when their actions are clearly detrimental to the interests of their nonfranchised constituents. What is more, Skerry maintains, "the officeholders who represent such districts are more likely to be responsive to the politicians who designed them than to the people who live in them."[17]

Efforts to create safe Hispanic districts in California illustrate Skerry's point. In one recent election, for example, only 28 people cast ballots in one Hispanic precinct, compared with an average of 146 votes in Anglo precincts in the same election.[18] The precinct was located in a district created specifically to give Hispanics a safe city council seat, one in which Hispanics constitute the majority of eligible voters, following a successful 1985 suit brought by the U.S. Justice Department under the Voting Rights Act. Gloria Molina was elected in 1986 to represent the new district. Like most efforts to create safe Hispanic seats, the drawing of district lines was based on population figures rather than figures based on the

16. *Ridge* v. *Verity*, 715 F. Supp 1308 (W.D. Pa. 1989); *Federation for American Immigration Reform* v. *Klutznick*, 486 F. Supp. 564 (D.D.C. 1980), appeal dismissed, 447 U.S. 916 (1980).

17. Peter Skerry, "Keeping Immigrants in the Political Sweatshops," *Wall Street Journal*, 6 Nov. 1989.

18. Marita Hernandez, "Toward Equality: Exploring a World of Difference," *Los Angeles Times*, 13 Feb. 1989.

number of citizens able to vote. Consequently, the district comprises about 200,000 residents—the same number as in non-Hispanic districts —but the number of registered voters in the district in 1989 was only about 38,000, compared with about 118,000 in a comparable Anglo district.[19] The discrepancy in registration is largely due to the presence of so many immigrants in Molina's district, about half of whom are illegal aliens. The effect, however, is to concentrate power in a handful of Hispanic elected officials who represent districts consisting of relatively few eligible voters. Nor do such "rotten boroughs" necessarily advance the interests of Hispanics seeking political office, as another Los Angeles voting rights case illustrates.

In 1988, MALDEF—later joined by the Justice Department—filed suit in federal court alleging that the L.A. County Board of Supervisors discriminated against Hispanic voters. Los Angeles County, the largest county in the nation with 8.7 million residents, is governed by a five-member board of supervisors. Even though 33 percent of the population of Los Angeles County is Hispanic, no Hispanic has been elected to the board in more than a hundred years. After a long trial in which Hispanic organizations testified that the failure to elect a Hispanic since 1875 constituted proof of discrimination, a federal court found that the board of supervisors had discriminated in drawing election district lines and ordered parties in the suit to submit

new plans that would redress Hispanic grievances. In an ironic twist, one day after the court declared that no Hispanic could be elected without creating a new, safe district, a Hispanic woman was the top vote-getter for a vacant seat on the board in an election held using the old, supposedly discriminatory district lines. These election results were voided, however, when the Ninth Circuit Court of Appeals upheld a lower-court decision and ordered a new election. The appeals court also accepted a redistricting plan drawn up by MALDEF, which was so badly gerrymandered that it looked contrived to include the largest number of Hispanic Democrats that it could.[20] One Hispanic whose residence was left out of the new district, however, was Sarah Flores, the Hispanic Republican who had placed first in the earlier election. Although the court ruled that Flores could still run in the new district even though she did not live within the new lines, her base of support had been eroded.

In a four-way race in January 1991, which included Councilwoman Molina and State Senator Art Torres, Flores came in third. Molina and Torres competed in a runoff the following month, which Molina won with 55 percent of the vote. Voter turnout was light, however; only 23 percent of those registered voted, but even this figure overestimates how few people actually participated in the election. The new district is made up of a population of about 975,000 persons of voting age, but fewer than 83,000

19. Interview with Carl Berry, Los Angeles Elections Division, 23 Oct. 1990.

20. "LA's Poodle District," *Wall Street Journal*, 21 Oct. 1990.

people voted. No doubt, participation was so low because many who live in the district are not U.S. citizens. Nonetheless, it is difficult to understand how Hispanic leaders could herald the election as a major victory in the fight for Hispanic political participation when fewer than 1 in 10 adults even voted.

Nor are ethnically gerrymandered districts the only method being used to guarantee Hispanic seats. In some areas where Hispanics are so residentially integrated that it is virtually impossible to create Hispanic districts, the courts have allowed cumulative voting in at-large elections to increase the likelihood that Hispanics will be elected. In Alamogordo, New Mexico, for example, a consent decree adopted in the wake of a vote-dilution lawsuit brought on behalf of Hispanic plaintiffs established cumulative voting for three at-large seats on the city council. Under the court-approved change, voters could cast all three of their votes for one candidate or split their votes among two or three candidates, under the assumption that minority voters would be more likely to cast multiple votes for a single minority candidate to ensure the election of someone of their own ethnic group. In the 1987 election following the consent decree, a Hispanic was elected to the Alamogordo city council even though fewer voters reported voting for the Hispanic candidate than for some of the losing non-Hispanic candidates. The winning results were obtained because more than half of those who voted for the Hispanic candidate cast more than one vote for her. Ironically,

even though Hispanics were overwhelmingly likely to have cast multiple votes for the Hispanic candidate, she would not have been elected without votes from non-Hispanic whites since Hispanics constituted barely 14 percent of the voters in the election (even though they represented about 21 percent of the voting-age population). Nearly 22 percent of the non-Hispanic whites who voted in the election voted for the Hispanic candidate, ensuring her election.[21]

WINNERS OR LOSERS?

The extension of the Voting Rights Act to Hispanic voters produced certain trade-offs. As with other ethnic entitlements, such as affirmative action in employment, voting rights protection grants certain benefits but at the expense of accepting what could become a self-fulfilling prophecy—that Hispanics are permanently disadvantaged. Under the act, Hispanics are treated as if they are now and will continue to be the victims of widespread, persistent, and systemic discrimination in the political arena, even though the facts suggest otherwise. Six Hispanics have been elected governor in three states in this century even though they do not constitute anything like a majority of voters in any state. In Florida, where Governor Bob Martinez was elected in 1986, Hispanics—mostly Cubans—

21. Richard L. Engstrom, Delbert A. Taebel, and Richard L. Cole, "Cumulative Voting as a Remedy for Minority Vote Dilution: The Case of Alamogordo, New Mexico," *Journal of Law and Politics*, 5(3):469-97 (Spring 1989).

made up only 11 percent of the population, less than one-third of whom voted in the election.[22] Clearly, these Hispanic candidates have been elected not as ethnic representatives but because a majority of voters believed the candidates' political qualifications—not their ethnicity—was relevant.

Even in places where Hispanics make up a large portion of the population, factors other than discrimination may explain why no Hispanics hold office. In Los Angeles County, for example, a Hispanic has run for the board of supervisors only once, in 1959 when Edward Roybal, now a member of the U.S. House of Representatives, lost the election in a runoff. The Voting Rights Act notwithstanding, it is still not possible to elect a Hispanic if Hispanic candidates do not run. Nor does it suffice to say that Hispanic candidates will be discouraged from running unless they can be guaranteed safe districts in which Hispanics constitute a majority of voters; that obviously did not stop the Hispanics who were elected governors of their respective states.

The notion of proportional representation that undergirds arguments in most voting rights cases is fraught with potential dangers. If Hispanics are entitled to Hispanic elected officials in areas where their proportion of the population is high, what about areas in which there are few Hispanics? The natural corollary to the notion that Hispanics can best represent the interests of Hispanics is that non-Hispanics can best represent the interests of non-Hispanics. This is a dangerous game for any minority to play.

The danger in buying into the notion of safe Hispanic districts is more than just the limiting effect it will have on the aspirations of those Hispanics who want to run for public office. There are more vital issues at stake. The success of the Hispanic voting rights strategy depends on dissuading Hispanics from integrating with the larger community. But this runs counter to the choices Hispanics are already freely making. As Douglas Massey and Nancy Denton point out, Hispanics are not highly segregated even in areas with large Hispanic populations, including Los Angeles, San Antonio, and Miami. "Indeed," they say, "a lack of high segregation on any dimension is the most common pattern for Hispanics."[23] Are Hispanic leaders prepared to argue that it is in Hispanics' interest to remain congregated in inner-city barrios in order to enlarge the roster of Hispanic elected officials? Those barrios now are occupied increasingly by new immigrants, many of them illegal. If middle-class Hispanics continue to choose to leave Hispanic neighborhoods, Hispanic organizations will be forced to rely even more heavily on noncitizens to demonstrate large concentrations of presumably underrepresented Hispanic voters.

22. U.S., Department of Commerce, Bureau of the Census, *Voting and Registration in the Election of November 1986*, Current Population Reports, series P-20, no. 414 (Washington, DC: Government Printing Office, 1987).

23. Douglas S. Massey and Nancy A. Denton, "Hypersegregation in U.S. Metropolitan Areas: Black and Hispanic Segregation along Five Dimensions," *Demography*, 26(3):383 (Aug. 1989).

The history of Hispanic involvement with the Voting Rights Act is a clear example of short-term gains purchased at the expense of long-range achievement. Hispanic leaders were quite successful in convincing legislators and the courts that Hispanics were politically powerless without the extraordinary intervention of the federal government. But in order to keep federal protection, Hispanics must continue to fail. If Hispanics move beyond the confines of inner-city barrios into middle-class suburbs, as they are already doing, will federal courts persist in creating gerrymandered districts that scoop up scattered Hispanic voters in a broad geographic area as the court did in Los Angeles County? And will Hispanics who have achieved middle-class status benefit from having their political fortunes tied to impoverished immigrants? At least one Hispanic activist suggests that that is exactly the point of the effort in Los Angeles County:

It ties the fortunes of the Latino middle class to those of lower-income Latinos. The Latino middle class, the chief beneficiary of the civil rights movement, can no longer cold-shoulder the interests of the Latino poor without paying a political price, because the two now constitute one political community.[24]

It is an odd reversal of the traditional ethnic model in the United States. Instead of encouraging those at the bottom to climb higher, it pulls down those who have already risen. There will be no winners if Hispanics accept this strategy.

24. Rodolfo Acuña, "The Fight for the Spoils," *Los Angeles Times*, 12 Aug. 1990.

ANNALS, *AAPSS*, 523, September 1992

Affirmative Action in the Labor Market

By DAVE M. O'NEILL and JUNE O'NEILL

ABSTRACT: One of the most controversial tools of federal antidiscrimination policy in the employment area is the affirmative action program conducted by the Office of Federal Contract Compliance Programs (OFCCP). The OFCCP requires firms holding federal government contracts to set numerical hiring goals for minorities and women. Firms that fail to meet their targets face the threat of contract cancellation. The setting of hiring goals requires estimation of available pools of qualified minorities and women, which in practice cannot be done with any precision. Studies show no clear positive link between gains in minority earnings and the affirmative action efforts of the OFCCP. Current earnings differentials between blacks and whites appear to be more closely tied to differences in work-related skills than to labor market discrimination. The growing premium on skill in our economy underscores the need for improvement in the schooling of blacks and other minorities suffering educational deficiencies.

Dave M. O'Neill received his Ph.D. in economics from Columbia University. Among his publications are The Federal Government and Manpower *(1973);* Discrimination against Handicapped Persons *(1976); and* Education in the United States: 1940-1983 *(1985).*

June O'Neill, professor of economics at Baruch College and the Graduate Center, City University of New York, and director of the Center for Business and Government, received her Ph.D. in economics from Columbia University. In 1986-87, she was research director of the U.S. Commission on Civil Rights.

NOTE: June O'Neill worked on this article while she was a recipient of a John M. Olin faculty fellowship.

A major goal of the sweeping federal antidiscrimination policies that were introduced in the 1960s was the elimination of discrimination in the hiring, promotion, and pay of minorities and women. Prior to the passage of the Civil Rights Act of 1964, many states had enacted fair employment practices laws.[1] These states were all outside the South, however. In the South, rigid racial separation prevailed and discrimination was openly practiced, often condoned by state and local governments.

In the decade following passage of the Civil Rights Act, blacks made rapid economic progress relative to whites. For example, the annual earnings of full-time black male workers increased from 63 percent to 73 percent of that of white male workers, while among women workers the black-white earnings ratio rose from 68 percent to 90 percent.[2] This was not the first period of black economic progress. The relative earnings of blacks had increased dramatically in the 1940s. The gains from the mid-1960s to the mid-1970s were large, however, and careful study has shown that federal civil rights policy had a substantial effect on the outcome.[3]

Proponents of affirmative action frequently point to the post-1964 gains of blacks as evidence of the beneficial effect of affirmative action. Affirmative action was only a part of the civil rights effort, however, and it was not fully implemented before 1972, when the period of rapid gains for blacks was beginning to wane.

In this article, we first examine the impact of federal affirmative action policy on the relative economic status of those it is intended to help, and we try to distinguish this effect from the influence of other civil rights policies as well as that of other factors such as skill differentials. We then discuss the extent to which current differentials in earnings reflect labor market discrimination as opposed to other explanations and address the question of whether the continuing economic progress of minorities and women requires an affirmative action policy.

The ultimate goals of the civil rights movement now have universal support. Few quarrel with the right of individuals to bring suit if they believe they have been discriminated against. Affirmation action, however, is one component of civil rights activity that has been the subject of intense and frequently divisive debate. It involves a degree of government regulation and supervision of private employment decisions that is unusual in the United States. Ironically, it can involve government sponsorship of racial preferences in employment that to many critics violates the fundamental rights of equality of treatment before the law. It is, there-

1. Thirteen states had enforceable antidiscrimination laws by 1959. See June O'Neill et al., *The Economic Progress of Black Men in America*, Clearing House Publication 91 (Washington, DC: Commission on Civil Rights, Oct. 1986), p. 108 and studies cited therein.

2. Calculated from data in U.S., Department of Commerce, Bureau of the Census, Current Population Reports, series P-60, published annually.

3. John J. Donohue III and James Heckman, "Continuous versus Episodic Change: The Impact of Civil Rights Policy on the Economic Status of Blacks," *Journal of Economic Literature*, 29:1603-43 (Dec. 1991).

fore, important to distinguish the effects of affirmative action from those of other less contentious aspects of civil rights policy, so that benefits can be weighed against costs.

ENFORCEMENT

The major federal program that enforces affirmative action in the private sector is administered by the Office of Federal Contract Compliance Programs (OFCCP). It has jurisdiction over all firms with federal contracts of $50,000 or more and with at least 50 employees. Federal contractors are a significant group of firms, accounting for about 30 percent of private sector employment.[4]

The OFCCP is not the only governmental body concerned with discrimination in employment. The Equal Employment Opportunity Commission (EEOC) has broad responsibility for investigating complaints of discrimination in all aspects of employment and compensation as prohibited by Title VII of the Civil Rights Act of 1964. Since 1972, the act has covered all organizations with 15 employees or more, in all sectors of the economy. The major enforcement weapon of the EEOC is the right to bring suit on behalf of plaintiffs. To help detect discrimination, the EEOC may review the racial and gender composition of firms as shown in the annual reports filed by all larger firms. Sometimes numerical hiring targets for minorities or women have been required as a result of court decisions. While some of the EEOC's activities resemble affirmative ac-

tion, however, it does not itself conduct ongoing regulation of the minority employment levels of firms in the same sense as the OFCCP, which is the focus of our discussion here.[5]

The Office of Federal Contract Compliance (OFCC) was established by President Johnson in the fall of 1965 under Executive Order 11246.[6] The order recognized the special leverage that the government might have over federal contractors by requiring not only that they do not discriminate but also that they take affirmative action and ensure that applicants and employees are treated without regard to race or ethnicity. Women were added to the list of protected groups in 1967 through Executive Order 11375. In 1973 and 1974, the disabled and Vietnam veterans were covered by affirmative action, and the OFCC became the OFCCP. In 1978, the OFCCP and 11 other contract compliance agencies were consolidated under the OFCCP and became a single agency within the Department of Labor.

Initially, affirmative action was narrowly interpreted as an exhortation to contractors to make an extra effort to recruit black workers. Although contractors were pressed to do more minority hiring, specific nu-

5. Many state and local governments have affirmative action programs similar to that of the OFCCP. The federal government also has a program for its own employees.

6. The first executive order prohibiting discrimination by federal contractors was signed by President Roosevelt in 1941. Presidents Truman and Kennedy also signed related executive orders. See Hugh Davis Graham, "The Origins of Affirmative Action: Civil Rights and the Regulatory State," this issue of *The Annals* of the American Academy of Political and Social Science.

4. O'Neill et al., *Economic Progress of Black Men*, p. 100.

merical hiring goals were not imposed. But, following court rulings that eased concerns about the legality of numerical standards, and modifications by the executive branch, the role of the OFCCP became more activist and the meaning of affirmative action was transformed. The setting of specific numerical employment goals for minorities became a central aspect of the program, and firms were required to adjust their hiring patterns to make a good-faith effort to achieve these goals. The OFCCP had the power to enforce compliance through its authority to cancel a firm's contract with the federal government. Thus the objective of affirmative action shifted from the attainment of a discrimination-free hiring process to attainment of specific employment outcomes.[7]

Reflecting on this change in the meaning of affirmative action and the role of the OFCC, Laurence Silberman, the Under Secretary of Labor from 1970 to 1973, later commented:

We wished to create a generalized, firm, but gentle pressure to balance the residue of discrimination. Unfortunately, the pressure numerical standards generate cannot be generalized or gentle; ... I now realize that the distinction we saw between goals and timetables on the one hand, and unconstitutional quotas on the other, was not valid. Our use of numerical standards in pursuit of equal opportunity has led to the very quotas guaranteeing equal results that we initially wished to avoid.[8]

Implementation

Since 1968, the OFCCP has required federal contractors to submit an affirmative action plan and to update it each year. The plan contains a narrative stating detailed numerical employment goals for minorities and women based on estimates of their availability in the relevant labor market. This availability analysis is crucial to the process.

In conducting the numerical analysis, a firm is required to divide workers into broadly homogeneous job groups corresponding roughly to major occupational categories. The OFCCP specifies eight factors that the firm should use in determining the availability of each minority and of women for each occupational category. The relevant labor market area is defined in terms of the reasonable area for recruitment for an occupational category. Typically, the more skilled and professional the occupation, the larger is the relevant geographic area.

To estimate the number of qualified minorities and women in a specific area and occupational category, a data source such as the most recent decennial census of population is used. However, the indicators of qualifications available in the census are quite general. They do not go beyond years of schooling completed, occupational category, and age. Information such as might be obtained

7. A similar development occurred in the EEOC's approach to the enforcement of Section VII. A Supreme Court ruling—*Griggs* v. *Duke Power* (1972)—held that a statistical disparity can be illegal even without discriminatory intent, if it results from any aspect of the firm's hiring procedures.

8. Laurence Silberman, "The Road to Racial Quotas," *Wall Street Journal*, 11 Aug. 1977. Used by permission.

from a qualifications test or a college or high school transcript is not available in the census and is not likely to be used in the OFCCP availability analysis.[9]

An indication of how general the concept of qualifications can be is revealed by the OFCCP's treatment of the construction industry. For this industry, the OFCCP, rather than the contractor, performs the availability analysis. Its method is simple—the proportion of minority workers in the local labor force is taken as the measurement of the availability of minorities qualified for construction occupations.[10]

After conducting an availability analysis, the firm must compare the availability of each protected group for each job category with the utilization of each group. If a significant discrepancy is revealed, the firm must present a "timetable" for closing the gap. Firms persistently out of compliance are first offered recommendations by the OFCCP for changing their recruitment procedures. If this effort fails, a hearing before an administrative judge is held, which

9. Even if available, information such as test scores or even schooling may be impermissible for determining qualifications. Both high school graduation and attainment of a particular score on two general intelligence tests were disqualified by the U.S. Supreme Court as requirements for admission into training programs for skilled crafts in *Griggs* v. *Duke Power Company*.

10. The goal for women in construction is a national constant, 6.9 percent. See Finis Welch, "Affirmative Action and Discrimination," in *The Question of Discrimination: Racial Inequality in the U.S. Labor Market*, ed. Steven Shulman and William Darity, Jr. (Middletown, CT: Wesleyan University Press, 1989), p. 144, n. 4.

will either resolve the dispute or lead to a recommendation to the Secretary of Labor to cancel the firm's federal contract. As a last resort, the firm can appeal the cancellation in a federal court.

Expected effects

The basic premise of affirmative action is that significant numbers of minority workers or women who can qualify for better and higher-paying jobs in the contractor sector are either working outside the contractor sector or in the contractor sector at lower-paying jobs, or they are unemployed. Because of ignorance or prejudice or both, federal contractors do not voluntarily hire or promote more of these qualified minority or women workers. The role of affirmative action is to provide both information, via the availability analysis, and incentive, via the threat of losing the government contract. It is expected that contractors will respond by increasing their employment of protected groups, and it is assumed that the increase in demand will result in higher wages for these workers. In addition, since these additional minority workers are assumed to have the productivity to match the higher wages, overall real gross national product is expected to increase due to a better allocation of resources.

The scenario sketched may not be valid, however. The situation could be one in which large numbers of qualified minority-group members or women are not underutilized, yet the OFCCP availability analysis, because it is based on crude indicators and methodology, will still indicate significant underutilization. Many federal contractors will then find themselves out of compliance. Voluntary attempts to hire more qualified minorities or women will be largely unsuccessful, and some contractors may hire unqualified workers to avoid pressures and penalties. This response is likely to be resisted because it would significantly reduce the firm's profits, especially if the firm is smaller and in a competitive industry. Another possible effect of this scenario is that qualified minority workers with good jobs in the noncontractor sector will be attracted to the contractor sector for immediate wage gains even though their long-run wage gains will not be large.

In both scenarios, the degree of compliance pressure that the OFCCP puts on contractors will be an important determinant of actual contractor behavior. Jonathan Leonard reports that process studies of the contractor program generally concluded that it was ineffective and weakly enforced in its early years, 1966-72.[11] The ultimate sanction—debarment from future federal contracts—seldom occurred;[12] the first disbarment applied to a contractor did not occur until 1974.[13] Even in 1980, when the OFCCP was at its peak in terms of resources,

and the incumbent administration believed strongly in "goals and timetables," only 2.5 percent of all federal contractors were subject to compliance reviews.

Enforcement of affirmative action is no easy matter. The task confronting both the contractors and the OFCCP is difficult if not impossible to accomplish without error. Productivity differences between workers cannot be measured with accuracy. Hence the pool of available minority and women workers who are qualified for specific jobs in an individual firm may not be knowable. Under these circumstances and without evidence of discriminatory behavior, a government agency in a democratic society may well be reluctant to take harsh measures against a firm just because it does not have the right numbers.

The two scenarios described illustrate different underlying situations. In the first, affirmative action would improve the relative economic status of women and minorities because there is an initial problem, namely, widespread discriminatory employment practices. In the second, although there is no substantial problem of underutilization, firms will still be prodded to increase their hiring of women and minorities—particularly for skilled jobs—because the crude measures of utilization available will tend to overestimate the number of qualified minorities.

Since it is possible for affirmative action to have a positive effect on the relative economic status of minorities under either scenario, we cannot readily distinguish between them on the basis of existing empirical evi-

11. Jonathan Leonard, "The Impact of Affirmative Action Regulation and Equal Employment Law on Black Employment," *Journal of Economic Perspectives*, 4:49 (Fall 1990).

12. Between 1978 and 1981, 27,000 compliance reviews at 11,000 different establishments resulted in only 26 debarments. Jonathan Leonard, "The Impact of Affirmative Action on Employment," *Journal of Labor Economics*, 2(4):447 (1984).

13. Leonard, "Impact of Affirmative Action Regulation," p. 49.

dence. Nonetheless, it seems plausible to assume that a finding of no effect on relative economic status is more consistent with the second scenario, while a finding of a positive effect is more consistent with the first scenario.

EMPIRICAL EVIDENCE

Two kinds of methodologies have been applied to study the effects of the affirmative action efforts of the OFCCP on the relative economic status of women and minorities. One uses administrative data from firms reporting to the EEOC and the OFCCP and compares changes in the distribution of minority and gender groups among employees in contractor and noncontractor firms. However, it is not possible with administrative data to determine directly if wage effects have occurred. The second approach uses economywide data on changes in the relative earnings of minorities and women and compares these changes with changes in program enforcement.

Studies using administrative data

If enforcement of numerical goals was effective in improving the relative economic status of groups protected by the OFCCP, one would expect to find that firms with federal contracts increased their relative employment of these groups by more than did firms that were not federal contractors. Moreover, the timing of the relative employment growth of minorities and women should coincide with

periods when the OFCCP was applying more resources to enforcement.

A finding of such employment effects is only a necessary condition for establishing the effectiveness of the OFCCP, however. Gains in employment of a minority group may reflect only a reshuffling from noncontractors to contractors without any relative wage gain. And even if some qualified minority individuals are upgraded by the shifts, the relative earnings of the entire minority group would not increase substantially unless the relative number affected was substantial.

Although the OFCC was established in the mid-1960s, significant enforcement of numerical minority hiring goals did not begin until the early 1970s. It took time for resources to be appropriated, for the concept of numerical hiring goals to evolve, and for the agencies to develop procedures for enforcing these goals. Leonard notes that enforcement activities by the OFCC became significantly more aggressive after 1973.[14] Data on the agency's resources also reveal relatively low levels of budget expenditures and positions in the early 1970s.[15]

After 1980, however, a sharp slowdown in real expenditures occurred, as OFCCP budget expenditures increased by less than the rate of inflation. Leonard argues that the Reagan administration, which was hostile to affirmative action as it had evolved

14. Ibid., p. 50.
15. In 1970, the OFCC had a staff of only 34 persons. In 1979, after consolidation of 11 agency offices with the OFCCP, positions numbered 1021. Donohue and Heckman, "Continuous versus Episodic Change," p. 1636, tab. 8.

TABLE 1

RATIO OF THE SHARE OF MINORITY OR FEMALE EMPLOYMENT TO THE SHARE
OF WHITE MALE EMPLOYMENT IN CONTRACTOR AND NONCONTRACTOR FIRMS

	Black Men		Black Women		White Women	
Year	Federal contractor	Noncontractor	Federal contractor	Noncontractor	Federal contractor	Noncontractor
1970	105.6	130.8	88.2	202.1	71.6	154.5
1974	118.3	132.4	112.1	224.3	74.2	157.4
1978	125.7	137.0	121.9	216.0	78.6	157.1
1980	123.5	137.7	134.5	218.0	81.5	142.6

SOURCE: Finis Welch, "Affirmative Action and Discrimination," in *The Question of Discrimination: Racial Inequality in the U.S. Labor Market*, ed. Steven Shulman and William Darity, Jr. (Middletown, CT: Wesleyan University Press, 1989), p. 177. Copyright 1989 by Wesleyan University Press by permission of University Press of New England. Reprinted by permission.

NOTE: Each ratio shown within the table is defined as follows: the numerator is the proportion of all minority (or women) workers employed by federal contractors (or noncontractors); the denominator is the share of white male workers employed by federal contractors (or noncontractors).

over the 1970s, almost stopped enforcement during the 1980s.[16] These historical developments suggest that if affirmative action did have an impact, it is most likely to be evident for the period 1974-80.

James Smith and Finis Welch have examined movements over time in the representation of black and female workers in firms that are federal contractors and in those that are not contractors. Their analysis is based on data filed by all firms required to report to the EEOC, and a summary of their findings is shown in Table 1. The ratios shown for each group are calculated so that a ratio of 100 signifies proportional representation; that is, the category of firms employs the same proportion of the minority group as it does of white males. As the ratios rise, the representation of the protected group increases relative to white males.

16. Leonard, "Impact of Affirmative Action Regulation," p. 58.

One key pattern to note is that while a significant shift in the distribution of black men toward federal contractors did occur between 1970 and 1974, the relative movement of black men to federal contractors slowed markedly between 1974 and 1980. Yet 1974-80 was the period when the OFCCP had a maximum of enforcement resources at its disposal and when we would expect to see maximum employment effects. The employment patterns for women, particularly black women, more closely coincide with the timing of changes in enforcement strength. Thus a simple comparison of changes in enforcement strength and changes in the employment of protected groups provides mixed evidence.

A number of studies have used administrative data to analyze patterns of employment change across the thousands of individual reporting firms, both contractor and noncontractor. The principle again is to compare the experience of federal contractors and noncontractors with respect to changes in their relative employment of protected groups. These studies, however, use multivariate analysis and therefore control for firm size, industry, and other factors that might contribute to employment changes. (The data shown in Table 1 are not adjusted for these factors.) In general, the studies find that federal contractors have increased their employment of black men relative to white men, and they have done so by more than the noncontractor firms that report to the EEOC. However, the measured effects differ in magnitude from study to study[17] and, although statistically significant, are not large enough to have produced any noticeable impact on the average relative earnings of black men.

It is difficult to draw any definite conclusions from the studies of administrative data. The aggregate data of Table 1 show a large relative increase in black male employment in the federal contractor sector, but only in the period prior to 1974, prior to the period of maximum OFCCP

enforcement power. The results of the multivariate analyses of microdata are not uniform, but some find an effect for the 1974-80 period. They do not eliminate the possibility that affirmative action had a positive impact, but neither do they provide strong evidence in favor of that possibility. It must be reiterated that the administrative data measure only employment gains in the federal contractor sector since data on wage gains are unavailable. As Donohue and Heckman stress, there is no close link between these employment shifts and overall improvements in the relative earnings of minorities.[18]

*Studies using
time-series data*

The second set of studies has the advantage of focusing directly on the changes over time in the relative earnings of protected groups and white males. Its major drawback, however, is that many different factors can influence the movement of earnings ratios over time, and it is therefore difficult to isolate the net effect of a particular influence, such as the OFCCP's affirmative action effort.

Figures 1-3 show trends over the period 1955-90 in relative earnings ratios for three comparison groups: black men to white men; black women to white women; and all women to all men. Examination of Figure 1 reveals a dramatic increase in the earnings of black men relative to white men between 1964 and 1974. (The relative earnings of black women also

---

17. Donohue and Heckman, "Continuous versus Episodic Change," pp. 1630-35, provides a review of the relevant studies, as does O'Neill et al., *Economic Progress of Black Men*, pp. 100-109. Some of the individual studies frequently cited are Orley Ashenfelter and James Heckman, "Measuring the Effect of an Anti-Discrimination Program," in *Evaluating the Labor Market Effects of Social Programs*, ed. Orley Ashenfelter and James Blum (Princeton, NJ: Princeton University, Industrial Relations Section, 1976), pp. 46-84; Leonard, "Impact of Affirmative Action on Employment," pp. 439-63; idem, "Employment and Occupational Advances under Affirmative Action," *Review of Economics and Statistics*, 66:377-85 (1984).

18. Donohue and Heckman, "Continuous versus Episodic Change," pp. 1630-35.

rose significantly, but for them the change represented a continuation of an ongoing increase.) The Civil Rights Act of 1964 made discrimination in employment illegal, and the time-series data suggest that it had a strong positive effect on the relative economic status of black men. Econometric studies by Richard Freeman, James Heckman, and others support this conclusion.[19] These authors attempt to measure other factors that might have influenced earnings ratios such as business cycles, economic growth rates, and black-white education differences. In a study of employment trends in South Carolina, Heckman and Paynor conclude:

Suddenly in 1964 blacks of both sexes became employed on a large scale. That year witnessed the implementation of Title VII of the 1964 Civil Rights Act. . . . Both the timing and the regression evidence suggest that government activity played an important role in integrating textiles.[20]

Some observers have taken this post-1964 increase in the ratio as evidence that the OFCCP's affirmative action program had a significant impact. However, both the timing of the effect—during the period 1964-74, during most of which the goals and

timetables approach had not yet been implemented—and its concentration in the South[21] strongly suggest it was the passage of the Civil Rights Act itself that produced the large increase in relative earnings.

Developments in the 1980s

The enforcement efforts of the OFCCP likely diminished during the 1980s. Adjusted for inflation, federal budget expenditures for this office declined by 28 percent from 1979 to 1989. The question then arises of whether the reduction in resources—as well as the lack of enthusiasm on the part of the Reagan administration—had negative consequences for the minorities and women targeted for affirmative action.

Figures 1-3 again show how three groups fared. Roughly speaking, black-white earnings ratios for men (Figure 1) and for women (Figure 2) reached a peak in the mid-1970s and since then have fluctuated, showing a slight tendency to decline. The ratio of women's earnings to men's, by contrast, which had failed to increase throughout the 1960s and 1970s, despite the anti-discrimination efforts, rose significantly during the 1980s (Figure 3).

Both the lack of convergence in the black-white earnings gap among men and the strong rise in the earnings of women relative to men appear to be the result of factors unrelated to affirmative action. During the 1980s, there was a sizable increase in the wage differential between skilled and unskilled workers. Studies have

19. Richard B. Freeman, "Changes in the Labor Market for Black Americans, 1948-1972", in *Brookings Papers on Economic Activity* ed. Arthur Okun and George Perry (Washington, DC: Brookings Institution, 1973), pp. 67-132; Donohue and Heckman, "Continuous versus Episodic Change," pp. 1603-43.

20. James Heckman and Brooks Paynor, "Determining the Impact of Federal Anti-Discrimination Policy on the Economic Status of Blacks: A Study of South Carolina," *American Economic Review*, 79(1): 173 (Mar. 1989).

21. Donohue and Heckman, "Continuous versus Episodic Change," pp. 1637-40.

FIGURE 1

BLACK-WHITE MALE EARNINGS RATIOS: YEAR-ROUND FULL-TIME WORKERS, 1955-90

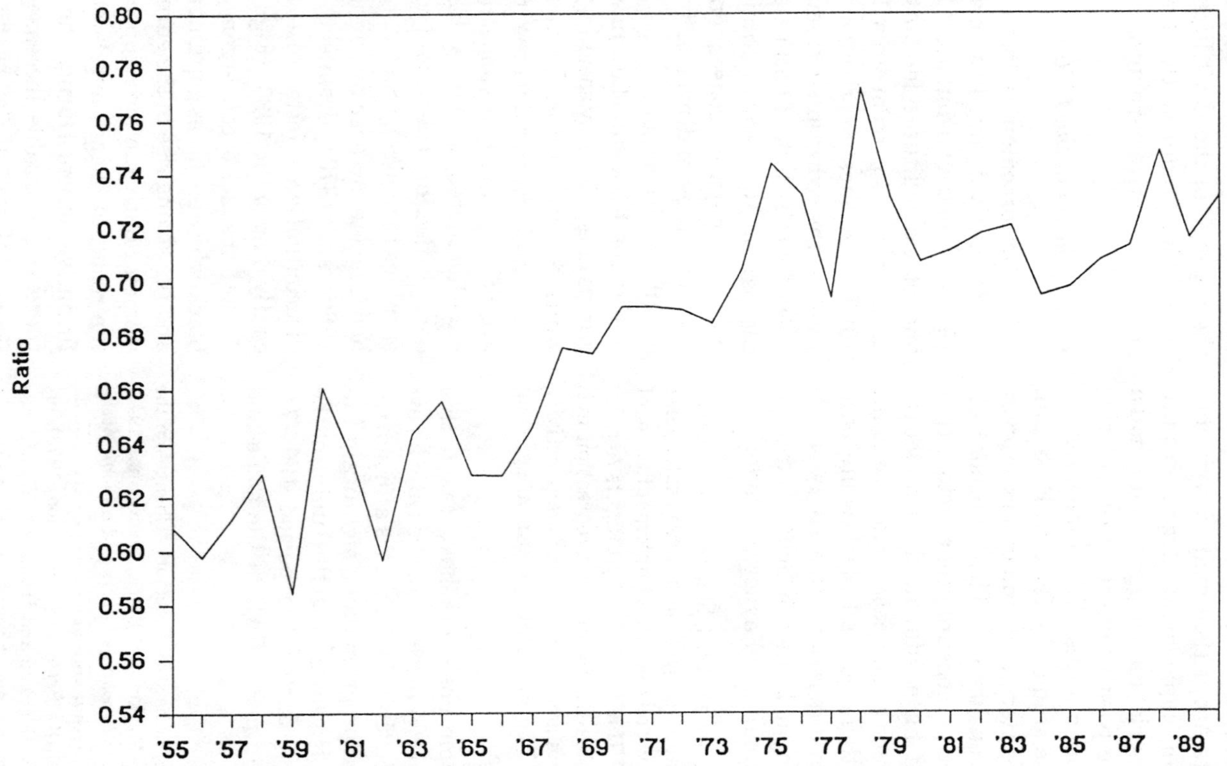

SOURCE: U.S., Department of Commerce, Bureau of the Census, Current Population Survey data.

FIGURE 2

BLACK-WHITE FEMALE EARNINGS RATIOS: YEAR-ROUND FULL-TIME WORKERS, 1955-90

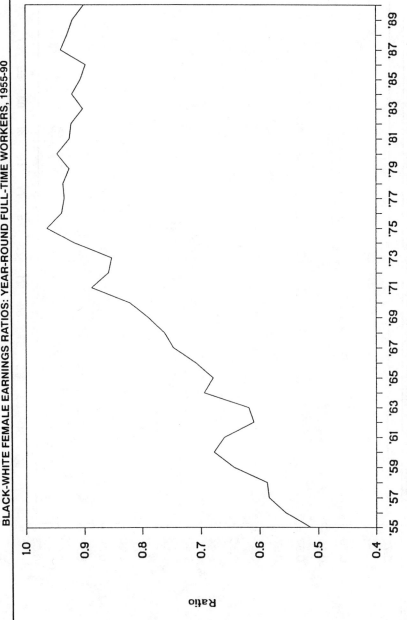

SOURCE: Bureau of the Census, Current Population Survey data.

99

FIGURE 3

FEMALE-MALE EARNINGS RATIOS: YEAR-ROUND FULL-TIME WORKERS, 1955-90

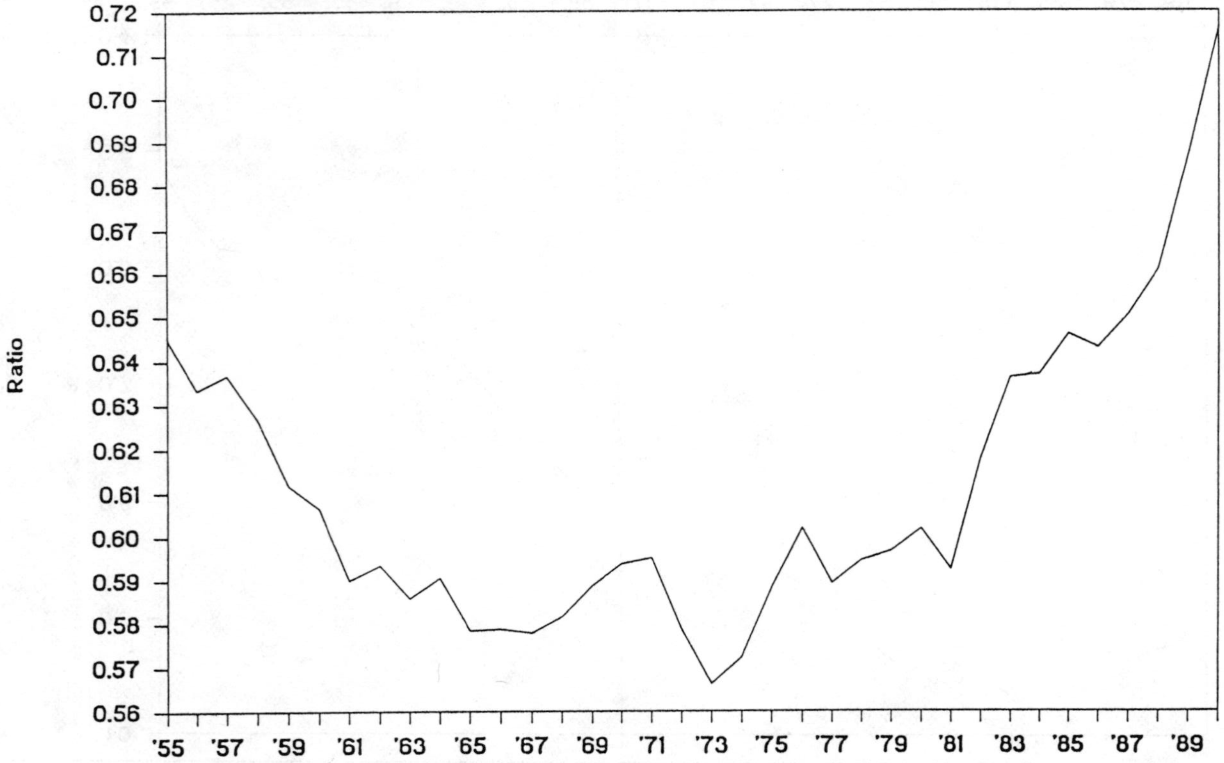

SOURCE: Bureau of the Census, Current Population Survey data.

TABLE 2

RATIOS OF HOURLY EARNINGS OF BLACK, HISPANIC, AND
ASIAN WORKERS TO THOSE OF WHITE NON-HISPANIC WORKERS, BY YEARS
OF SCHOOL COMPLETED AND GENDER, FOR WORKERS AGED 20-59 (1988-89)

Years of Schooling	White	Black	Hispanic	Asian
Men				
Total	1.000	.724	.743	1.024
8-11	1.000	.819	.809	.938
12	1.000	.777	.820	.887
13-15	1.000	.814	.859	.937
16 or more	1.000	.801	.843	.927
Women				
Total	1.000	.903	.864	1.141
8-11	1.000	.928	.929	1.082
12	1.000	.942	.927	1.045
13-15	1.000	.942	.963	1.064
16 or more	1.000	1.011	.964	1.022

SOURCE: Calculated from the microdata files of U.S., Department of Commerce, Bureau of the Census, Current Population Survey, Mar. 1989; ibid., Mar. 1990.

NOTE: Hourly earnings ratios are averaged over calendar years 1988 and 1989.

shown that this structural shift in labor market demand can account for most of the trends in the racial earnings ratio since the mid-1970s.[22] Blacks, on average, are less skilled than whites and consequently suffer disproportionately from a shift in demand against low-skilled labor. Women's earnings rose relative to men's in the 1980s largely because women's skills increased relative to men's. Recent cohorts of working women are relatively more educated and have acquired more continuous years of work experience than was true of women in the past.[23]

22. Chinhui Juhn, Kevin M. Murphy, and Brooks Pierce, "Accounting for the Slowdown in Black-White Convergence," in *Workers and Their Wages: Changing Patterns in the United States*, ed. Marvin Kosters (Washington, DC: American Enterprise Institute Press, 1991), pp. 107-45.

23. June O'Neill and S. Polachek, "Why the Gender Gap in Wages Narrowed in the 1980s," *Journal of Labor Economics* (in press).

IS AFFIRMATIVE ACTION
NEEDED IN THE 1990s?

It is now almost thirty years since the passage of the Civil Rights Act. Although earnings differentials between blacks and whites have narrowed, they have by no means disappeared. Earnings differentials of varying sizes are still found between other groups as well—men and women, Hispanics and whites. The extent to which these differentials reflect underlying differences in work-related skills as opposed to discriminatory hiring and employment practices is clearly important in any debate over the need for such policies as affirmative action.

Table 2 summarizes recent data comparing the hourly earnings of black, Hispanic, and Asian workers to those of white non-Hispanic workers of the same gender. The observed patterns in the ratios suggest the complexity of the factors at work in the labor market. For example, Asian men, a group subjected to a considerable amount of prejudice and discrimination, actually have higher earnings than white men. But they also have more education. Within schooling categories, the earnings of Asian men are less then white men's, but not by much, especially considering the special language problems of recent Asian immigrants.

Strikingly different patterns are observed among women. The earnings of minority women are all very close to those of white women. Asian women's earnings actually exceed those of white women within education categories; this pattern is in sharp contrast to the situation among males.

The most serious concerns about the effects of labor market discrimination on earnings, however, relate to minority males, especially black males. Black-white earnings ratios within schooling categories are considerably higher than they were in 1964, but they are still significantly below parity. However, differences in the quality of schools attended and in family background result in differences in achievement among those who have completed the same nominal amount of schooling. Substantial differences between blacks and whites have been found in scores on tests measuring school achievement.[24] For example, at the same age

and schooling level, black men score well below white men on the Armed Forces Qualification Test (AFQT). It has been demonstrated that the earnings of both blacks and whites are positively associated with AFQT scores.[25] It follows that, on average, blacks and whites with the same education level may not be viewed as equally productive by nondiscriminating firms.

How much of the racial differential in earnings between blacks and whites with the same educational level can be explained by the AFQT differential? Results derived from analysis of data on individual black and white male earners in 1987 show that after controlling for AFQT differentials by race—as well as years of schooling and region—the earnings ratio increases from 83 percent to 90-96 percent.[26] Among those with college training, the ratio rises above 100 percent. These results suggest that deprivation related to school, home, and neighborhood are more serious obstacles to the attainment of black-white equality in earnings than current labor market discrimination.

CONCLUDING COMMENTS AND IMPLICATIONS

We could find no good evidence that the federal program of affirmative action with numerical hiring goals, which reached its full force between 1974 and 1980, had a significant and lasting effect on the relative

24. O'Neill et al., *Economic Progress of Black Men*, pp. 54-77; June O'Neill, "The Role of Human Capital in Earnings Differences between Black and White Men," *Journal of Economic Perspectives*, 4(4):25-45 (Fall 1990); Abigail Thernstrom, "The Drive for Racially Inclusive Schools," this issue of *The Annals* of the American Academy of Political and Social Science.

25. O'Neill, "Role of Human Capital," p. 43 and tab.

26. Ibid., tab. 5, p. 41.

economic status of black men. This may seem an unlikely conclusion given the amount of controversy surrounding the program. If it had little effect, then why all the shouting? Our conjecture is that the program may have had significant effects on individual firms and workers even though its net effect in the aggregate was small.

For example, Jonathan Leonard has found that the OFCCP focused its compliance reviews on large firms with relatively large representations of black workers—in other words, on firms that were least likely to be discriminating.[27] Such a strategy, while generating highly visible enforcement activity, may not lead to significant increases in the relative economic status of black men.[28] Public perceptions of government programs are usually based on anecdotal evidence from newsworthy cases. Thus the complaints of a few individuals about reverse discrimination can shape public attitudes even if, in the aggregate, only a tiny percentage of qualified nonminority workers have been displaced by less qualified minority workers. Indeed, in a democracy like ours the possibility seems remote that an affirmative action program could force large numbers of private sector contractors to hire large numbers of unqualified minorities over a long period of time.

This does not mean that affirmative action bears no ill effects. The implementation of numerical goals and timetables by the OFCCP in the 1970s may have done little either to raise the relative economic status of black men or to lower the economic status of white men. Rather, its main impact may have been to generate divisiveness and ill will. A cost that is still harder to measure is the possibly negative impact that affirmative action may have had on the self-image of minority youths or on their incentives for self-help.[29]

27. Jonathan S. Leonard, "Affirmative Action as Earnings Redistribution: The Targeting of Compliance Reviews," *Journal of Labor Economics*, 3:363-84 (July 1985). Leonard labels the OFCCP targeting strategy as "leaning on open doors."

28. If firms subject to compliance reviews are not in fact discriminating, then relative gains by blacks can be made only at the expense of more qualified white workers. Such a situation would be difficult to force upon employers for any period of time or on a large scale.

29. See Glenn C. Loury, "Incentive Effects of Affirmative Action," this issue of *The Annals* of the American Academy of Political and Social Science.

ANNALS, *AAPSS*, 523, September 1992

Split Visions:
Minority Business Set-Asides

By GEORGE R. LaNOUE

ABSTRACT: In the 1970s and 1980s, programs assisting and preferring businesses owned by women and certain minority group members mushroomed at every level of government. For most of this period, they remained relatively uncontroversial and almost totally unstudied. In 1989, however, the Supreme Court in *City of Richmond* v. *Croson* invalidated the use of racial classifications in local public contracting programs unless they were used as temporary narrowly tailored remedies for identified discrimination. *Croson* has triggered a flurry of litigation across the country and an avalanche of studies commissioned to help jurisdictions preserve their minority business programs. The outcome of the conflict over these programs may define the limits of using racial classifications in a variety of public policy areas.

George R. LaNoue is professor of political science and director of the Policy Sciences Graduate Program, University of Maryland, Baltimore County. His most recent books are Academics in Court: The Consequences of Faculty Discrimination Litigation *with Barbara Lee (1987) and* Minority Business Programs and Disparity Studies *(1991).*

P ROGRAMS benefiting minority business enterprises (MBEs) and women's business enterprises (WBEs) represent the clearest form of quotas, the largest expenditures, and one of the most frequent causes of litigation of all forms of affirmative action, but until 1989 they received the least scholarly attention.

Buoyed by a powerful rhetoric of sharing the economic pie and targeted mainly on the construction industry, where employment discrimination was well documented,[1] these programs expanded dramatically in the 1970s and 1980s. With bipartisan support and the backing of a 1980 Supreme Court decision, they seemed well on the way to reallocating business ownership by race, ethnicity, and gender.

Then, in 1987, three federal circuit courts ruled that state or local MBE programs violated the equal protection clause of the Fourteenth Amendment. In 1989, in *City of Richmond* v. *Croson*, the Supreme Court made a similar ruling.[2]

The *Croson* decision has led to an intense analysis of the sources, rationales, and effects of MBE programs. These findings promise to be widely litigated in the next decade and may result in a definitive determination of the allowable use of racial classifications in business and elsewhere. This article will examine the origins, legal status, and consequences of federal, state, and local M/WBE programs.

1. See, for example, Ray Marshall and Vernon M. Briggs, *The Negro and Apprenticeship* (Baltimore: Johns Hopkins University Press, 1967); I. Dubinsky, *Reform in Trade Union Discrimination in the Construction Industry* (New York: Praeger Press, 1973).

2. 488 U.S. 469 (1989).

FEDERAL PROGRAMS

In fiscal year 1989, about $8.65 billion was awarded to MBEs in federal set-asides, including $3.5 billion in a Small Business Administration (SBA) program. Yet Congress's decision to create such programs was unusually haphazard. They evolved from Section 8 of the Small Business Act of 1953, which never mentioned set-asides or minorities.

The SBA initiated its program administratively in response to the 1967 Report of the Commission on Civil Disorders. The Kerner Commission concluded that one cause of the unrest was that minorities did not own many small businesses and so were excluded from the economic mainstream. Consequently, SBA adopted regulations requiring federal contracts to be allocated to firms owned by "socially or economically disadvantaged" persons (DBEs). In theory, that could be a person of any race or ethnicity, but all blacks, Hispanics, Asian Americans, American Indians, Eskimos, and Aleuts were ruled presumptively eligible. By 1978, over 96 percent of the firms in the program were owned by members of those groups, and two-thirds, by blacks.

In 1978, Congress enacted Public Law 95-507, which furnished a statutory basis for the SBA program and required all federal agencies to set percentage goals for procurement contract awards to small minority-owned businesses. The law also amended the Small Business Act to require prime contractors with federal contracts over $500,000 or $1 million in certain construction categories to set percentage goals for DBEs. The new law emphasized the social and economic disadvantage of owners rather than their race or ethnicity, but few poor white owners received awards. The program had already built up a minority clientele, and businesses begun by poor persons were often risky investments.[3]

Minority set-asides were first authorized in the 1977 Public Works Employment Act (PWEA), which mandated expenditures of $4 billion to stimulate a sluggish economy, particularly in the construction industry. The language—"Except to the extent that the Secretary of Commerce determines otherwise, . . . ten per centum of . . . each grant shall be expended for minority business enterprises"—originated as a floor amendment by Representative Parren Mitchell, Democrat of Maryland, and generated remarkably little debate. Discussion in the House of Representatives filled only six pages of the Congressional Record; that in the Senate, two pages. Congress was apparently impressed by the fact that minorities were 15-18 percent of the population, but MBEs received less than 1 percent of federal contracts.

Drew S. Days III, an Assistant Attorney General for Civil Rights during the Carter administration, who successfully defended the PWEA set-aside before the Supreme Court in the landmark decision of Fullilove v. Klutznick, remarked:

One can only marvel at the fact that the minority set-aside provision was enacted into law without having a committee report and with only token opposition. . . .

Without a careful examination of the facts and alternatives, the legislation may be misdirected and fail to assist those most deserving of aid, may harm others unjustifiably, and may operate . . . longer than necessary.[4]

Federal efforts to assist women-owned businesses began in 1979 when President Carter issued Executive Order 12138, designed to discourage discrimination against female entrepreneurs. The Women's Business Ownership Act of 1988 (Public Law 100-533) authorized the federal promotion of WBEs, which received $1.75 billion in contracts that year.

The pattern set by the SBA and the PWEA has been followed in many federal programs. The most notable are programs of the Departments of Transportation and Defense. The 1982 Surface Transportation Assistance Act (Public Law 97-424) required that at least 10 percent of all Federal Highway Administration and other transportation agencies' expenditures go to disadvantaged businesses. Under this program and its 1987 successor, Public Law 100-17, the Transportation Department distributes highway construction funds—currently, about $1.5 billion a year—through state departments of transportation, which become responsible for the set-asides.[5] The 1987 National Defense Authorization Act set a 5 percent goal for Defense procurement contracts to DBEs; in fiscal 1989, $5.3 billion was set aside for exclusive bidding by DBEs.

The 1977 PWEA precedent has been extended to other public works

3. Daniel Levinson, "A Study of Preferential Treatment: The Evolution of Minority Business Enterprise Assistance Programs," George Washington Law Review, 49:61, 70-71 (1980).

4. Drew S. Days III, "Fullilove," Yale Law Journal, 96:453, 469 (1987).

5. Tom Ichniowski, "Justice by the Number," ENR, 2 Sept. 1991, p. 26.

programs. For example, recent legislation set aside 10 percent of the construction value of U.S. embassies abroad, 10 percent of international development grants, 10 percent of the development, construction, and operation of the Superconducting Super Collider, and 8 percent of National Aeronautics and Space Administration contracts, including those for the space station that may be operational in July 1997, for MBEs.

Other statutes seek to help minority firms without set-asides. The Competitive Equality Banking Act of 1987 is designed to help minority-owned savings and loan institutions; 1986 and 1989 laws—Public Laws 99-499 and 101-73—ensure the participation of minority firms in the cleanup of hazardous-waste sites and in federal responses to failed savings and loan institutions.[6]

In addition, 130 federally financed Minority Enterprise Small Development Investment Companies provide equity funds, long-term loans, and management assistance to MBEs; 95 Minority Business Development centers advise prospective minority entrepreneurs.

Legal challenges to federal programs

The set-asides under the Public Works Employment Act of 1977 were examined by the Supreme Court in *Fullilove* v. *Klutznick* in 1980.[7] The case began in November 1977, when several contractor associations filed a complaint in a New York federal court seeking to enjoin the set-aside.

In a six-to-three decision, the Supreme Court found the set-aside facially constitutional but offered no single rationale for the statute's validity. Chief Justice Burger, writing for Justices White and Powell, conceded that the PWEA contained no findings of discrimination, but "Congress had abundant historical basis from which it could conclude that traditional procurement practices, when applied to minority businesses, could perpetuate the effects of prior discrimination."[8] Consequently, Congress could enact a remedy.

For the Chief Justice, the validity of racial and ethnic criteria was decided by the goal of remedying past discrimination, the flexible waiver and exemption provisions, and the program's limited extent and duration. He repeatedly stressed that "Congress must proceed only with programs narrowly tailored to achieve its objectives."[9]

Justice Marshall, joined by Justices Brennan and Blackmun, created the majority by arguing more expansively that such programs need only be "substantially related"[10] to a remedial purpose.

Justice Stewart, dissenting with Justice Rehnquist, found the legislative record deficient and the act overbroad, providing benefits to groups without justification and to businesses that include

6. For a current list of federal set-asides, see Mark Eddy, *Federal Programs for Minority and Women-Owned Businesses* (Washington, DC: Congressional Research Service, 1990), pp. CRS-10-11, tab. 4, p. 7.

7. 448 U.S. 448 (1980).

8. Ibid., p. 478.

9. Ibid., p. 490.

10. Ibid., p. 519.

(1) those minority owned firms that have successfully obtained business in the past on a free competitive basis and undoubtedly are capable of doing so in the future as well; (2) firms that have never attempted to obtain any public business in the past; (3) firms that were initially formed after the Act was passed, including those that may have been organized simply to take advantage of its provisions; (4) firms that have tried to obtain public business but were unsuccessful for reasons that are unrelated to the racial characteristics of their stockholders; and (5) those firms that have been victimized by racial discrimination.[11]

Federal support for minority firms came to the Supreme Court again in 1990 in *Metro Broadcasting, Inc.* v. *FCC.*[12] A *Harvard Law Review* commentator termed the *Metro* decision, the last majority opinion authored by Justice William Brennan, "the last hurrah of a dying liberal order."[13]

Metro was two distinct cases consolidated for decision. The first concerned an appeal from a Federal Communications Commission (FCC) decision selecting one of three applicants to operate a new television station in Orlando. The successful applicant—which was 90 percent Hispanic-owned—was the beneficiary of an FCC policy giving a competitive plus to minority applicants for television and radio stations. The second involved the FCC distress-sale policy permitting transfer of a station to minority owners in circumstances not applicable to others.

The two preferential policies were evaluated on three criteria: equal protection, correct standard of review, and burden imposed on non-minorities. As in many affirmative action cases, the 5-4 *Metro* decision turned on the proper standard of review.

Brennan's majority deemed appropriate the easily satisfied intermediate scrutiny test, which requires only that race-conscious measures "serve important governmental objectives within the powers of Congress and which are substantially related to achievement of those objectives."[14] Brennan noted that in *Fullilove* the majority did not apply strict scrutiny and that *Metro* involved the important governmental objective of broadcast diversity. The connection between expanded minority ownership and increased broadcast diversity "has been repeatedly recognized by both the [FCC] . . . and the courts."[15] The majority felt that the two preferential policies were not only acceptable but inevitable since the FCC had tried to encourage diversity of programming consideration of race and had failed. The burden on nonminorities was slight. Distress sales represented less than 0.4 percent of all broadcast sales.

Justice O'Connor, joined by Chief Justice Rehnquist and Justices Scalia and Kennedy, wrote a lengthy, often acrimonious dissent. *Metro*, according to the dissenters, marked a "repudiation of our recent affirmation [in *Croson*] that the Constitution's equal protection guarantees extend

11. Ibid., p. 540.
12. 110 S.Ct. 2997 (1990).
13. Patricia J. Williams, "Metro Broadcasting, Inc. v. FCC: Regrouping in Singular Times," *Harvard Law Review*, 104:525 (1991).

14. 110 S.Ct. at 3009.
15. Ibid., p. 3015.

equally to all citizens."[16] *Fullilove* involved congressional attempts to remedy identified past discrimination, while the *Metro* majority conceded that the FCC preferential policies were not necessarily remedial but were justified by general public policy.

The dissenters argued that race-conscious measures should be used only to remedy the specific effects of identified racial discrimination. They believed that the nexus between race and programming was unproven, unprovable, and ultimately stereotypical. It would be far better for the FCC to evaluate applicants individually to determine which could provide whatever programming the commission believed to be underrepresented. Justice Kennedy, joined by Justice Scalia, stated, "I cannot agree . . . that the Constitution permits the Government to discriminate among its citizens on the basis of race in order to serve interests so trivial as 'broadcast diversity.' "[17]

Evaluation of federal programs

MBE programs raise several questions. One of the thorniest is, Which ethnic groups should receive the preferences? No systematic study of this issue has been conducted. The groups chosen seem to have been drawn from other affirmative action programs without assessing the validity of these choices in the business world. Indeed, several Hispanic and Asian groups are at or above the national average in business success.[18] When the Small Business Act was amended in 1978 to put emphasis on "socially and economically disadvantaged business concerns," Asian Americans were not initially included. After inquiries from several Western senators and passage of a House amendment restoring their status, the SBA ruled persons from most Asian countries eligible[19] but, in another decision, excluded Hasidic Jews.[20]

Altering the low-bid process has evidently fostered some fraud. From Wedtech, which began as an 8(a) Hispanic-owned company and ended in a scandal enmeshing politicians and businessmen of many ethnic backgrounds,[21] to less visible frauds, MBE programs have had a great many problems.

By creating a sheltered market for firms that may be less efficient competitors, the programs raise the cost

16. Ibid., p. 3029.
17. Ibid., p. 3045.

18. Frank A. Fratoe and Ronald L. Meeks, *Business Participation Rates of the 50 Largest U.S. Ancestry Groups: Preliminary Report*, (Washington, DC: Department of Commerce, Minority Businesses Development Agency, 1985); Timothy Bates, "Impact of Preferential Procurement Policies on Minority-Owned Businesses," *Review of Black Political Economy*, Summer 1985, pp. 51, 54.

19. U.S., Commission on Civil Rights, *Competing in the Marketplace: A Look at Minority Business Enterprises in the State of Washington* (Washington, DC: Government Printing Office, 1979), pp. 5-7.

20. U.S., *Federal Register*, 15 Apr. 1980, p. 25563.

21. Marilyn W. Thompson, *Feeding the Beast: How Wedtech Became the Most Corrupt Little Company in America* (New York: Charles Scribner's, 1990); William Steinberg and Matthew C. Harrison, Jr., *Feeding Frenzy: The Inside Story of Wedtech* (New York: Henry Holt, 1989).

of public contracts. One informed witness testified that disadvantaged firms submit quotes 10.7 percent higher than firms owned by white males. An Abt Associates evaluation concluded that the Department of Transportation DBE program cost an extra 15 percent, or $180 million a year.[22] The programs may prop up firms that cannot or should not survive. The General Accounting Office noted that the SBA supported far more MBE janitorial services than the private sector could ever absorb.[23] From 1968 to 1977, after $2.2 billion was awarded to 3726 MBEs, only 149 had graduated from the program and only 33 showed a positive net worth. A Senate committee found that for the lucky few the 8(a) program was "a gravy train of immense proportions."[24]

The ultimate test is whether setasides promote the growth of targeted firms. Though the failure rate of MBEs is 60 percent above that of other firms,[25] the growth in their num-

ber has been impressive. From 1982 to 1987, the number of black-owned firms rose from 308,260 to 424,165; of Hispanic-owned firms, from 233,975 to 422,373; and of women-owned firms, from 2.6 to 4.1 million.[26]

What part of this growth was caused by a good economy, what part by the rise in general economic opportunities for women and minorities, and what part by M/WBE programs is unknown. These programs have provided training, capital, and networks for new M/WBEs and have obliged older businesses to share opportunities with them. They have also induced new entrepreneurs to enter fields for which they were ill prepared and that may not have had room for them.[27]

Unless the Supreme Court overturns *Fullilove* and *Metro*, federal setasides appear secure. They reward important groups in the Democratic coalition, while Republicans have long supported them on the theory that the new entrepreneurs are useful citizens and may become Republicans. At the same time that President Bush was opposing "employment quotas" in various civil rights bills, he approved the 10 percent set-aside in the Highway Transportation Act.

STATE AND LOCAL MBE PROGRAMS

Federal set-asides have been widely copied by state and local gov-

22. Robert Jerrett III et al., *An Assessment of Program Impacts of the Disadvantaged Business Enterprise (DBE) Requirement in the Federal-Aid Highway Construction Program* (Washington, DC: Department of Transportation, 1986), pp. 127-38.

23. Legislative History, P.L. 95-507, p. 3845.

24. U.S., Congress, Senate, Committee on Governmental Affairs, Subcommittee on Federal Spending Practices and Open Government, *Reports Based on Hearings and Inquiries Conducted on the Small Business Administration Involving Abuses in the 8(a) Program and Irregularities Concerning Minority Businesses*, 95th Cong., 2d sess., 1978.

25. U.S., Department of Commerce, Minority Business Development Agency, internal study memo, Feb. 1984, figure reprinted in James H. Lowry, "Set-Aside Programs: Viable Vehicles for Change or Threats to the Free Enterprise System?" in *Selected Affirmative Action Topics in Employment and Business*

Set-Asides (Washington, DC: Commission on Civil Rights, 1985), 1:119.

26. U.S., Department of Commerce, Census Surveys of Minority and Women-Owned Businesses, 1982; ibid., 1987.

27. Jerrett et al., *Assessment of Program Impacts*, pp. 77 ff.

ernments. In 1989, at least 234 jurisdictions—states, cities, counties, and special districts—had an MBE program and most included WBEs.[28] Areas with large black populations often had the strongest programs; usually, they also covered Hispanics, Asian Americans, Native Americans, Eskimos, and Aleuts. This inclusiveness was later to embarrass the programs as critics and courts faulted preferences for groups that owned no business and may never have lived in the jurisdictions.

Diverse programs

Nearly uniform in group coverage, the programs varied in their methods. Some emphasized race-neutral techniques such as training, funding, and bonding opportunities, better publicity about contracts, and smaller subcontracts to facilitate competition. The effectiveness of such options is yet unknown. Other programs began with set-asides or phased them in when race-neutral methods seemed ineffective or politically unsatisfactory.

A set-aside or quota on prime contracts or subcontracts is common. In Maryland, 10 percent of all procurement is set aside for M/WBEs; in Washington, D.C., 50 percent of construction contracts. Seattle and Hillsborough County, Florida, require that when three or more M/WBEs exist in a construction subcontract category, the total dollar amount of the relevant subcontracts must go to M/WBEs. San Francisco and King County, Washington, grant M/WBEs a 5 to 10 percent advantage in bid competition or award point preferences to joint ventures, contracts, or proposals with substantial M/WBE participation. Programs have different degrees of flexibility. Some use goals with waivers; others use quotas.

While genuine mentorships or partnerships have occurred, other relationships between MBEs and non-MBEs have resulted in switches, fronts, or conduits. Switches commonly occur when ownership is transferred from husband to wife to create a WBE. White males often set up a front company with a woman or minority who has little or no operating control. A white prime may subcontract the required amount to a conduit M/WBE that does no real work. Thus, in a major Seattle bridge project, the MBE bought machinery and resold it at a small profit to the prime.

There have been problems determining who is a minority, since many people are of mixed descent. Los Angeles has highly detailed rules, yet controversy has arisen over $19 million in contracts to an MBE whose owner is 1/64 Cherokee.[29]

Diverse motives

The first local program began in Atlanta in 1971. In part, it was to secure biracial support for building a rapid transit system. In 1986, the Baltimore City Council's black cau-

28. *The Effect of Richmond v. Croson on MBE Programs Nationwide* (Washington, DC: Minority Business Enterprise Legal Defense and Educational Fund, 1989).

29. John Hurst and Ronald B. Taylor, "Fraction of Indian Blood Worth Millions in Business," *Los Angeles Times* 27 Dec. 1990.

cus persuaded the mayor to establish an MBE program by threatening to withhold funding for a practice facility for the Baltimore Colts. Programs have often been adopted after pressure from federal agencies or a campaign by local minority groups.

As with most social legislation, set-asides were thought to be necessary or desirable for various reasons. Program sponsors had different rationales:

— to remedy current contract discrimination against specific minority firms;
— to overcome the present effects of past contract discrimination against minority firms in general;
— to compensate for current or for past societal discrimination;
— to establish new economic strength in minority communities generally;
— to stimulate general business competition;
— to meet the political demands of particular individuals or groups; or
— to create new political coalitions.

The overwhelming impetus for local programs has been the desire to reallocate public contracts to reflect new political realities. As long-repressed blacks or new ethnics came to power, it seemed unfair to permit companies owned by those who had achieved success earlier to receive more than their fair share of public contracts, even if they were low bidders.

For example, the average age of the 25 largest construction companies in San Francisco is 50 years, but only one is minority-owned. Bechtel, founded in 1898, is larger than all the minority construction companies combined. In 1940, the median founding year of these 25 companies, 90 percent of the city's population was white; in 1990, under 47 percent. Despite two adverse court decisions, San Francisco has fought vigorously for MBE preferences.

From the outset, local MBE programs have been politically contentious. A few have been tainted by scandal. The programs breach the lowest-responsible-bidder anticorruption and antidiscrimination principles of the reform movement. Consequently, to make them palatable to voters and courts, they are sold as discrimination remedies even if other motivations are at work.

Supporters counter that set-asides create jobs, especially for minorities; add economic vitality and competition; and are needed to overcome past and present discrimination against minority firms. Without them, such firms might never be integrated into the economic mainstream.

Court decisions

The quest for social justice, conflicting views of civil rights, and raw politics have made a difficult mix for courts to adjudicate. By 1986, at least a dozen cases on the legality of set-asides had been decided by federal and state courts, with very inconclusive results. Though the programs share some similarities with affirmative action programs in employment and education that courts had often upheld, the low-bid public contracting system was, on its face, race neutral. There were many allegations that white contractors were reluctant to subcontract with M/WBEs, but no documented case where a minority or female low bidder had not received a prime contract. Evidence of discrimination in contracting was weaker than in such areas as education, employment, or voting.

That fact began to trouble the increasingly conservative federal courts. After three circuit courts struck down state and local set-aside laws in 1987, it was only a matter of time before the Supreme Court became involved.

City of Richmond v. *Croson* began over a minor incident. In 1983, J. A. Croson Co., a plumbing contractor, submitted a low bid of $126,530 to install urinals in the Richmond jail. A Richmond ordinance required an MBE subcontractor for at least 30 percent of the total dollar amount of all public contracts. The only feasible subcontract was supply of the urinals, and only one MBE was interested. Its price was $7633 higher than Croson had anticipated. Croson applied for a waiver and, when it was denied, petitioned for the extra $7633 cost. When that, too, was rejected, it sued. In 1989, after six years in litigation, Croson found itself before the Supreme Court.

Six justices were convinced the Richmond program violated the Fourteenth Amendment's equal protection clause. The plurality opinion, written by Justice O'Connor, joined by Chief Justice Rehnquist and Justice White, agreed that the proper test for evaluating racial classification in MBE programs was strict scrutiny:

The Richmond Plan denies certain citizens the opportunity to compete for a fixed percentage of public contracts based solely upon their race. To whatever racial group these citizens belong, their "personal rights" to be treated with equal dignity and respect are implicated by a rigid rule erecting race as the sole criterion in an aspect of public decision making.

Absent searching judicial inquiry into the justification for such race-based measures, there is simply no way of determining what classifications are "benign" or "remedial" and what classifications are in fact motivated by illegitimate notions of racial inferiority or simple racial politics.[30]

Not all MBE programs were unconstitutional. If a state or local jurisdiction could show through "proper findings" that it had participated in contract discrimination against minority firms, it could, in limited circumstances, use racial classifications to remedy the situation. O'Connor declared:

Where there is a significant statistical disparity between the number of qualified minority contractors willing and able to perform a particular service and the number of such contractors actually engaged by the locality or the locality's prime contractors, an inference of discriminatory exclusion could arise.[31]

O'Connor asserted, however, that

— finding discrimination in one market does not permit an assumption that discrimination exists in all markets;
— finding discrimination against one minority group does not permit an assumption that discrimination exists against all such groups;
— if discrimination exists, nonra-

30. *City of Richmond* v. *Croson* at 493.
31. Ibid., p. 509.

cial remedies must be utilized first; and
— if racial classifications are necessary in extreme cases, they should be narrowly tailored.

The *Croson* decision was vigorously denounced by civil rights leaders. They had endorsed set-asides and knew that the strict scrutiny test affirmed by *Croson* might endanger other forms of affirmative action. Consequently, Senator Paul Simon, Democrat of Illinois, introduced legislation proposing a federal finding of continuing societal discrimination to legitimate all reasonable local set-asides to remedy discrimination,[32] but it has not received much attention.

Disparity studies

Increasingly, jurisdictions have sought to assemble the proof Justice O'Connor suggested was necessary to support an MBE law. Few jurisdictions had such information; they usually commissioned external studies. Many consultants appeared—professors, lawyers, companies specializing in affirmative action issues, and accounting firms. By 1 March 1991, 29 jurisdictions had completed studies costing $5.5 million, and another 37 studies costing $7 million had been commissioned.[33]

The results of these evaluations are controversial.[34] Some consulting companies have moved from city to city providing justifications for the jurisdictions' MBE programs with a mixture of social science, pseudoscience, and racial politics. The government paying the piper has called the tune.

Justice O'Connor asked for statistical evidence of disparity between the availability of M/WBEs and their utilization in public contracts, but many studies neglect that point. They detail the historical context of local discrimination and argue that, without it, many more M/WBEs would exist. Or they compile anecdotal evidence of discrimination from minority and women owners.

It is not certain either of these approaches will be successful. The historical evidence of discrimination against Richmond's blacks was well documented, but Justice O'Connor insisted it was "sheer speculation" as to how many MBEs there would be "but for" that discrimination. Since perceptions of business discrimination are subjective and M/WBEs have a vested interested in claiming discrimination to preserve set-asides, anecdotal evidence is not necessarily persuasive.

Yet statistical evidence has also proved elusive. Few jurisdictions kept records of the proper data. M/WBEs have proliferated in the 1980s but are relatively small. Over 90 percent of black businesses have no employees. Set-aside goals were

32. U.S., Senate, Committee on Governmental Affairs, *Hearings to Amend the Civil Rights Act of 1964: Permitting Set-Asides*, 101st Cong., 2d sess., 16 May 1990.

33. *Factors Affecting the Cost and Performance of MBE Disparity Fact-finding Studies* (Washington, DC: Minority Business Enterprise Legal Defense and Education Fund, 1991).

34. George R. LaNoue, *Minority Business Programs and Disparity Studies* (Washington, DC: National League of Cities, 1991).

usually set above actual availability. Statistical analyses have often shown that set-asides caused overutilization of M/WBEs or that there is no discrimination in at least some markets for some groups.

Such analyses are usually politically unacceptable. Few jurisdictions have pruned their programs to match their analyses. Consequently, the next round of litigation will focus on the validity of the studies and the obligation of jurisdictions to "narrowly tailor" their programs to accord with research findings.

THE FUTURE OF M/WBE PROGRAMS

The outcome of the legal and political conflict over set-asides is uncertain. By May 1991, these programs had been struck down 16 times and successfully defended 15 times, mostly on procedural grounds. Some 35 cases were pending.

The programs have minority business constituencies and public bureaucracies that are dependent on them and ideologically committed to them. While the Associated General Contractors of America (AGC), a formidable opponent with 101 chapters and an annual budget of $8 million, has won important victories in New Haven, Philadelphia, and San Francisco, it is unlikely to sustain a protracted fight. In a contest conducted by expensive litigation, the party financed by taxpayers has a decisive advantage over the party financed by dues payers. Further, the major national civil rights organizations stand ready to assist the defendant's litigation, while AGC has not built a broader business alliance and is backed only by a few small conservative litigation agencies and subcontractor organizations.

Ironically, the *Croson* decision may have made AGC's task more difficult. By changing the focus of litigation from the facial constitutionality of set-asides—involving inexpensive petitions for summary judgment—to detailed, expensive trials about the validity of disparity studies, *Croson* has increased the plaintiff's burden. If a particular study and law are successfully challenged, it is relatively easy to amend the law and commission a new study.

Croson may do little more to end set-asides in contracting than the *Bakke* decision did to end them in university admissions. The lesson may be that racial classifications can be terminated only when government agencies and interest groups unite to do so and financial rewards or penalties enforce the policy. That was how the traditional civil rights coalition attacked discrimination against minorities. A similar strategy to protect the rights of white males from the new majority coalition of minorities and women might work but appears politically unlikely now.[35]

History does not inevitably repeat itself, however. There seems to be growing opposition to racial classifications in public programs and suspicion that many affirmative action programs have become vehicles for discrimination. That, coupled with conservative changes in the federal judiciary, may force a reexamination

35. The problem is discussed in *Associated General Contractors of California* v. *City and County of San Francisco*, 813 F.2d 922, 932 (9th Cir. 1987).

of set-asides and a termination of those not remedying discrimination.

A plausible argument can be made that reallocating economic shares among ethnic groups is better done by the federal government, as suggested by *Fullilove* and *Metro*, than by more parochial state and local governments, as decided in *Croson*. But that does not resolve the fundamental moral or constitutional issues. To some, set-asides are a just remedy for discrimination; to others, unjust favoritism. As long as this split vision persists, neither public policy nor the law will rest easily.

ANNALS, *AAPSS*, **523**, September 1992

Affirmative Action
in Government Employment

By J. EDWARD KELLOUGH

ABSTRACT: Affirmative action in government is important not only for the equitable distribution of employment opportunities but as a symbol of the nation's commitment to end discrimination against minorities and women and to make government more responsive to their interests. This article examines the development of affirmative action policy in employment at the federal, state, and local levels. Recent federal political appointments are noted. Research that has attempted to assess the effects of affirmative action is discussed.

J. Edward Kellough, assistant professor of political science at the University of Georgia, teaches in the graduate program in public administration and conducts research on public personnel issues and policy evaluation. He received the Ph.D. from Miami University and has taught at Texas A&M University. He has published in a number of scholarly journals and is the author of Federal Equal Employment Opportunity Policy and Numerical Goals and Timetables *(1989).*

IN the 1970s, affirmative action emerged as one of the most contentious issues facing government and private sector managers. Recently, dissension has risen to new heights with the struggle over civil rights legislation in 1990 and 1991, the emergence of affirmative action as a political campaign issue, and the debate over Supreme Court nominee Clarence Thomas's view on the subject.[1] Controversy over affirmative action reflects a fundamental conflict between two core values: a belief in individual rights that prohibits drawing distinctions along racial, ethnic, or gender lines, and an acknowledgment that social equity may demand compensation for groups that have suffered past discrimination.[2]

This article will discuss the development and impact of affirmative action in federal employment and to a lesser extent in state and local governments. Analysis will focus on the civil service, but the article will also briefly consider federal political appointees. Affirmative action is defined here as systematic effort to increase the employment representation of groups who have borne the brunt of discrimination and have historically been denied opportunities for employment or advancement. As such, it requires more than merely responding to discrimination complaints.

1. See Thomas B. Edsall, "A Political Powder Keg," *Washington Post National Weekly Edition*, 14-20 Jan. 1991, p. 6.
2. John Nalbandian and Donald E. Klingner, "Conflict and Values in Public Personnel Administration," *Public Administration Quarterly*, Spring 1987, pp. 17-33.

FROM NONDISCRIMINATION TO NUMERICAL GOALS

Affirmative action emerged from a concern for equal employment opportunity (EEO). Although the concept of equal opportunity is central to American political values, the first conscious attempt by government to address the issue did not come until the early 1940s, when it became unlawful to withhold federal employment on the basis of race or ethnicity. Soon after that action, procedures were adopted enabling individuals who had suffered racial or ethnic discrimination in the federal service to lodge complaints that could lead to investigation and resolution.

In the late 1940s, additional affirmative steps were taken. Eventually, these included the active recruitment of minorities and women as well as white males; training and upward-mobility programs for lower-level employees, who were disproportionately women and minorities; and such practices as the collection and publication of data on the distribution of women and minorities in public service.

Despite these early approaches, growth in minority and female employment, especially in higher-level positions, remained slow. In response, advocates of EEO pushed for and secured the authorization of numerical goals and timetables for the employment of minorities and women. That approach was designed to facilitate managerial planning to address the underrepresentation of women and minorities in certain job categories.

Goals and timetables, however, represented a significant policy departure since they sanctioned the consideration of race and sex in personnel practices.[3] Earlier EEO efforts, consisting of statements prohibiting discrimination, procedures for complaint processing, and recruitment and training efforts designed to reach all segments of society, were formed on the principle of nondiscrimination. Plainly, that principle is compromised by numerical goals and timetables developed on the basis of race, ethnicity, and gender. Since the 1970s, goals and timetables, sometimes referred to as quotas, have probably become the most commonly thought of approach to affirmative action.

AN EQUITABLE, REPRESENTATIVE BUREAUCRACY

All affirmative action programs are intended as a force for justice in employment policy. EEO efforts in general are designed to guarantee that people who have historically been barred from employment or promotion because of race, ethnicity, or sex are no longer denied opportunities for such reasons. In both public and private employment, the objective is a more equitable distribution of job opportunities. As Krislov has written, "We cannot with justice say

to a man compelled to carry a burden on his back for a long way in a race, and therefore miles behind, 'you may drop the pack; the race is now equal.' Amends must be made."[4]

In addition, affirmative action in government has important symbolic value. If government is to promote equity in the private sector successfully, it must set its own house in order. If discrimination cannot be eliminated and the full participation of women and minorities achieved in the public service, it is unlikely to be achieved elsewhere.[5] A commitment to affirmative action in government sends the message to other segments of society that discrimination against minorities and women is no longer tolerable.[6]

Furthermore, it is likely that a government bureaucracy more representative of the people will be more responsive to the people's needs. Shielded from political pressure by merit system rules, civil servants exercise considerable discretionary authority. By controlling policy implementation, public agencies, within the range of permissible interpretations, determine how government goals are translated into programmatic activity. Executive supervision and legislative oversight may not al-

3. J. Edward Kellough, *Federal Equal Employment Opportunity Policy and Numerical Goals and Timetables* (New York: Praeger, 1989); see also David H. Rosenbloom, *Federal Equal Employment Opportunity* (New York: Praeger, 1977).

4. Samuel Krislov, *The Negro in Federal Employment* (Minneapolis: University of Minnesota Press, 1967), p. 77.

5. Ibid., p. 5.

6. David H. Rosenbloom, "Equal Employment Opportunity, Affirmative Action, and Public Personnel Management," in *Public Personnel Update*, ed. Michael Cohen and Robert T. Golembiewski (New York: Marcel Dekker, 1984), p. 33.

ways suffice to ensure accountability and responsiveness to the public.[7] A representative bureaucracy, however, may be more likely than an unrepresentative one to serve the interests of all groups, assuming that the values influencing a bureaucrat's policy preferences derive at least in part from racial or ethnic background and gender.[8]

The concept of representative bureaucracy has been much discussed.[9] Some research suggests that bureaucratic recruitment and socialization activities may overwhelm the effects of social characteristics. Meier and Nigro, for example, found little agreement between high-level federal employees and members of their racial or ethnic groups in the general population on questions of domestic spending priorities.[10] Rosenbloom and Featherstonhaugh, however, found substantial differences between black and white federal employees regarding attitudes toward political participation—views that were congruent with differences found between blacks and whites in the general population.[11]

Additionally, a thorough review of the literature by Thompson concluded that under certain circumstances minority public servants do actively represent the interests of their racial or ethnic groups. Thompson noted, for example, that minority police officers were less likely than white officers to characterize minority citizens as hostile or indifferent to law and order. Also, black social workers were more likely than their white coworkers to perceive black clients favorably.[12]

Thompson's observations have been reinforced by Meier, Stewart, and England, who demonstrated that discrimination against minorities in the public schools diminished as the number of minority teachers increased.[13] A recent examination of Equal Employment Opportunity Commission district offices also showed that decisions benefiting minorities filing complaints of discrimination were positively associated with minority representation on the district staff. That is, decisions favorable to minorities occurred more frequently in offices with greater minor-

7. See Charles Gilbert, "The Framework of Administrative Responsibility," *Journal of Politics*, 21:373-407 (1959).

8. Grace Hall Saltzstein, "Representative Bureaucracy and Bureaucratic Responsibility," *Administration & Society*, 10(4):465-75 (Feb. 1979).

9. For an excellent literature review, see Kenneth J. Meier, Joseph Stewart, Jr., and Donald Menzel, "Active Representation in Educational Bureaucracies: Policy Impacts" (Paper delivered at the annual meeting of the American Political Science Association, Washington, DC, 1991).

10. Kenneth J. Meier and Lloyd G. Nigro, "Representative Bureaucracy and Policy Preferences," *Public Administration Review*, 36:458-69 (July-Aug. 1976).

11. David H. Rosenbloom and Jeannette G. Featherstonhaugh, "Passive and Active Representation in the Federal Service," *Social Science Quarterly*, 57:873-82 (Mar. 1977).

12. Frank J. Thompson, "Minority Groups in Public Bureaucracies," *Administration & Society*, 8:201-26 (Aug. 1976).

13. Kenneth J. Meier, Joseph Stewart, Jr., and Robert E. England, *Race, Class, and Education* (Madison: University of Wisconsin Press, 1989); see also Meier, Stewart, and Menzel, "Active Representation in Educational Bureaucracies."

ity representation.[14] Findings such as these suggest that a more representative bureaucracy may be a more responsive bureaucracy, at least in certain social policy areas.

HISTORY OF FEDERAL EEO

The Pendleton Act of 1883 and the system of open competitive examinations it established for the federal service seemed clearly to endorse the concept of equal opportunity. Unfortunately, discrimination prevented minorities and women from fully participating in the selection process.[15] Not until 1940 did the Ramspect Act prohibit discrimination on the basis of race, creed, or color in the establishment of salaries, the allocation of positions to grades, and the issuance of transfers and promotions.[16] Shortly before, President Roosevelt's Executive Order 8587 had prohibited racial discrimination in the federal service in general terms.[17] But, as little was done to enforce the act or the order, the policy of nondiscrimination was more a sentiment than a reality.

Fair Employment Practice Committee, 1941-46

In 1940, blacks, 9.8 percent of the U.S. population, held 4.2 percent of federal jobs, almost all in the lowest levels.[18] The black leader A. Philip Randolph planned a mass march and rally in Washington to protest discrimination in defense industries and federal employment. On 25 June 1941, a week before the march was to take place, Roosevelt signed Executive Order 8802, establishing a substantive EEO program for the federal government and defense contractors.[19] The march was canceled.

The Fair Employment Practice Committee (FEPC), created by the order, could investigate complaints of discrimination and make recommendations for their resolution, but it had no enforcement power. For the most part, the committee focused on discrimination in defense industries. Though disbanded in 1946 due to opposition of southern congressmen, the FEPC documented and aroused public awareness of discrimination in government employment.[20] A continuing series of subsequent executive orders reaffirmed the federal EEO commitment.

14. John J. Hindera, "Representative Bureaucracy" (Paper delivered at the annual meeting of the American Political Science Association, Washington, DC, 1991).

15. For an excellent account of the development of the federal EEO program, see Rosenbloom, *Federal Equal Employment Opportunity*; Krislov, *Negro in Federal Employment*. This section relies heavily on these sources.

16. U.S., *Statutes at Large*, vol. 54, pt. 1, p. 1211.

17. U.S., *Federal Register*, 13 Nov. 1940, pp. 4445-48.

18. Don Hellriegel and Larry Short, "Equal Employment Opportunity in the Federal Government," *Public Administration Review*, 32:851-58 (Nov.-Dec. 1972).

19. U.S., *Federal Register*, 27 June 1941, p. 3109.

20. Krislov, *Negro in Federal Employment*, p. 34.

Fair Employment Board, 1948-55

President Truman's Executive Order 9980, issued in July 1948, established a Fair Employment Board (FEB) in the Civil Service Commission to investigate discrimination complaints much as the FEPC had done.[21] All complaints, however, were to be given a hearing at the agency level before an appeal could be made to the FEB. When the board investigated appeals, it required appointing officials to demonstrate that selections were made entirely on the basis of merit.[22]

In addition to complaint processing, the FEB initiated "constructive action," a precursor to affirmative action programs. Constructive action consisted of establishing contacts with minority organizations, encouraging minorities to apply for federal jobs, improving training programs for low-level employees, and conducting periodic surveys of the distribution of minorities in the federal service.[23]

President Eisenhower's committee, 1955-61

In January 1955, the federal EEO effort received President Eisenhower's imprimatur with the issuance of Executive Order 10590. This order reaffirmed the policy of nondiscrimination, endorsed the recruitment of

more minorities, and established the President's Committee on Government Employment Policy to supervise federal EEO efforts.[24] The committee reviewed complaints of discrimination, conducted investigations, and issued recommendations to departments and agencies.

President Kennedy's committee, 1961-65

Federal EEO programs were again reorganized by President Kennedy, whose March 1961 Executive Order 10925 created the President's Committee on Equal Employment Opportunity.[25] This committee was decidedly more aggressive than its predecessors. It endorsed the concept of representative bureaucracy, stressed the importance of affirmative recruitment and training efforts, initiated an annual census of minority employment, and cultivated close ties with civil rights groups. When discrimination was found, the committee reviewed all agency appointments or promotions for a period of time to ensure that corrective measures were being implemented.[26]

During the Kennedy administration, blacks slightly exceeded proportional representation in the federal service, holding 13.1 percent of federal jobs by 1963.[27] They remained

21. U.S., *Federal Register*, 28 July 1948, pp. 4311-13.

22. Rosenbloom, *Federal Equal Employment Opportunity*, p. 64.

23. Ibid.

24. U.S., *Federal Register*, 19 Jan. 1955, pp. 409-11.

25. Ibid., 8 Mar. 1961, pp. 1977-79.

26. Rosenbloom, *Federal Equal Employment Opportunity*, pp. 68-69.

27. U.S., Civil Service Commission, *Study of Minority Group Employment in the Federal Government: 1965* (Washington, DC: Government Printing Office, 1965).

concentrated in the lowest positions, however. As a result, concern began to focus on increasing minority representation in the higher bureaucracy.

Civil Service Commission, 1965-79

The more aggressive approach to EEO followed by the President's Committee on Equal Employment Opportunity provoked opposition from conservative members of Congress and concomitant appropriation difficulties. President Johnson's response, in his landmark Executive Order 11246 of September 1965, was to transfer responsibility for federal EEO back to the Civil Service Commission, where it would be somewhat shielded from congressional opponents.[28]

Johnson's order authorized the Civil Service Commission to investigate individual complaints of discrimination in federal employment and issue binding EEO directives to agencies and departments.[29] As of 1967, the Civil Service Commission was also to enforce Executive Order 11375, which prohibited employment discrimination on the basis of sex and placed women under the federal EEO program for the first time.[30]

But progress remained slow in middle- and higher-level jobs, and discussion ensued about transferring responsibility for the government's internal program to the Equal Employment Opportunity Commission (EEOC), which enforced EEO in the private sector. Legislation requiring such a transfer was introduced in 1970.[31] In response, the Civil Service Commission strengthened its program. In May 1971, it authorized but did not require departments and agencies to use numerical goals and timetables. The Labor Department had required goals and timetables for government construction contractors as early as 1969.[32]

The need to base federal EEO policy on presidential orders finally ended with passage of the 1972 Equal Employment Opportunity Act.[33] This law amended the 1964 Civil Rights Act by expanding restrictions on discrimination in the private sector and prohibiting discrimination by state and local governments and in federal employment. The Civil Service Commission remained responsible for the federal program. The statute required it annually to review and approve departmental and agency affirmative action plans and to issue EEO regulations.

Equal Employment Opportunity Commission, 1979 to the present

Though the 1972 Equal Employment Opportunity Act reaffirmed the federal affirmative action program

28. Krislov, *Negro in Federal Employment*, pp. 42-45.

29. U.S., *Federal Register*, 28 Sept. 1965, pp. 12319-25.

30. Ibid., 17 Oct. 1967, pp. 14303-4.

31. U.S., Congress, S. 2453, H.R. 17555, 91st Cong., 2d sess., 1970.

32. Arthur A. Fletcher, "Whatever Happened to the Philadelphia Plan?" *Business and Society Review / Innovation*, 5:24-28 (Spring 1973).

33. U.S., *Statutes at Large*, vol. 86, pt. 1, p. 103.

implemented by the Civil Service Commission, the number of minorities and women in upper grades remained modest. President Carter, who strongly supported affirmative action, transferred federal EEO responsibility to the EEOC under a reorganization order coinciding with the 1978 Civil Service Reform Act.[34] The act itself endorsed the idea of representative bureaucracy, calling for "a work force reflective of the Nation's diversity"; established a new EEO recruitment program; and mandated that achievement of affirmative action goals be one basis for evaluating the performance of members of the new Senior Executive Service.

The EEOC placed emphasis on numerical goals and timetables in agency affirmative action plans. Detailed instructions were developed for determining minority and female underrepresentation in higher-level positions, and goals and timetables were required when underrepresentation was documented. During the Reagan years, however, the EEOC backed away from this approach; regulations issued in 1987 permitted but no longer required agencies to utilize numerical goals.[35]

IMPACT OF FEDERAL EEO

An examination of federal employment patterns over time indicates that the process of integrating women and minorities into middle and higher levels of the federal service has been, for the most part, gradual and incremental. Data on the representation of women and minorities for selected years are presented in Table 1.

Although minority and female employment has increased over the years, we cannot be certain how much of that increase is due to affirmative action. Time-series analysis of annual employment data shows little significant change in black federal employment trends in middle- and higher-level grades attributable to the policy.[36] Black employment expanded steadily in those grades from the early 1960s to 1984 with almost no perceptible increase in the rate of employment following the 1971 authorization of goals and timetables.

The growth of female employment in middle and higher grades did increase following the 1971 intervention, however. In grades 7-12, for example, female employment grew at an average rate of 0.54 percent per year from 1968 to 1971 but at 1.25 percent per year from 1972 to 1984. In grades 13-18, female employment increased by 0.1 percent per year before and 0.6 percent per year after the authorization of goals and timetables.[37]

The gap between the average grades of white men and women in the General Schedule also narrowed slightly during the 1970s and early 1980s, but it was not eliminated.[38] The extent to which such progress can be

34. U.S., Congress, House, Committee on Government Operations, *Reorganization Plan No. 1 of 1978: Message from the President of the United States*, 95th Cong., 2d sess. House Document 95-295.

35. U.S., Equal Employment Opportunity Commission, *Management Directive 714*, 6 Oct. 1987.

36. Kellough, *Federal Equal Employment Opportunity Policy*, pp. 27-37.

37. Ibid., pp. 36-39.

38. Gregory B. Lewis, "Changing Patterns of Sexual Discrimination in Federal Employment," *Review of Public Personnel Administration*, 7(2):1-13 (Spring 1987).

TABLE 1

**THE PERCENTAGE OF WOMEN, MINORITIES, AND
BLACKS AMONG FEDERAL CIVILIAN EMPLOYEES, 1970, 1980, and 1990**

Total and Selected Grades	Women	Minorities*	
		Total	Blacks
1970			
Total GS	33.2	14.7	11.1
GS 9-12	15.3	7.4	4.7
GS 13-15	4.1	3.9	2.3
Executive grades	1.7	2.2	1.5
1980			
Total GS	45.3	20.8	14.5
GS 9-12	27.2	14.8	9.1
GS 13-15	8.3	8.5	4.8
Executive grades	6.2	7.0	5.0
1990			
Total GS	50.2	26.4	16.5
GS 9-12	39.0	21.3	8.4
GS 13-15	18.7	12.7	6.4
Executive grades	11.1	7.7	4.7

SOURCES: U.S., Civil Service Commission, *Study of Minority Group Employment in the Federal Government*, 30 Nov. 1970; idem, *Study of Employment of Women in the Federal Government*, 31 Oct. 1970; U.S., Office of Personnel Management, *Equal Employment Opportunity Statistics*, 30 Nov. 1980; idem, *Affirmative Employment Statistics*, 30 Sept. 1990.

NOTE: Federal civilian employees are those in General Schedule (GS) and equivalent grades; executive grades include the Senior Executive Service and GS 16-18.

*Blacks, Hispanics, Asians, and Native Americans.

attributed to affirmative action is an open question given the number of other political and social changes since the 1960s.

Analysis of the effects of the transfer of authority to the EEOC in 1978 produces similar, somewhat mixed conclusions. No increase occurred in the employment rate of blacks in middle- and higher-level positions; in fact, the rate of growth in black employment declined beginning in 1981. In grades 13-18, for example, black employment increased at an average rate of 0.21 percent per year before the 1978 reforms and subsequently at only 0.13 percent per year.

For Hispanics, there were no substantial long-term changes in employment patterns after the reforms; the rate before and after was essentially the same. For women, however, the rate of gain in grades 13-18 rose from an average annual increase of 0.34 percent prior to the 1978 reforms to 0.83 percent after.[39]

Considerable variation in racial, ethnic, and gender employment pat-

39. J. Edward Kellough and David H. Rosenbloom, "Representative Bureaucracy and EEOC," in *The Promise and Paradox of Bureaucratic Reform*, ed. Patricia W. Ingraham and David H. Rosenbloom (Pittsburgh: University of Pittsburgh Press, 1992).

TABLE 2

FEDERAL CIVILIAN EMPLOYEES, 30 SEPTEMBER 1990: NUMBER AND PERCENTAGE OF WOMEN, MINORITIES, AND BLACKS IN SELECTED AGENCIES (All pay plans)

| | Number (thousands) | | | | Percentage* | | |
| | | | Minorities | | | | Minorities | |
Agency	Total	Women	Total	Blacks	Women	Total	Blacks
All agencies	2150	927	588	357	43.1	27.3	16.6
Agriculture	132	52	23	11	39.4	17.2	8.3
Commerce	50	26	15	11	52.0	30.0	22.2
Defense	994	368	252	143	37.0	25.4	14.4
Education	5	3	2	2	58.5	45.8	38.7
Energy	18	7	4	2	37.5	20.0	11.9
HHS	123	79	46	28	64.8	37.4	23.0
HUD	14	8	6	4	58.0	40.8	31.1
Interior	79	29	21	4	36.4	26.9	5.3
Justice	84	33	25	15	39.8	29.2	17.4
Labor	17	8	5	4	46.4	31.4	23.9
State	16	7	4	3	44.3	23.3	16.3
Transportation	67	17	12	7	25.6	17.5	10.8
Treasury	157	88	49	34	55.8	31.4	21.9
Veterans Affairs	252	138	84	58	54.8	33.3	23.0
EPA	17	8	5	3	48.7	26.2	19.0
EEOC	3	2	2	1	64.2	63.2	50.7
FDIC	18	9	4	2	52.3	20.6	13.0
GSA	20	8	7	6	40.9	36.3	29.0
NASA	25	8	4	2	30.4	16.5	9.2
OPM	7	4	2	1	61.9	32.4	26.9
SBA	5	3	2	1	51.5	34.5	22.5

SOURCE: Office of Personnel Management, *Affirmative Employment Statistics*, 30 Sept. 1990, tab. 1.

NOTE: The acronyms stand for agency names as follows: HHS, Department of Health and Human Services; HUD, Department of Housing and Urban Development; EPA, Environmental Protection Agency; EEOC, Equal Employment Opportunity Commission; FDIC, Federal Deposit Insurance Corporation; GSA, General Services Administration; NASA, National Aeronautics and Space Administration; OPM, Office of Personnel Management; SBA, Small Business Administration.

*Percentages were calculated from unrounded numbers.

terns has occurred across departments and agencies. Some made more progress than others in minority and female employment following the authorization of goals and timetables, and some are better integrated along racial/ethnic and gender lines.[40] Table 2 displays data on

the representation of minorities and women in selected departments and agencies.

Several factors contribute to the numbers of minorities and women employed. The proportion of an

40. J. Edward Kellough, "Federal Agencies and Affirmative Action for Blacks and Women," *Social Science Quarterly*, 71(1):83-92 (Mar. 1990); idem, "Integration in the Public Workplace," *Public Administration Review*, 50:557-66 (Sept.-Oct. 1990).

agency or departmental work force located in Washington, D.C., for example, greatly influences the level of black employment. The extent to which the agency mission is concerned with social justice and equity issues is also positively associated with black employment, as is the rate of new hires and the extent of blue-collar and clerical employment. For women, the prevalence of clerical positions is the most important variable associated with higher employment numbers, but agency mission and the rate of new hires are also salient. The major determinant of Hispanic employment is the proportion of agency positions located in areas of the country with large Hispanic populations.[41]

POLITICAL APPOINTEES

Because political appointees occupy many of the top policymaking positions in the federal government, it is important to look briefly at the record of past administrations on the appointment of minorities and women to those jobs. Frances Perkins, the first woman appointed to a cabinet position, served as Franklin Roosevelt's Secretary of Labor from 1933 to 1945. The first black in the cabinet, Robert C. Weaver, was Lyndon Johnson's Secretary of Housing and Urban Development in 1966.[42] Johnson also appointed Thurgood Marshall as the first black Supreme Court justice. Presidents Nixon and Ford appointed minorities to a number of subcabinet posts.

The Carter administration was evidently the first to maintain a computerized list of all presidential appointees by race, sex, and ethnicity. By the end of Carter's term, 22 percent of his appointments had gone to women and 21 percent to minorities.[43] Carter appointed Andrew Young, the first black person to serve as U.S. Representative to the United Nations, and two black department heads: Donald F. McHenry, Secretary of the Army, and Patricia Roberts Harris, Secretary of Housing and Urban Development and, later, Secretary of Health, Education, and Welfare. Carter also appointed Juanita Kreps, the first female Secretary of Commerce, and Shirley Hafstedler, Secretary of the new Department of Education.

During Ronald Reagan's tenure in office, fully 37 percent of all presidential appointees were women, but only approximately 9 percent were minorities,[44] presumably because of the heavy identification of prominent black leaders with the Democrats. Reagan nominated Sandra Day O'Connor, the first woman Supreme Court justice, and Jeane Kirkpatrick, U.N. Representative; Elizabeth Dole and Margaret Heckler were named

41. J. Edward Kellough and Euel Elliott, "Demographic and Organizational Influences on Racial/Ethnic and Gender Integration in Federal Agencies," *Social Science Quarterly*, 72(1) (Mar. 1992).

42. See Romeo B. Garrett, *The Presidents and the Negro* (Peoria, IL: Bradley University, 1982).

43. U.S., Commission on Civil Rights, *Equal Opportunity in Presidential Appointments* (Washington, DC: Government Printing Office, June 1983), p. 2. Data for the Carter years reflect all political appointments, full-time and part-time, requiring and not requiring Senate approval. Subsequent data from the Reagan and Bush administrations are equally comprehensive.

44. Data provided by the Ronald Reagan Presidential Library.

Secretary of Transportation and of Health and Human Services, respectively, and Samuel Pierce was named Secretary of Housing and Urban Development.

The increased appointment of women has apparently continued under President Bush. As of September 1991, 39 percent of his appointees were women and 12 percent, minorities.[45] Bush named two women, Elizabeth Dole in 1988 and Lynn Martin in 1990, to head the Department of Labor. One black, Louis W. Sullivan, former president of Morehouse School of Medicine in Atlanta, was confirmed as Secretary of Health and Human Services. Two Hispanics received cabinet appointments, Lauro Cavazos at Education and Manuel Lujan at Interior.

One of Bush's most contested choices was conservative black judge Clarence Thomas, former head of the EEOC, to replace Thurgood Marshall on the Supreme Court; one of his least contested was the selection of black General Colin Powell as chairman of the Joint Chiefs of Staff, clearly one of the most important government posts ever held by a black American.

AFFIRMATIVE ACTION IN STATE AND LOCAL GOVERNMENT

Though federal EEO programs began in the 1940s, state and local programs developed much later. In fact, a 1967 Commission on Civil Rights survey found pervasive discrimination against minorities in state and local government.[46] Minority employees held mainly lower-level blue-collar positions as common laborers; in some jurisdictions, particularly in the South, certain jobs were considered appropriate only for minorities.

In the 1960s, the only significant EEO requirements imposed on the states, beyond the Fourteenth Amendment, were in federal standards requiring merit systems of employment in state programs receiving federal financial assistance and in Housing and Urban Development programs administered by local government development agencies.[47] The merit system standards, developed originally in 1939, required selection, promotion, and compensation practices based on merit principles in agencies receiving federal funds. Discrimination on the grounds of religious or political opinion or affiliation was prohibited. A prohibition of racial discrimination was added in 1963. That year, the Department of Housing and Urban Development required local development authorities to "take affirmative action to ensure that applicants are employed and employees are treated during employment, without regard to race, creed, color, or national origin."[48] According to the Commission on Civil Rights, however, these programs had little effect on state and local employment.

In 1972, federal requirements were considerably expanded. As noted, the

45. Data provided by the White House Office of Presidential Personnel.

46. U.S., Commission on Civil Rights, *For All the People . . . by All the People* (Washington, DC: Government Printing Office, 1969).

47. Ibid., pp. 91-92.

48. Ibid., p. 108.

1972 Equal Employment Opportunity Act placed state and local governments, as well as the federal service, under the nondiscrimination provisions of Title VII of the Civil Rights Act of 1964. The 1972 legislation gave the EEOC responsibility for supervising state and local employment practices and authorized legal action against government units charged with discrimination. State and local governments were required to adopt affirmative action programs and to collect and report data on minority and female employment.

The lack of early data has limited empirical research on state and local EEO to the period after 1972. In general, studies show increasing proportions of minorities and women in state and local positions, but the extent to which those trends are attributable to affirmative action is, again, uncertain because of other political and social developments.

Cayer and Sigelman suggested that the first few years of state and local affirmative action following the 1972 act produced gains for women and minorities, although the act was most beneficial for white women. They found substantial variation in the status of positions held by minorities and women in different functional areas of government service, however.[49] More recently, Kelly et al. have reported progress in the employment of women in higher-level jobs in state government, but it should be noted that women still dis-

proportionately occupy lower-echelon positions.[50]

At the municipal level, an examination of a sample of 134 large cities suggested that the proportion of minorities in the work force is positively related to the size of the minority population and, in lesser measure, the presence of a minority mayor and relatively low unemployment.[51] A much larger survey indicated that minority council members are more important than minority mayors.[52] This study also found that minority employment was greater in unreformed municipal governments, that is, mayor-council systems and where there was ward rather than at-large representation. The presence of strong municipal unions has been found to repress minority employment.[53]

The employment of women has been positively associated with the growth of government, the presence of traditionally female clerical positions, and the election of a female mayor.[54]

CONCLUSION

Affirmative action in government represents an attempt to respond to

49. N. Joseph Cayer and Lee Sigelman, "Minorities and Women in State and Local Government: 1973-1975, *Public Administration Review*, 40(5):443-50 (Sept.-Oct. 1980).

50. Rita Mae Kelly et al., "Public Managers in the States," *Public Administration Review*, 51:402-12 (Sept.-Oct. 1991).

51. Lana Stein, "Representative Local Government," *Journal of Politics*, 48:694-713 (Aug. 1986).

52. Kenneth R. Mladenka, "Blacks and Hispanics in Urban Politics," *American Political Science Review*, 83:165-91 (Mar. 1989).

53. See Frances F. Piven, "Militant Civil Servants in New York City," in *Politics in America*, ed. Walter D. Burnham (New York: Van Nostrand, 1973), pp. 297-326.

54. See Grace Hall Saltzstein, "Female Mayors and Women in Municipal Jobs," *American Journal of Political Science*, 30:140-64 (Feb. 1986).

past and current employment discrimination against women and minorities. The most visible approach relies on goals and timetables for minority and female employment. Because that approach transcends nondiscrimination by establishing minority and female preferences, it has generated significant controversy and must usually be defended in terms of compensatory justice.

Goals and timetables were adopted because earlier approaches were not seen as particularly efficacious. Efforts to understand the impact of affirmative action in government have not produced definitive conclusions, however. Minority and female employment has increased and gains have been made at the higher levels, but the extent to which they can be attributed to affirmative action is not clear. Research has shown that, at both federal and local levels, political, economic, demographic, and organizational factors influence the employment of women and minorities and may at times constrain the effectiveness of affirmative action.

ANNALS, *AAPSS*, 523, September 1992

The Drive for Racially Inclusive Schools

By ABIGAIL THERNSTROM

ABSTRACT: Disproportionate numbers of black students do poorly on standardized tests; strategies to improve American education thus frequently target inner-city schools. These strategies often have an unrecognized affirmative action component. A search for more minority students or teachers is clearly an affirmative action effort, but the elimination of all tracking or competency grouping is another matter. It is normally viewed as nothing more than a pedagogical strategy, but in fact, like other affirmative action efforts, it amounts to a conscious effort to alter the low-track status of minority pupils. Similarly, the demand for curricular reforms, racial sensitivity training, and more culturally appropriate tests, while not obviously affirmative action strategies, are in fact precisely that. They attempt to broaden the definition of excellence and to create a more racially inclusive educational system. Such well-meaning strategies are not likely to close the racial gap in school performance. That task may call for quite a different approach.

Abigail Thernstrom received her Ph.D. in government from Harvard University. She is the author of Whose Votes Count? Affirmative Action and Minority Voting Rights *(1987), which won awards from the Policy Studies Organization and the American Bar Association, among others. With Diane Ravitch, she has edited a collection of documents entitled* The Democracy Reader *(1992). She writes frequently for such journals as* The New Republic, The Public Interest, *and* Commentary.

REPUBLICANS and Democrats alike have only one clearly good idea to solve the problems of the black underclass: better schools—the traditional ticket out of poverty. Education, they say, creates opportunity. The children of inner-city black families will escape from the ghetto if they receive decent schooling.

Better schooling for black students means different things to different advocates. Strategies abound: smaller classes, more nurturing, higher expectations, accelerated learning . . . the list is long. Some of these strategies aim to improve education in general; they rest on the notion that better schools will benefit all students. Others, however, focus specifically on the perceived needs of minority children, especially black children.

Many of the programs that target minority children have an affirmative action component, although one that is not so obvious. Thus, while an admissions quota at an academically elite school such as Boston Latin is unmistakably an affirmative action effort, other reforms appear quite different at first glance. Insisting that students with different levels of academic achievement work together rather than in separate tracks, for instance, would seem to contain no element of racial preference. In fact, however, the currently fashionable attack on competency or ability grouping is but one expression of a larger movement to institute policies that ignore differences in educational achievement in the name of racial and ethnic equality, and that is precisely what affirmative action is all about.

That is, these minority-targeted programs are, in general, leveling efforts. They label as discriminatory traditional methods of sorting and selecting minority students and minority teachers. They assume inevitable tension between equity and rigorous academic standards—between racial justice, on the one hand, and policies that result in clear distinctions between better and worse students, on the other. And they resolve that tension by opting for a form of affirmative action—erasing or modifying, in the name of equity, the hierarchy into which high and low performers fall.

All affirmative action programs are a response to minority underrepresentation by the standard of ethnic and racial proportionality. In the case of schooling, blacks are indeed underrepresented in faculty and other staff positions, as well as in schools, classrooms, and other tracks that admit only high performers. Have they been "segregated" or unfairly "excluded," as affirmative action and other equity advocates claim? If so, they are entitled to remedial action—affirmative inclusionary efforts.

"Segregation" no longer has the clear meaning it once had. Take the question of student placements. Separating students on the basis of their performance on standardized exams can be viewed as a segregative act given the disproportionate concentration of blacks at the low end of the scale. Alternatively, it can be seen as a constructive response to the unfortunate fact of low academic achievement. Different perceptions demand different policies.

RACIAL DIFFERENCES IN ACADEMIC ACHIEVEMENT

It is beyond dispute that disproportionate numbers of black students indeed do poorly on standardized exams. At every age level, black students today lag far behind their white peers in the most important subjects that have been tested by the National Assessment of Educational Progress.[1] The 1990 data indicate that in reading, for example, black 13-year-olds, typically in the eighth grade, are about as adept at handling written material as whites who are almost two—1.8—years younger. By the age of 17, the gap has widened to 3.4 years, so that on reading tests, black students about to graduate from high school score only a few points ahead of whites in the eighth grade. In fact, it is clear that a very large and troubling difference in reading competence is present not long after children first start school and that the gap does not diminish notably with prolonged exposure to the educational system.

The results of the assessment of mathematics skills are much the same. But if the disparities in reading and mathematical competence seem shockingly large, they are modest in comparison with the immense racial gap in science and writing. In science, blacks in their final year of high school demonstrate much less command of the subject than whites back in the eighth grade. Even greater disparities show up on tests of writing skills. Here blacks in the

eleventh grade perform just a few points ahead of whites in grade four.

The only good news in all this is that the racial gap in reading and math proficiency used to be far greater than it is now. The first tests by the National Assessment of Educational Progress in 1971 showed blacks to be 3.3 years behind whites in reading at age 13, and fully 6.0 years behind at age 17. This gap has narrowed almost to half by 1990. In mathematics, the picture is similar. In science, though, there appears to have been far less progress. Black 17-year-olds were seven years behind whites in 1969 and almost six today.[2]

As a consequence of the racial gap in performance, few blacks are eligible for admission by traditional standards to elite institutions, whether private or public, and a paucity of black students are in the top tracks in schools that assign classes on the basis of proven academic competence. Such results were once acceptable; today they are not. The absence of Catholics or Swedes in academically exclusive settings would raise no eyebrows. But in the case of blacks, relatively low scores on standardized tests are not generally interpreted simply as bad news. Instead, the news conveyed is viewed as an indictment of the tests themselves and those who devise and use them. The results are seen as a wrong that demands a remedy—a way of sorting

---

1. For the statistical work on student achievement, I am indebted to Stephan Thernstrom.

2. National Center for Education Statistics, *Trends in Academic Progress: Achievements of U.S. Students in Science, 1969-70 to 1990; Mathematics, 1973 to 1990; Reading, 1971 to 1990; and Writing, 1984-1990* (Washington, DC: Office of Education, 1991), pp. 26, 64, 112, 152.

and grouping students that is more racially fair. Such a remedy would reject the academic hierarchies in which blacks cluster at the bottom. It might rely significantly on qualities other than standardized test performance. It would be, in short, an affirmative action remedy.

THE AFFIRMATIVE ACTION ARGUMENT AGAINST TESTING AND TRACKING

Varied arguments are used against interpreting black students' average scores on standardized tests as simply bad news—not welcome, but providing useful information and thus a legitimate basis upon which to sort students for instructional purposes. For instance, those who attack the validity of the standardized tests argue that the scores are worthless, that they do not tell authorities what they should want to know. Federal district judge Skelly Wright put the point succinctly in a 1967 Washington, D.C., desegregation decision. "When standard aptitude tests are given to low income Negro children . . . ," he said, "test scores become practically meaningless. Because of the impoverished circumstances that characterize the disadvantaged child, it is virtually impossible to tell whether the test score reflects lack of ability— or simply lack of opportunity."[3]

Actually, critics argue, black students' results on standardized tests are meaningless for two reasons. It is not only that socioeconomic disadvantage handicaps these test takers. The students are asked the wrong questions. The exams are racially

and culturally biased. They measure nothing worthwhile—or nothing appropriate to blacks.

Perhaps the most consequential formulation of this point was contained in *Larry P.* v. *Riles*, the 1979 decision that banned the use of I.Q. tests in California schools—although only for blacks. The state had relied, in part, on the results of such tests in determining placement in the EMR track—those classes designated for the "educable mentally retarded." "Black children's intelligence may be manifested in ways that the tests do not show," Judge Peckham ruled.[4] In so doing, he cited the testimony of Georgia State professor of education Dr. Asa Hilliard, best known subsequently for his advocacy of Afrocentric curricular material for black children. Hilliard had stated that blacks have "a cultural heritage that represents an experience pool which is never used" or tested by standardized tests.[5] The point was not Hilliard's alone. For instance, Harvard University professor of education Charles Willie has argued that standardized testing is flawed when it fails "to recognize that in social organization there always are at least two norms, the norm of the dominant people of power and the norm of the subdominant people of power."[6]

3. *Hobson* v. *Hansen*, 269 F. Supp. 401, 485 (D.D.C. 1967).

4. *Larry P.* v. *Riles*, 495 F. Supp. 926, 957 (1979).

5. Ibid., p. 959.

6. Charles V. Willie, "The Unfair Effects of Standardized Testing on Blacks and Other Minorities," in *The Prices of Secrecy: The Social, Intellectual and Psychological Costs of Current Assessment Practice*, ed. Judah L. Schwartz and Katherine A. Viator (Cambridge, MA: Harvard Graduate School of Education, Educational Technology Center, 1990), p. 24.

The "norm of the subdominant people" is said to include nonstandard English—a fact that tests routinely ignore, Hilliard complained in his court testimony. "Vocabulary is not standard," he said, "even when people use the same word."[7] Syntax is not standard. Nor are cultural references—to Shakespearean plays, historical events, or even recreational scenes—Judge Peckham noted. The black child "uses language requiring a wide use of many coined interjections (sometimes profanity)," states material given to teachers in Portland, Oregon.[8] Again, in the literature on testing, the point is a familiar one. FairTest calls such questions as, What do you call a baby cow? unfair to inner-city children.[9] Carol Chomsky, a Harvard colleague of Charles Willie's, argues that labeling such constructions as "he didn't want to ride in no cars" as mistakes is an objectionable value judgment. "Students are asked to . . . classify their own speech as error-ridden." Standardized tests, or at least those portions that assess spoken language, should reflect community language norms.[10]

The point will often take a more radical form. It is not simply that black children do not know and should not know who Columbus was; blacks think differently from the way whites do. " 'African-American students and European-American students have very different learning styles,' " educational consultant Jawanza Kunjufu has said.[11] Likewise, a 1987 New York State Board of Regents booklet argued that "children's racial, ethnic and emotional backgrounds and cultures influence the manner in which they learn concepts and process information." It enumerated a number of "qualities noted in African-Americans"—among them, a "preference for inferential reasoning rather than deductive or inductive reasoning" and a "tendency to approximate space, number and time instead of aiming for complete accuracy."[12]

If black children learn differently, they must be tested for different skills. Indeed, Nancy Amuleru-Marshall, on the research staff for the Atlanta public schools, has argued that "any tests that emphasize logical, analytical methods of problem solving will be biased against minorities."[13] In the same vein, Thelma Mumford-Glover, director of Atlanta's gifted and talented program, has stated that "multicriteria are essential to the identification of gifted and talented African-American children."[14] Her office discourages all use of I.Q. and achievement tests.

7. *Larry P.* v. *Riles*, 495 F. Supp. at 958.

8. David Nicholson, "Afrocentrism and the Tribalization of America," *Washington Post National Weekly Edition*, 8-14 Oct. 1990, p. 23.

9. Michelle Guido, "Californians Debate Halting Use of IQ Test," *Chicago Tribune*, 18 Aug. 1991.

10. Carol Chomsky, "Language and Language Arts Assessment," in *Prices of Secrecy*, ed. Schwartz and Viator, p. 74.

11. Dirk Johnson, "Milwaukee Creating 2 Schools Just for Black Boys," *New York Times*, 30 Sept. 1990. Copyright © 1990 by The New York Times Company. Reprinted by permission.

12. Mark A. Uhlig, "Learning Style of Minorities to Be Studied," *New York Times*, 21 Nov. 1987, p. 29.

13. Carol Innerst, "Definition of 'Intelligence' Grows in the Name of Diversity," *Washington Times*, 28 May 1990.

14. Ibid.

As Judge Peckham implies, given the clash of cultures, the problem of test bias cannot be solved by eliminating certain items and substituting others.[15] Removing the offensive items would not rid a test of its pervasive cultural bias, critics agree.[16]

Culturally inappropriate tests mean that blacks will do worse than whites, and, at bottom, that seems to be the main concern of critics: the tests' disparate racial and ethnic impact. "The consequences of testing . . . constitute the most damning evidence against the fairness of tests. Poor and minority students consistently score lower than do whites," University of California at Los Angeles education professor Jeannie Oakes has written in a widely quoted book on tracking.[17] In a similar vein, Charles Willie has argued that "standardized testing . . . is particularly dangerous for individuals in subdominant power groups," since such testing disproportionately excludes members of those groups.[18] Most recently, a civil rights coalition has argued against the Bush administration's national-testing proposal on the ground that a disproportionate number of black—and other minority—students are likely to score low.

By implication, tests are legitimate only when the distribution of black and white scores is identical.[19]

The assumption seems to be that such a disparate racial impact is inexplicable except as the consequence of discrimination, a point that Judge Peckham made explicitly. In an earlier ruling in the same case, he had called the concentration of black children tracked in EMR classes an "unmistakable sign of invidious discrimination" and had gone on to argue that academic potential—or the lack thereof—is surely distributed randomly across racial and ethnic groups.[20] There is "no basis for assuming otherwise than that the ability to learn is randomly spread about the population," he said.[21] Peckham's 1979 decision contained much the same statement.[22]

Of course, "the ability to learn" may be randomly distributed while academic performance is not. For the purposes of sorting and grouping students, what counts would seem to be performance. But the sorting and grouping process itself has a discriminatory impact, test and tracking critics generally argue. Tracking is a self-fulfilling prophecy; students labeled as less competent quickly become so. The concern is well-founded when tracking means back-of-the-bus education for children who are academically behind. But dumbed-down school-

15. This is certainly the implication contained in his approving citation of the Asa Hilliard testimony arguing that blacks and whites disagree over the meaning of common words.

16. Guido, "Californians Debate."

17. Jeannie Oakes, *Keeping Track: How Schools Structure Inequality* (New Haven, CT: Yale University Press, 1985), p. 11.

18. Willie, "Unfair Effects," p. 22. Willie was referring to Scholastic Aptitude Tests, but he would obviously extend the point to standardized tests in general.

19. Kenneth J. Cooper, "Exams Opposed over Potential Harm to Minorities," *Washington Post*, 12 June 1991.

20. *Larry P. v. Riles*, 343 F. Supp. 1306, 1310 (1972).

21. Ibid.

22. *Larry P. v. Riles*, 495 F. Supp. at 944 (1979).

ing and inflexible assignments—so that children are condemned to inferior education in every subject for the life of their time in school—are not necessary consequences of grouping students according to their level of academic performance. In any case, the problem of educational quality is only one of the questions that anti-tracking spokespersons raise—and not one of concern to this article. These spokespersons make another point, which is the topic here. Identifying students as academically inadequate, they say, has a special impact on black children; minority status lowers teachers' expectations, with the result that students learn less. Ghetto kids, upon whom teachers look down, inevitably do poorly.[23] That was an argument that Judge Skelly Wright made in the District of Columbia desegregation case, in turn cited approvingly by Judge Peckham in his first *Larry P.* decision.[24]

Judge Wright refers to teachers' "misjudgments" about the ability of black students. Other tracking critics are not so kind. They make the very serious charge that racism, not poor judgment, determines who ends up in what level of classes. Racists initially designed the tests, and racists determine who goes where.[25] Judge Peckham concluded that no nonracial rea-

sons could possibly explain the concentration of blacks in EMR classes; "overenrollments" could not have "resulted under a color-blind system of placement."[26] In a September 1990 newscast, an ABC News reporter stated flatly that "throughout the nation schools are sorting students into high- and low-ability groups, often with racial bias regardless of their test scores." The program went on to quote Jeannie Oakes. "Often you'll see high-scoring kids in low tracks, low-scoring kids in high tracks and often that relates to ethnicity and social class," she said.[27]

Sorting based on racism is, of course, appalling. But no evidence suggests that what Oakes "saw" is common. Nevertheless, her perception is widespread and has, on occasion, triggered organized parent protest. This was the case in early 1990 in Selma, Alabama, when parents took to the streets in part over the tracking issue. "We have black children who are high achievers, who have high test scores, who have not been allowed to take algebra," an attorney and activist with a high school daughter complained.[28] A year later,

experts have from the beginning been willing to tolerate or even encourage tests that portray minorities, especially blacks, as intellectually inferior." He rested his conclusion on the work of Professor L. J. Kamin. See Kamin, *The Science and Politics of IQ* (Potomac, MD: Lawrence Erlbaum, 1974).

26. *Larry P.* v. *Riles*, 495 F. Supp. at 944.

27. ABC News, 4 Sept. 1990. The reporter quoted was Bill Blakemore. See also Chun, "Sorting Black Students," p. 100: "Even high-achieving blacks tend to be placed in low ability groups or tracks, while low-achieving white, middle-class students tend to be placed in high tracks or ability groups."

28. *Washington Post*, 14 Feb. 1990.

23. The point is made by many commentators. See, for example, Eva Wells Chun, "Sorting Black Students for Success and Failure: The Inequity of Ability Grouping and Tracking," in *Black Education: A Quest for Equity and Excellence*, a special edition of *Urban League Review*, 11(1-2):93-106 (Summer 1987-Winter 1987-88).

24. *Larry P.* v. *Riles*, 343 F. Supp. at 1312.

25. On the assertion that racists designed the tests to begin with, see, for example, Judge Peckham in *Larry P.*, 495 F. Supp. at 955: "The

parents in the Richardson, Texas, school district charged that black children were put in special education classes not only because they spoke, dressed, and acted differently but also because whites did not want any academic competition from blacks.[29]

That charge hinted at a broader point. It is not only racism but also its corollary, a desire to reinforce the existing hierarchical structure of power in the society, that drives the assignment of students to the various tracks, it is often argued. Thus Boston political scientist James Jennings describes tracking as a "mechanism by which to reinforce the racial and social hierarchy in our society that places blacks and the economically disadvantaged at the bottom."[30] Jeannie Oakes makes the same point. "The differentiated curriculum has served to reinforce the racial and socioeconomic stratification of society," she has written.[31] In fact, FairTest argues, children are different but none have academic "deficits."[32] Schools should promote "a sense of community and social justice, not privilege or definitions of 'deserving' and 'undeserving,'" the report on tracking by the Massachusetts Advocacy Center explains.[33]

POLICY IMPLICATIONS

I have reviewed the varied arguments against standardized tests and ability or performance grouping at some length. The point should be clear: critics of such tests do not see them as basically fair, as a legitimate means of measuring a student's academic progress. On that, all antitesting, antitracking advocates agree. Different ways of arguing the point, however, have different policy implications. For instance, the contention that standardized tests misjudge blacks' ability is an argument for substantially ignoring scores in admissions and sorting policies. Students whose record and performance on standardized tests show minimum qualifications should thus be admitted to academically selective schools —in unspecified numbers. In general, hierarchical arrangements should be modified or eliminated; cooperative learning or heterogeneous grouping within individual schools should replace academic tracking.[34]

These are classic affirmative action strategies; meritocratic standards, as traditionally defined, and differences in educational achievement are ignored in the interest of

29. Jonathan Eig, "Black Parents Decry Remedial Program," *Dallas Morning News*, 19 Feb. 1991.

30. Diego Ribadeneira, "'Tracking' Cheats Needy Students in City, Study Says," *Boston Globe*, 27 Mar. 1990.

31. Oakes, *Keeping Track*, p. 153.

32. FairTest: National Center for Fair and Open Testing (Cambridge, MA), "K-12 Testing Fact Sheet" (Brochure, n.d.).

33. *Locked in / Locked Out: Tracking and Placement Practices in Boston Public Schools* (Cambridge: Massachusetts Advocacy Center, Mar. 1990), p. 11.

34. In theory, antitracking advocates could recognize the need for some differentiation between students but insist on racial quotas in the different academic levels. In fact, that is what the plaintiffs in *Larry P.* demanded: racial quotas in the EMR classes. The judge rejected that notion, however. In addition, in 1971 a Californian legislative declaration prohibited disproportionately high numbers of students who were members of any racial or ethnic group in EMR classes, but the legislation had no teeth. These California demands and declaration are unique, to the best of my knowledge.

racial justice. The instructional playing field is made more level, but the arguments that black children think and learn differently, that the questions asked on the exams are racist or inappropriate, that teachers and administrators make racist assumptions about the capability of black children and sort them accordingly, and that schools have a duty to create an egalitarian society call for something more. They suggest the need for entirely different curricular materials, "culturally appropriate" assessment processes, more black teachers and racial sensitivity training for those who are white, and the abolition of all academically selective classes and schools. They call for familiar strategies that have arrived as corollaries to affirmative action policies in other settings.

Arguments for the elimination of tracking have gained wide acceptance. No one knows how many schools have actually replaced ability grouping—more accurately described as performance or competency grouping—with some sort of nonhierarchical way of organizing students, but certainly the desirability of doing so is frequently articulated. The notion that students—particularly minority students—should not be judged, sorted, and labeled seems widely accepted in orthodox education circles.

That idea has had a clear impact on admissions policies in elite schools —those that accept students on the basis of some sort of performance testing. Under affirmative action pressure, these special schools have altered their admissions criteria in order to enroll minority students.

Thus in Alexandria, Virginia, the Thomas Jefferson High School, specializing in science and technology, has adopted entirely new admissions standards that emphasize motivation and grades rather than scores on standardized tests in order to raise the number of minority students.[35] In Fairfax County, Virginia, four gifted and talented programs were reported in 1990 to be considering nonverbal tests for admission—tests that would "tap all the intelligences"—in order to increase their minority enrollments.[36]

The California Academy of Mathematics and Science, a high school that opened in 1990, decided not to rely on an entrance test in order to achieve a diverse student body. A student who scores above the sixty-fifth percentile on one of the mathematical achievement tests, who has taken eighth-grade algebra, and who has maintained a B average in math classes is eligible for admission. The result is a school that approximately mirrors the local population: 15 percent white, 85 percent minority, with even numbers of blacks, Hispanics, and a combination of Asians and Pacific Islanders.[37] Boston's three elite high schools now have, in effect, racial and ethnic quotas—judicially mandated as part of a desegregation plan.[38] In other cities affirmative ac-

35. *Los Angeles Times*, 9 Nov. 1990.

36. Frank Wolfe, "Fairfax Schools Hunt for Gifted Minorities," *Washington Times*, 8 Aug. 1991.

37. Telephone conversation with staff at the school, 9 Jan. 1992.

38. *Morgan* v. *Kerrigan*, 401 F. Supp. 216 (1975). No school was forced to take students that scored below the fiftieth percentile on the Secondary Scholastic Aptitude Test, however.

tion plans are supplemented by mentoring and other programs; Bronx Science in New York, for instance, has both a special admissions program for disadvantaged students and a summer program for students whose entrance examination scores fall short of the necessary mark.[39] Private schools, too, have altered admissions requirements in order to enroll black—and Hispanic—students.

Thus those who would ignore differences in educational achievement in the name of racial and ethnic equality have won at least a partial victory in the widespread commitment that schools have made to modifying tracking. Ability or competency grouping within schools has become increasingly unfashionable; cooperative learning is the current buzzword. In addition, elite, or top-track, schools are everywhere altering admissions policies to acquire a greater racial and ethnic mix of students. But neither form of tracking has disappeared entirely, and, indeed, most of the more radical proposals made by reformers—implied or explicit—have met considerable resistance. For instance, the Massachusetts Advocacy Center and others who see schools as engines for egalitarian social reform argue for the elimination of all exclusive schools, given their disproportionate racial and ethnic impact.[40] Those schools remain, however, ironically due in part to pressure from minority parents, who see such schools as an avenue of social mobility.[41]

A lesser degree of skepticism has greeted proposals to institute more culturally appropriate curricular materials and to train teachers in racial sensitivity—familiar by-products of affirmative action programs. In fact, it seems safe to say that no major urban school system has been unaffected by demands for curricular revision. Some schools are using or discussing the use of multicultural history and English texts that tell a racially and ethnically inclusive story; others have adopted an Afrocentric curriculum that extends to math and science and places the contributions of Africans and African Americans at the center of all instruction. In general, these are local school district decisions, but in California and New York the curriculum is being revised at the state level.

Thus California has adopted a new social studies series that weaves the story of non-European civilizations and non-European peoples into both the world and the American history texts. On the other hand, Atlanta, Detroit, Washington, D.C., and other cities are teaching Egyptian hieroglyphics, discussing the work of black inventors, and telling African stories.[42] New York State, too, appears

39. Los Angeles Times, 9 Nov. 1990.

40. Locked in / Locked Out, p. 58.

41. Thus in San Francisco in early 1970s, the National Association for the Advancement of Colored People opposed making admissions at an elite magnet school noncompetitive. In Boston there has been similar resistance.

42. The literature on multicultural and Afrocentric curricular revisions has become very large. See, for instance, Mary Lefkowitz, "Not out of Africa," New Republic, 10 Feb. 1992, p. 29; Nathan Glazer, "In Defense of Multiculturalism," ibid., 2 Sept. 1991, p. 18; Diane Ravitch, "Multiculturalism: E Pluribus Plures," American Scholar, 59(3):337-54 (Summer 1990); Molefi Kete Asante and Diane Ravitch, "Multiculturalism: An Exchange," American Scholar, 60:267-76 (Spring 1991).

headed in an Afrocentric direction.[43] In other jurisdictions, a commitment to multicultural education has been made, with the details yet to be worked out; thus Minnesota has embraced the idea of a new statewide graduation requirement that would assess students' ability to live in a culturally diverse society, but it has not yet arrived at a consensus on what the measure might be.[44] Private schools, too, are taking a second look at curricular materials that seem Eurocentric in tone and are adding courses on subjects such as black music.[45] Indeed, some that serve only black students have fully embraced the Afrocentric notion. At Shule Mandela Academy in East Palo Alto, California, for instance, pupils are asked to "think black, act black, speak black, buy black, pray black, love black and live black."[46]

It is not students alone, of course, who are said to need a different education; affirmative action advocates would like to see an extensive process of retraining for teachers as well. Such retraining is much talked about—with unknown results. In

Portland, Oregon, all teachers are encouraged to use the "Baseline Essays" that are the bible of the Afrocentrists and that trace all knowledge and culture back to ancient Egypt, which is depicted as a black-African civilization. Afrocentric conferences that provide workshops and lectures for teachers are a regular feature of the educational landscape. Elite private schools are also asking teachers to rethink the messages they deliver; thus the Phillips Academy, in Andover, Massachusetts, has an Office of Community Affairs and Multicultural Development that runs staff as well as student workshops and generally promotes multiculturalism.[47]

The demand for increasing the number of black teachers, particularly in heavily black urban school systems, has also been well received, at least to the extent that the market has allowed. School systems across the nation are on a determined search for more black teachers, despite the fact that there is a substantial racial gap in black and white teachers' scores and no evidence that black children learn better from black instructors.[48] New York City, for example, adopted an affirmative action plan in 1990 that includes a directive to find teachers in southern black colleges. The city has plenty of company in its search. Recruiters are competing in a seller's market. " 'When you go to teacher fairs,' " one Minnesota official has complained,

43. See New York State Social Studies Review and Development Committee, "One Nation, Many Peoples: A Declaration of Cultural Interdependence" (Report, June 1991).

44. Bob Hotakainen, "Desegregation Plans Sought: State Will Require Action by Suburban Districts," *Star Tribune* (Minneapolis), 14 May 1991.

45. For a description of private school efforts, see, for instance, Phyllis Coons, "National Association of Independent Schools Pilots Multicultural Plan," *Boston Globe*, 29 July 1990; Sharon Britton, "A Fast-Changing Andover Rethinks Its View of the World," ibid., 2 June 1991.

46. "A Is for Ashanti, B Is for Black," *Newsweek*, 23 Sept. 1991, p. 45. © 1991, *Newsweek*, Inc. All rights reserved. Reprinted by permission.

47. Britton, "Fast-Changing Andover."

48. Gerald David Jaynes and Robin M. Williams, Jr., eds., *A Common Destiny: Blacks and American Society* (Washington, DC: National Academy Press, 1989), p. 364.

" 'you'll see some of the best-qualified teachers of color walking around with five and six contracts in their pocket, just ready to choose.' " Those contracts may include college loan forgiveness and other such enticements.[49]

CONCLUSION

Affirmative action in elementary and secondary education often takes forms that may not be immediately recognized as such. Efforts to increase minority representation in elite schools and to recruit more black teachers are business as usual. But heterogeneous classroom grouping—sometimes called cooperative learning—is another matter. Normally viewed as nothing more than a pedagogical strategy, it, like other affirmative action efforts, amounts, in fact, to a conscious effort to alter the low-track status of minority pupils. De-tracked students, by definition, become part of the high-track group. Their representation among the elect is increased. Similarly, the demand for curricular reforms, racial sensitivity training, and more culturally appropriate tests, while not obviously affirmative action strategies, are precisely that. They attempt to broaden the definition of excellence and to create a more racially inclusive educational system.

Are these affirmative action policies an answer to the inadequate performance of black students? Not all educators think they are. There is " 'a lot of knee-jerk, Band-Aid response,

especially when it comes to minority achievement,' " a Montgomery County, Maryland, administrator has said. " 'We are under pressure to have the right numbers: not too many black kids suspended, get more in honors courses,' " he went on. " 'It's all about looking good and not dealing with the real problems.' " Shuffling kids, instituting leveling policies that disguise differences in academic competence, adopting a multicultural or Afrocentric curriculum, hiring black teachers, running sensitivity workshops—these are all solutions on the cheap. They cost taxpayers almost nothing and, in urban school districts in which almost all pupils are members of minority groups, they affect relatively few whites. Thus they are both financially and politically palatable.

A serious attack on the racial gap in performance may take more, however. Indeed, it may call for recognizing—rather than ignoring—different levels of educational attainment, not with programs that are boring and academically worthless, of course, but with different work, approached and paced differently, for different kids. Moreover, for those inner-city students who are now performing especially poorly, it may take expensive intervention in their out-of-school lives. In 1992 the educational landscape is dotted with experiments focused for the most part on disadvantaged children. It is not yet clear what will truly work. It is clear, how-

49. Bob Hotakainen, "Incentives Urged to Attract Minority Teachers to State," *Star Tribune* (Minneapolis), 14 Aug. 1991.

50. Patrick Welsh, "A Lesson in Reading, Writing—and Red Tape: The Problem Our School Bureaucracies Create," *Washington Post*, 2 Dec. 1990.

ever, that the best reformers know that so-called white academic standards are not racist, that the failure to meet those standards is meaningful, and that real progress will have occurred when whites and blacks, by a common measure, perform the same.

ANNALS, *AAPSS*, 523, September 1992

Affirmative Action in Higher Education

By HAROLD ORLANS

ABSTRACT: Affirmative action in higher education has sought to increase the number of women and minority students and faculty in most educational fields, levels, and ranks. Voluntary measures to recruit black students and faculty began in the 1960s, before the government, in the early 1970s, imposed elaborate requirements to promote the employment of women and minority faculty. Women's groups pressing to change admission and employment practices they judged discriminatory have made far greater gains than blacks. In the last decade, Asians have also done surprisingly well as graduate students, faculty, and research staff in the sciences and engineering. The higher-educational status of blacks remains troublesome. In small part, this reflects many black students' preference for the professions over graduate school and academic life; in larger part, the consequences of slum life and schools.

Harold Orlans has a Ph.D. in anthropology from Yale (1949). Since 1954, he has conducted studies of policy and administration in Washington. His books include The Effects of Federal Programs on Higher Education *(1962),* Contracting for Knowledge *(1973), and* Private Accreditation and Public Eligibility *(1975). In 1984-86, he directed an aborted study of affirmative action in higher education at the U.S. Commission on Civil Rights.*

EFFORTS to increase the number of minority and women students and faculty in higher education have been much debated but inadequately studied. Because opinion is so polarized, objective study is difficult, perhaps impossible. The same statistics accompanied by different quotations support contrary conclusions of discrimination or preference. Actual practices in admitting, aiding, tutoring, and grading students and in hiring, paying, and tenuring faculty can be so disguised that it is hard to know what they really are. Words like "racism," "standards," "quality," "equity," "equal opportunity," and "quota" can mean opposite things to those who like and dislike affirmative action. However, their use and adverbs like "only" before innocent numbers quickly betray a writer's position.

AFFIRMATIVE ADMISSIONS

Many northern institutions began to recruit black students during the 1960s, especially after the disturbances following the 1968 assassination of Martin Luther King, Jr. Political pressures and government and private programs spurred their initiatives; whether colleges lead or follow the clamor of events is often hard to determine.

Since 1973, federal court orders in *Adams* required 19 southern and border states, including Ohio and Pennsylvania, to enroll more blacks in historically white, and more whites in historically black, state colleges.[1]

Governors, legislatures, state higher education authorities, and private boards have pressed institutions to enroll more "underrepresented" minorities—usually blacks and Hispanics. Thus California legislative bodies have repeatedly adjured community colleges and the state's two university systems "to approximate . . . the general ethnic, gender, economic, and regional composition of recent high school graduates, both in first-year classes and . . . graduating classes."[2]

Special aid and enrollment-driven appropriations have induced many institutions to recruit minority students. Federal and private programs also seek to increase the number of women, blacks, and Hispanics in the sciences and engineering.

Except in *Adams*, courts have evidently not ordered student recruitment to rectify past discrimination. The 1972 law barring educational discrimination against women, however, contributed to the upsurge in their admission to medical, law, and other professional schools.

Selective institutions

The wisdom of special standards for black and Hispanic applicants has

---

1. *Adams* was initiated in October 1972, when the NAACP Legal Defense Fund filed suit charging Health, Education, and Welfare Secretary Elliot Richardson with failure to compel 10 states, which he had found to maintain segregated colleges, to desegregate their colleges or lose their federal funds. Federal District Court Judge John H. Pratt ordered successive Health, Education, and Welfare Secretaries to comply. See Jean Preer, *Lawyers v. Educators* (Westport, CT: Greenwood Press, 1982).

2. *Freshman Admissions at Berkeley* (Berkeley: University of California, Academic Senate, Berkeley Division, Committee on Admissions and Enrollment, May 1989), p. 13.

been much debated, especially at selective institutions.

Once, multiple-choice tests were said to make admission decisions fairer than subjective judgments based on essays, photographs, interviews, and family background that favored well-to-do and well-mannered applicants. Today, such tests are said to be biased against blacks and Hispanics, for whom greater reliance is placed on interviews, separately ranked test scores, extracurricular interests, and elusive or illusory factors like personal determination or the contribution of diversity to educational quality.

Critics say that admitting academically poor minorities is unfair to better-qualified applicants who are excluded. It can lead to high dropout rates, lower academic standards, remedial instruction, and a separate track with easier courses, grades, and degrees for below-par students. Those who need tutoring and grants and take longer to graduate are costly, per degree, so their retention is closely tied to money. Protests at callous revolving-door policies—when, to boost minority enrollment, colleges admit many students who soon drop out—are most cheaply met by promoting and graduating them.

It is charged that, at elite colleges, mediocre minority students are patronized and suffer anxiety and self-doubt they would not feel at less selective colleges and that lowered standards stigmatize able minority students who do not require them. Advocates of affirmative admissions respond that they prefer favorable to unfavorable discrimination. There have been special admission standards for the children of alumni, faculty, donors, politicians, celebrities, athletes, and local residents, and easy degrees for students who buy term papers, cheat on exams, and take a gentleman's C with little study and much beer. Why not for blacks and Hispanics?

Elite colleges have social as well as academic functions. The inclusion of formerly excluded minorities among their graduates and, thereby, among our future leaders is a more important service than the preparation of more scholars and scientists. As blacks and Hispanics are a rising proportion of the population, their higher education is vital to social peace and to the quality of the work force and economy.

Eliminating special admissions would greatly reduce the number of blacks and Hispanics at selective colleges and raise it at state and community colleges, where they are already concentrated. It would revive the discarded idea of educating them only for jobs at the lower rungs of the economic and social ladder. It would restore the lily-white complexion of prominent colleges, exposing them to political and financial retribution.

Nathan Glazer has made the case for special admissions at selective colleges:

If colleges and universities remain . . . the major means by which a rough status is distributed among men, they cannot maintain the primacy of tested academic ability, except in those areas where they have a strong case that tested academic talents . . . are necessary . . . —particularly in the sciences. . . . [Academic abilities] are only doubtfully suited for determining the distribution of status and power in society. There is now a powerful drive to have blacks play a larger role in society. It is inconceivable that academic standards . . . will be allowed to stand in the way.[3]

Asian students

The academic status of Asian Americans contrasts sharply with that of blacks and Hispanics. Though designated a minority and included in government minority statistics and policies, their academic qualifications usually equal or, in science, excel those of whites.

Yet many selective institutions admit proportionately fewer Asian than black and Hispanic applicants. Asians call that a quota or ceiling, as it must be; like whites, they must have their overrepresentation reduced if other groups are to have their underrepresentation raised.

In the early 1980s, the proportion of Asian applicants admitted to Harvard, Brown, Yale, Princeton, and Stanford was below the average for all applicants,[4] a plain case of discrimination against superior students. The proportion of applicants admitted from each ethnic group is seldom reported; for the class entering Amherst in September 1991, it was as follows: blacks, 55 percent; Hispanics, 53 percent; Asians, 31 percent; whites, 18 percent.[5]

At Berkeley, the admission chances of applicants with a 3.5 high school grade average and 1200 Scholastic Aptitude Test score were put at " 'nearly a hundred percent' " for blacks and " 'about five percent' " for whites or Asians.[6] As the University of Virginia admissions dean explained, " 'We take more in the groups with weaker credentials and make it harder for those with stronger credentials.' "[7]

The head of a Connecticut preparatory school tells the following story. Two of his students, both Californians, applied to Berkeley.

Student A was ranked in the top third of his class, student B in the bottom third. Student A had College Board scores totalling 1,290; student B's scores totaled 890. Student A had a record of good citizenship; student B was expelled . . . for breaking a series of major school rules. Student A was white; student B was black. Berkeley refused student A and accepted B.[8]

Determining fair and proper representation is an insoluble dilemma. Should a model college class reflect the ethnic composition of comparable colleges? of all or the best seniors in high schools from which the college recruits? of the present or future local, state, or national population? An Education Commission of the

3. Nathan Glazer, "Are Academic Standards Obsolete?" in *Inside Academe* (New Rochelle, NY: Change, 1972), p. 160.

4. Sucheng Chan and Ling-chi Wang, "Racism and the Model Minority: Asian-Americans in Higher Education," in *The Racial Crisis in American Higher Education*, ed. Philip G. Altbach and Kofi Lomotey (Albany: State University of New York, 1991), p. 54.

5. *Amherst Student*, 3 Apr. 1991, pp. 1-2. Of the 973 students admitted 103, or 10.6

percent, were black; 102, or 10.5 percent, Hispanic; 146, or 15 percent, Asian; and 622, or 64 percent, white or unidentified.

6. As Ernest Koeningsburg, professor of business, who has served on Berkeley admission committees, is quoted in Dinesh D'Souza, "Illiberal Education," *Atlantic*, Mar. 1991, p. 54.

7. Quoted by Thomas Edsall and Mary Edsall, "Race," *Atlantic*, May 1991, p. 73.

8. Donald Werner, "College Admissions: Shaky Ethics," *New York Times*, 4 June 1988. Copyright © 1988 by The New York Times Company. Reprinted by permission.

States report wants minority enrollment "at least proportionate to the minority population of each state."[9]

If affirmative efforts are to improve, not perpetuate, the educational status of blacks and Hispanics, colleges should raise their enrollment above present levels. To do so, they must dip deeper into their scholastic ranks. Blacks were 5 percent and Hispanics, 3 percent of the Massachusetts population yet 8 and 7 percent, respectively, of the fall 1990 entering class at Harvard, which may have sought targets closer to the 12 and 8 percent of the national population that blacks and Hispanics then constituted.

Of course, selective colleges cream the crop, leaving poorer students to crowded public colleges.

Unselective institutions

Colleges need students as sawmills need logs. Since government student aid benefits the college as well as the student, a tacit collusion can arise whereby both share the money and neither cares overmuch about education—or even about attendance, as the House Veterans' Affairs Committee once learned:

We found no attendance policies, no standards in grading [at Florida Junior College, Jacksonville]. . . . 6,000 veterans enrolled, innumerable examples of individuals who . . . had never passed one single, solitary course . . . being carried in good standing . . . and paid by the U.S. Government. . . . this pattern emerges across the country. . . . these people

. . . are not even on the campus. They are simply carried on the rolls.[10]

Whatever may have happened in the 1960s and 1970s, blacks and Hispanics at selective institutions now tend to be serious, full-time students, often from middle-class families. At urban community colleges and large public universities where low-income students congregate, the situation can be grim. Those who must work and/or care for children attend part-time. Many need financial and personal help, advice, and encouragement and instruction in grammar, spelling, expository writing, reading with discernment, and study skills. All this they must get from overburdened, underpaid, and undervalued teachers, teaching assistants, tutors, and advisers, the untenured proletariat serving hard-pressed students.[11]

High dropout and loan-default rates result, along with feeble grades in serious courses or decent grades in feeble courses, long years of attendance, and low rates of graduation and graduate study. At every educational level, a similar pattern recurs: relatively more blacks and Hispanics do poorly in school, withdraw, or do poorly there and do not finish or proceed further.

Parity for the poor

Our schools and colleges necessarily reflect the society that sustains

9. Mary Crystal Cage, "Government Officials Urged to Create Incentives for Colleges to Increase Minority Enrollment," *Chronicle of Higher Education*, 12 Dec. 1990, p. A17.

10. U.S., Congress, House, Committee on Veterans' Affairs, Subcommittee on Education and Training, *Overpayments and Enforcement of Standards in the Veterans' Education Program*, 94th Cong., 2d sess., 1976, pp. 1965-66.

11. See Harold Orlans, "Changing Conditions, Minority Education at Oakes College," *Thought and Action*, 6(1):21-34 (Spring 1990).

them. The report of an august council to improve the education of minorities correctly concludes, "We must have not only better schools, we must also have better housing, health, nutrition, job opportunities, and adequate student financial assistance."[12] That is, we must make the slum life of the poor resemble middle-class suburban life.

In 1977, obedient to the judge's order in *Adams*, Health, Education, and Welfare Secretary Joseph Califano issued guidelines for states to eliminate the "vestiges of racial segregation" in their colleges and universities. They are among the most comprehensive affirmative action goals for black students—and faculty—prepared by any agency: the proportion of black high school students who enter state institutions should at least equal that of white graduates; the proportion of black graduates of state colleges who enter state graduate and professional schools should at least equal that of white graduates in each major field; annual goals should be set and "all reasonable steps" taken "to reduce any disparity between the proportion of black and white" graduates of state institutions at all levels—two-year, four-year, and graduate; parity in all these and other goals should be reached "not later than within five years."[13]

Of course, these goals have not been met. An official can decree parity in black and white physics doctorates, in the number of poor black and

affluent white students who read at home in quiet and comfort, who travel, study hard, get good grades in good schools, and then go to college instead of to work, childbearing, the army, or prison. He can decree educational parity as did the good king, standing on his palace balcony, arm extended above his assembled people: "It is my wish that this be the most educated country in the world, and toward that end, I hereby ordain that each and every one of my people be given a diploma."[14] Would that it were that simple to achieve parity for all people in all fields and levels of education, to escape history, economics, and the injustice of being born in the wrong family and the wrong circumstances.

AFFIRMATIVE HIRING

About 1100 institutions with $50,000 or more in federal contracts must set numerical goals for hiring more women and minority faculty and other employees in areas where they are "underutilized," or not employed in proportion to their "availability."

The program has been enforced more rigidly under some officials, like Health, Education, and Welfare Secretaries Elliot Richardson (1970-73) and Joseph Califano (1977-79), than others, like Caspar Weinberger (1973-75). Under Presidents Reagan and Bush, enforcement apparently became weaker, yet neither president rescinded hiring goals and the Labor Department continues to impose them.

12. Quality Education for Minorities Project, *Education That Works* (Cambridge: Massachusetts Institute of Technology, 1990), p. 4.

13. *Federal Register*, 11 Aug. 1977; ibid., 15 Feb. 1978.

14. *New Yorker* cartoon in John Valley, *Increasing the Options* (Princeton, NJ: Educational Testing Service, 1972), p. 4.

In any case, most campuses would probably retain similar policies voluntarily. The rising enrollment of minorities and women—now 54 percent of all students—has often led to demands for more minority and women faculty. Carnegie and Sloan Foundation commissions have endorsed affirmative action as have many college boards; accrediting agencies have pressed for it with varying force.

When President Reagan considered dropping employment goals, American Council on Education President Robert Atwell protested: "Higher education administrators have come to accept affirmative action. . . . [It has] transformed our faculty . . . with the infusion of individuals with new ideas and backgrounds. . . . [it has provided] role models for many of our students. . . . Overall, [it] . . . has worked."[15]

When the diversity standard in Middle States accreditation—requiring a college's board, administrators, faculty, curricula, and services to reflect its student body in ways not clearly specified—was attacked by Education Secretary Lamar Alexander, Atwell defended it. Such a standard, he correctly stated, "represents not a unanimous view but a strong consensus on the part of the leaders of our colleges and universities."[16]

Affirmative action regulations were formally imposed in October 1972, when Office for Civil Rights (OCR) Director Stanley Pottinger informed all colleges and universities that those with federal contracts

15. Letter to President Ronald Reagan, 18 Sept. 1985.

16. U.S., Department of Education, National Advisory Committee on Accreditation and Institutional Eligibility, Transcript, 22 Nov. 1991.

must comply. To cite a typical case, the University of North Carolina had done little until then; its first affirmative action officer was hired in September 1973 and department chairmen received their first instructions soon after. Harvard's first affirmative action plan was adopted in 1973.

Woman power

Women were the main force behind OCR's action and the main beneficiaries of hiring goals in higher education.

In 1970, the Women's Equity Action League (WEAL) began to file class-action complaints charging academic institutions with a pattern of discrimination against women. President Johnson's Executive Order 11375, extending contractor affirmative action to women as of October 1968, supplied the vital lever. In a well-organized national campaign, academic women wrote their congressmen to ask why the Secretaries of Labor and Health, Education, and Welfare did not enforce this order.

The Secretaries received too many congressional letters to ignore. Before long, WEAL brought charges against over 250 institutions under Executive Order 11375 and 1972 legislation barring sexual discrimination in "any education . . . activity" receiving federal funds.

Women's charges of discrimination were countered by some 150 charges of reverse discrimination against white men, preferential hiring of blacks, and quotas that OCR received by October 1973. Many were brought by the Anti-Defamation

League and other organizations reflecting the views and interests of Jewish faculty.[17] They had suffered from past restrictive quotas and, being now "overrepresented" at many universities, could suffer again from demographically representative employment. The Anti-Defamation League complained that OCR investigated charges of discrimination more diligently than those of reverse discrimination.

Testifying for the American Jewish Committee in favor of affirmative action, Bernice Sandler, who led WEAL's effective campaign, said:

I am concerned and dismayed at the opposition to affirmative action [by] . . . many Jewish groups. . . . many Jewish women feel that these groups are concerned about Jewish men and . . . are not speaking for the Jewish women . . . who suffer far more in academia because of their sex than their religion.[18]

Staff incompetence

Everyone criticized OCR. It did too little to please affirmative action supporters, too much to please opponents, and both sides agreed it was incompetent.

Sandler called criticism of OCR "inefficiency, incompetence and inconsisten[cy] . . . more than justified."[19] OCR staff were "largely drawn from the black civil rights

movement. . . . [They were] mostly male, and seemed . . . in questionable sympathy with . . . women activists."[20] Their concentration on the concerns of blacks, especially in *Adams* states, prompted successful suits and court orders directing OCR to give more attention to women, Hispanics, and disabled persons. By 1977, the orders of federal judges served to allocate 80 percent of OCR staff time.

Academic officials and faculty were appalled at the ignorance of higher education exhibited by OCR and Labor staff. Many did not even have a college degree. They used inapplicable or meaningless words ("firm," "job group"), forms, and ideas ("availability," "utilization"); demanded vast amounts of nonexistent, fabricated, or confidential data; equated low numbers with discrimination; questioned hallowed hiring practices such as private recommendations and the Ph.D. requirement, indeed any requirement that might reduce the number of female or minority appointments.

It took years before affirmative action plans were approved; endless "deficiencies" were found and changes required in statistics, hiring goals, and procedures. By September 1976, four years after the first OCR directive, only 33 of 863 institutional plans had been approved.

Matters did not improve when, in 1978, enforcement moved to the Labor Department's Office of Federal Contract Compliance Programs

17. Richard Lester, *Reasoning about Discrimination* (Princeton, NJ: Princeton University Press, 1980), p. 165.

18. U.S., Congress, House, Committee on Education and Labor, Special Subcommittee on Education, *Hearings, Federal Higher Education Programs, Institutional Eligibility, Civil Rights Obligations*, 93d Cong., 2d sess., 19 Sept. 1974, p. 282.

19. Ibid., p. 280.

20. Joyce Gelb and Marian Palley, *Women and Public Policies* (Princeton, NJ: Princeton University Press, 1982), p. 112.

(OFCCP). Labor staff often rejected the OCR format for higher education plans, insisting on senseless industrial terms and categories—for example, "sales workers." To this day, they talk of "firms," not "institutions," since colleges occupy perhaps 5 percent of their staff time.

In 1982, Purdue was in the eleventh year of a continuing compliance review. At Johns Hopkins, OFCCP conducted eight reviews in four years; a Hopkins spokesman attributed many of the "deficiencies" charged by OFCCP staff to their "failure to read . . . and comprehend the massive documents . . . they had demanded" or to the university's obeying regulations that OFCCP then altered. Staff often changed; documents were often lost—the university had to supply some of them nine times.[21]

After long years of combat, opponents and proponents of affirmative hiring, like exhausted buck with locked horns, have had to put up with an unsatisfactory system they have failed either to end or improve.

In Washington and on campus, the line between real and pedantic, meaningful and formal enforcement, desirable and undesirable hiring is contentious and difficult to document objectively. Hence the constant resort to statistics and debates over their adequacy, relevance, and meaning.

The composition of faculty

The pressure to employ women and minority faculty comes not only

21. Estelle Fishbein, General Counsel, Johns Hopkins University, U.S., Congress, Senate, Committee on Labor and Human Resources, *Hearings*, 97th Cong., 1st sess., 29 and 30 July and 29 Oct. 1982, pt. 1, pp. 260-62.

from Washington and state capitals but campuses where the number of women or minority students has risen markedly. Windows need not be broken or the media air student grievances. Ultimately, the pressure is the same that audiences exert on movie houses and producers: play to, indeed arouse public taste or risk empty seats while your rivals enjoy packed houses.

The tendency of the social composition of faculty to follow that of students is shown in Table 1, which reports the number of students and faculty by sex and ethnicity at the beginning and end of the decade from 1978-79 to 1988-89. Since it takes four years to replace a student body but perhaps thirty for a faculty, the statistics are not ideal; statistics seldom are.

Nonetheless, a comparison of the changes in the student and faculty populations is illuminating. In every ethnic group, the relative increase of both women students and faculty exceeded that of men. However, despite a small decline in the number of black male students, the number of black male faculty rose by 1900 (toward the end of the decade).

The lower ranks of assistant professors, instructors, and short-term, temporary, and part-time faculty, who can readily be hired—even after registration—and fired as the student body fluctuates, doubtless reflect the student population more closely than the tenured professoriat.

The comparative mobility of students and turgidity of faculty are evident in the institutional distribution of blacks. In the era of segregation, most black students and almost all

TABLE 1
**NUMBER OF STUDENTS AND FACULTY AND
PERCENTAGE CHANGE, 1978-88 AND 1979-89, BY SEX AND ETHNICITY**

| Sex and Ethnic Group | Number (thousands) | | | | Percentage Change | |
| | Students* | | Faculty† | | Students | Faculty |
	1978	1988	1979	1989	1978-88	1979-89
Total	11,231	13,043	451.3	514.7	16.1	14.0
Men	5,621	5,998	335.3	358.6	6.7	6.9
Women	5,609	7,045	116.1	156.1	25.6	34.5
White	9,194	10,284	410.9	455.6	11.9	10.9
Men	4,613	4,712	308.5	319.3	2.1	3.5
Women	4,581	5,572	102.5	136.3	21.6	33.0
Black	1,054	1,130	19.5	23.2	7.2	19.1
Men	453	443	10.6	12.5	−2.2	18.0
Women	601	687	8.9	10.7	14.3	20.5
Hispanic	417	680	6.8	10.1	63.1	48.8
Men	213	310	4.9	6.8	45.5	38.7
Women	205	370	1.9	3.3	80.5	74.5
Asian	235	496	13.1	24.1	111.1	84.4
Men	126	259	10.6	19.0	105.6	78.8
Women	109	237	2.5	5.1	117.4	108.3

SOURCES: For the data on students, *Minorities in Higher Education* (Washington, DC: American Council on Education, 1990), p. 27; for faculty data, ibid., 1991, p. 63.

NOTES: Details may not add to totals due to rounding. Totals include Native American students and faculty and several hundred thousand resident-alien students.

*Full- and part-time.

†Full-time.

black faculty were concentrated in about 105 traditionally black colleges. When segregation ended, black students dispersed more rapidly than black faculty. By 1982-83, only 16 percent of black students but 44 percent of full-time black faculty were still located at these colleges.

Black students at traditionally white institutions complain that they have too few black teachers, especially tenured professors; some accreditors want the proportion of black faculty to approximate that of black students in each institution; while the Labor Department envis-ages an identical proportion of black faculty—one equal to their national "availability"—in every institution. These conflicting views of affirmative employment are irreconcilable. Faculty cannot be concentrated at black and urban colleges where black students concentrate and also dispersed in equal proportions among 3700 institutions.

Women faculty

Historically, the proportion of faculty who were women has greatly exceeded the proportion of women among Ph.D. recipients (Table 2).

TABLE 2

PERCENTAGE OF WOMEN FACULTY AND PH.D.'s, 1890-1989

	Percentage of Women among	
Year	Faculty*	Ph.D.'s Awarded
1890	19.6	1.3
1900	19.8	6.0
1910	20.1	9.9
1920	26.3	15.1
1930	27.2	15.4
1940	27.6	13.0
1950	24.5	9.6
1960	22.0	10.5
1970	23.1	13.3
1980	29.0	29.7
1989	30.3	37.7[†]

SOURCES: 1890-1980, *Digest of Education Statistics 1989* (Washington, DC: National Center for Education Statistics, 1989), p. 166; 1989, *Minorities in Higher Education* (Washington, DC: American Council on Education, 1991), pp. 59, 63.

*Based on number of different individuals, not full-time equivalents.

[†]The growing number of Ph.D.'s earned by predominantly male foreign students affects the figures for recent years. Thus, in 1989, women received 42.7 percent of the Ph.D.'s awarded to U.S. citizens.

Only in the early 1980s did the flood of women into graduate and professional schools change that situation. Women faculty and advanced-degree recipients have been concentrated in education, the humanities, and what have been called semiprofessions such as home economics, library science, nursing, and social work.

Women have also been concentrated in the lower faculty ranks and salaries, in teaching rather than research activities, and in two- and four-year colleges and universities with lesser reputations. Affirmative action has sought to change this distribution to resemble that of men and to produce more women Ph.D's in predominantly male fields like the physical sciences, math, and engineering.

The dubious success of substantial resources devoted to this effort can be judged by comparing the degrees awarded to women in various sciences with those in professional fields (Table 3).

One might see the rise in the number of women's engineering Ph.D.'s and the doubling of their physics Ph.D.'s in the 1978-88 decade as a great success, but few degrees were actually awarded and the number in mathematics declined. The continued growth in the life sciences, traditionally the sciences of greatest interest to women, seems more significant.

The real revolution occurred in the professions, especially law and medicine. Including 24,600 master's of business administration degrees, the terminal business degree, which the Education Department does not regard as professional, women received four times more professional than doctoral degrees in 1988. From 1958 to 1989, the proportion of M.D.'s

TABLE 3
ADVANCED DEGREES AWARDED TO WOMEN
IN SELECTED SCIENCES AND PROFESSIONS, 1978-88

Degree and Field	Number of Degrees Awarded				Percentage Change	
	1978		1988		1978-88	
	Total	Women	Total	Women	Total	Women
Ph.D.*	25,291	7,355	23,172	9,505	−8.4	29.2
Science and Engineering*	13,086	2,792	12,847	4,114	−1.8	47.3
Physics	804	29	721	57	−10.3	96.6
Math	619	91	341	59	−44.9	−35.2
Life sciences	3,522	778	3,658	1,285	3.9	65.2
Engineering	1,261	30	1,778	178	41.0	493.3
Professional*	66,581	14,311	70,735	25,251	6.2	76.4
Dentistry	5,189	566	4,477	1,177	−13.7	108.0
Medicine	14,279	3,069	15,358	5,080	7.6	65.5
Law	34,402	8,945	35,397	14,330	2.9	60.2

SOURCES: For Ph.D.'s (to U.S. citizens only): *Science & Engineering Indicators—1989* (Washington, DC: National Science Board, 1989), p. 226; for professional degrees: *Digest of Education Statistics 1991* (Washington, DC: National Center for Education Statistics, 1991), pp. 280-81, and *Digest of Education Statistics 1980* (Washington, DC: National Center for Education Statistics, 1980), p. 128.
　　*Including fields not listed below.

awarded to women rose from 5 to 33 percent and the number, from 347 to 5128; the proportion of law degrees, from 3 to 41 percent and the number, from 272 to 14,519: a genuine invasion and occupation of formerly male domains.

The Asian-black contrast

Affirmative action was instituted for blacks but, in advanced degrees and faculty appointments, Asians have prospered.

The contrast between the relatively stable number of Ph.D.'s awarded to and faculty positions held by blacks since the mid-1970s and the sharp increase in those of Asians is striking. The 1990 census reported four times as many blacks as Asians in the U.S. population; the 1980 census, eight times as many. Yet from 1975 to 1985, the number of full-time Asian faculty rose 9300 and black faculty, 500. By 1990, there were more Asian than black faculty—24,250 and 23,225, respectively.

In 1987, six times more Asian than black scientists and engineers with Ph.D.'s were engaged in academic research and development, a source of income beloved by academic administrators (Table 4). That helps to explain why, at Harvard in a recent year, six times more Asians than blacks held faculty appointments, including many postdoctoral training and research positions.[22]

22. See John B. Williams, "Affirmative Action at Harvard," this issue of *The Annals* of the American Academy of Political and Social Science, tab. 5.

TABLE 4

**NUMBER OF BLACK AND ASIAN SCIENTISTS AND ENGINEERS
WITH Ph.D.'s ENGAGED IN ACADEMIC RESEARCH AND DEVELOPMENT, 1987**

Sciences	Total[#]	Blacks	Asians
Physical*	22,407	192	2,179
Mathematical[†]	9,172	62	995
Computer	3,491	. . .**	348
Environmental[‡]	6,348	30	331
Life	51,918	736	4,456
Biological	34,138	459	2,857
Agricultural	7,040	97	347
Medical	10,740	180	1,252
Engineering[§]	19,059	119	3,381
Psychological	13,012	230	319
Social[‖]	29,179	736	1,834
Total	154,586	2,111	13,843

SOURCE: *Science & Engineering Indicators—1989* (Washington, DC: National Science Board, 1989), p. 320.

*Chemistry, physics, astronomy.
[†]Mathematics, statistics.
[‡]Earth and atmospheric science, oceanography.
[§]Aeronautical, chemical, civil, electrical, materials, mechanical, nuclear, systems, and so on.
[‖]Economics, political science, sociology, anthropology.
[#]Including whites, Hispanics, Native Americans.
**Less than 20.

The contrast in the academic record, credentials, and employment of these two minorities shows the folly of seeking identical employment patterns for groups whose social, economic, and educational experience differs so radically.

Many Asians received their early education in nations where schools provide academic preparation, not detention, entertainment, or a battlefield where teachers and students fight for attention and control. Asian Ph.D. and faculty statistics are magnified by foreign students who eventually remain. Of the 5150 Asians awarded Ph.D.'s in 1989, only 624 were citizens; 631 held permanent visas, and 3877, temporary visas.

Both foreign and American-born Asians come from intact families, study earnestly, and are not mocked or harassed for doing so. The longer they live here, the more they may relapse toward the American academic mean.

Many black students suffer the ills of distressed neighborhoods, turbulent schools, and broken homes. In 1989, 60 percent of those in higher education and 53 percent of those awarded Ph.D.'s were women, compared to 29 percent of Asians and 41 percent of whites. Many men had left school for work, unemployment, the military, crime, and other nonacademic pursuits.

Asians have clustered in the sciences and engineering, where academic employment prospects remain good; blacks, in softer graduate fields. Historically, black graduates could find work in segregated colleges and school systems; education still accounted for 48 percent of the Ph.D.'s earned by black citizens in 1989.

By margins as high as 6 to 1, blacks have preferred professional degrees in such fields as law, medicine, dentistry, and business to Ph.D.'s. Who but universities trying to placate protesting students and Labor inspectors can say they are wrong to choose the rewards of private practice over the aggravations of the academy?

Enduring forces and effects

It is impossible to separate the employment of women and minority faculty in an era of government affirmative action from the employment that might otherwise have occurred. Independent affirmative action would have persisted,[23] though most measures took their present form in response to government pressure. Some say that, under Presidents Reagan and Bush, only the independent measures have persisted with any force.

Without gainsaying the altruism of higher education administrators, other forces have impelled them in the same direction. Women students, now the dominant market for academic wares, are a powerful economic force; another is the Asian labor pool, which has become vital for the operation of the rich academic research complex.

Affirmative action has brought enduring changes in personnel record systems and employment procedures.

In the early 1970s, campus record systems could seldom provide the labor force statistics that government agents demanded. In many states, it had been illegal to record an employee's race or ethnicity; now it became mandatory. Rules against nepotism and the appointment of a department's own Ph.D.'s, once regarded as desirable protection against favoritism and intellectual inbreeding, were now considered discriminatory against women and obstacles to a university's growing its own minority faculty.

Personal contact with friends and colleagues, perhaps supplemented by informal scouting at professional meetings, was the traditional way to fill faculty positions. Labeled "the old boys' network" that intentionally or unwittingly excluded many women and minorities, that has completely changed. Public notice must now be given, contacts made with organizations serving women and minorities, and advertisements placed; the *Chronicle of Higher Education* and other publications have fattened on the revenue.

A trail of paper is laid down for every appointment. The key to who will eventually be chosen may or may not be found in a close reading of the position description. Efforts are made to identify the minority status of applicants by forms sent to the affirmative action officer—not the search committee—by scrutiny of vitae, or by private inquiry. Special funds

23. John Williams describes two programs that Harvard instituted to recruit minority faculty and administrators; other universities have tried similar programs. See Williams, "Affirmative Action at Harvard."

may be allotted to bring "underrepresented" candidates to interviews; special explanations may be required if these candidates are rejected. In many searches, that may suffice. In others, when political pressure builds, a dean might approve only statistically satisfactory appointments.

As confidential files have been disclosed in hearings and suits on charges of discrimination, written evaluations may have become more formal and less frank. What is said and thought privately, the reality as distinct from the records of faculty searches and appointments, is known only to close participants. Affirmative action officers who monitor the formalities and produce mountains of rebarbative statistics may know as little as most candidates. Applicants are screened, a few are interviewed and ranked, a dean accepts or revises the ranks, and an offer follows.

The process is so slow that it can be futile; the campus and candidates' situations can change so much that a new search must begin. All that emerges are statistics in which affirmative action critics see quotas and advocates, institutional racism and sexism. A task force of academic women concludes, "By and large, the tenure system, based on a confidential, subjective analysis, has remained untouched. . . . That is to say, during the second decade [of affirmative action] . . . , many departments were willing to *hire* women, but not necessarily to tenure them."[24]

Battles over affirmative appointments can occur only where affirmative candidates—in the painful language of the trade, members of "protected" or "target" groups—exist. In the physical sciences and engineering, they are mainly Asians; in the life sciences, the humanities, and, increasingly, the professions, women; in education and some social sciences, women and blacks.

The question of quality can be dodged by redefining the necessary qualifications, giving more weight to life experience—to sex and color—and less to scholarly publications. Like other industries, the academy must cater to its public; purely academic standards have seldom governed more than a fraction of the higher—often more properly called "postsecondary" —educational enterprise. As Kenneth Clark, the prominent black psychologist, remarks, "Mediocrity is the norm in most of our institutions controlled by white males. It can't be any more so than it has been."[25]

An institution's faculty will seldom precisely reflect the sex and ethnicity of its students. To expect this is to expect a glacier to flow like a river. However, in slow-moving places—such as seminaries and perhaps some black colleges—and also in fast-changing institutions and fields highly responsive to their markets, where courses are more fashionable than difficult, that situation may be approximated.

24. Mariam K. Chamberlain, ed., *Women in Academe* (New York: Russell Sage Foundation, 1988), p. 178.

25. *Consultations on the Affirmative Action Statement of the U.S. Commission on Civil Rights* (Washington, DC: Commission on Civil Rights, 1981), 2:63.

ANNALS, *AAPSS*, 523, September 1992

Work for Americans with Disabilities

By WALTER Y. OI

ABSTRACT: The available data indicate that less than a third of disabled working-age adults are employed, and, when they are, they are paid lower wages. Their incomes are low even after including transfer payments. The problem of identifying a disabled person and the nature of the labor market are reviewed in this article. It is argued that in addition to imposing functional limitations, disability steals time and shortens life expectancy. The Americans with Disabilities Act is intended to improve the plight of the disabled by mandating equal employment rights, a rights approach that worked well for race and gender but will not do for the task at hand. People with disabilities do not constitute an identifiable minority. They move into and out of a state of being disabled and exhibit different degrees of limitation and different life expectancies. The aim of eliminating labor market discrimination is important, but equal access to jobs and public places will not significantly improve the well-being of disabled persons unless it is integrated into a larger disability policy program including rehabilitation, medical care, and income transfers.

Walter Y. Oi is the Elmer B. Milliman Professor of Economics at the University of Rochester. He holds a Ph.D. from the University of Chicago. In addition to publications in labor economics and price theory, he has worked on the elimination of the military draft, the Occupational Safety and Health Administration, transport economics, and consumer product safety.

NOTE: The author wishes to thank the H. B. Earhart Foundation for financial support of his research.

THE Americans with Disabilities Act, called by sponsors an Emancipation Act for those with disabilities, eventually will affect all employers with fifteen or more workers and all places of public accommodations and services." This is how the Bureau of National Affairs began its summary of Public Law 101-336, the Americans with Disabilities Act (ADA).[1] Disabilities are conditions that place bounds on the range of work and activities that an individual can perform. The incomes of disabled persons are low, an outcome that the ADA attributes to labor market discrimination. The ADA proposes to improve the plight of the disabled by mandating rights to equal employment opportunities. It is a policy that was adopted to raise the economic well-being of racial minorities and women. I shall argue, however, that disability is not like race or gender. A civil rights policy that was designed to eradicate racial and gender discrimination cannot be taken off the shelf and applied to disabled individuals.

THE EMPLOYMENT GOAL

Work is sought not only for the earnings that it yields but also for the dignity and product that go along with it. Some individuals are unable to secure suitable employment because of discrimination or ignorance on the part of the employers. Although it took many years, legislation was enacted to guarantee equal employment opportunities for women and racial minorities. Title I of the

1. Bureau of National Affairs, 18 July 1990.

ADA mandates strong civil rights for people with disabilities. The main provisions were summarized by the Bureau of National Affairs:

A covered entity is prohibited from discriminating against a *qualified individual* with a disability in regard to job application, hiring, discharge, compensation, training, or other terms, conditions, or privileges of employment. Employers are required to make reasonable accommodations to the known physical or mental limitations of an otherwise *qualified individual* unless to do so would impose an *undue hardship*. Included in the prohibition is the use of qualification standards, employment tests, or selection criteria that tend to screen out individuals with disabilities unless the standard is job related.[2]

The language is fuzzy. No bright line separates a person with a disability from the rest. Who decides when an applicant is qualified? A reasonable accommodation is to be determined by the need for it and whether or not it imposes an undue hardship. Operational definitions and the resolution of disputes are important in enforcing the act to assure the attainment of the employment goal.

CHARACTERISTICS AND SIZE
OF THE TARGET POPULATION

Most of us have an idea of what constitutes a disabling condition, but rough ideas are not enough. The definition adopted in the ADA was taken from the Rehabilitation Act of 1973:

Disability means with respect to an individual (1) a physical or mental *impairment* that *substantially limits* one or more of the *major life activities* of such individual, (2) a *record* of such an

2. Ibid.

impairment, or (3) *being regarded* as having such a substantially limiting impairment.

Reasonable individuals and even experts can disagree about the meaning of the key terms in italics. The absence of a consensus standard among researchers testifies to the difficulties of identifying and measuring the target population.

Estimates of the number of disabled persons are ordinarily obtained from surveys that rely on self-assessments.[3] The context and wording of questions differ across surveys. Not surprisingly, estimates of the prevalence of disability vary across surveys, ranging from 8.5 to 17.2 percent of the population.[4] The prevalence

rate for severe disability—the percentage unable to work—is less variable, 3.2 to 5.1 percent of all working-age adults.[5]

Although overall incidence rates vary, different surveys exhibit close agreement on the patterns of differences in disability rates by age, gender, education, and race. Men report a higher work disability rate, 9.3 percent, compared to 8.6 percent for women (see Table 1). The incidence rate is inversely related to years of schooling: 16.0 percent for men with less than 12 years of education to 4.3 percent for college graduates. Aging raises the disability rate; for men, it climbs from 5.9 percent for 25- to 34-year-olds to 23.1 percent for 55- to 64-year-olds. When age and schooling are jointly considered, the work disability falls from 44.6 percent for 55- to 64-year-old male high school dropouts to 2.4 percent for young (25- to 34-year-old) college graduates. The corresponding range for women was 34.3 to 2.5 percent.

These striking differences conform to the implications of Michael Grossman's health capital model.[6] Less educated individuals have fewer resources for medical care, nutrition,

3. In the annual March Supplement to the Current Population Survey, the basic household survey, an individual is classified as having a work limitation if one or more of the following conditions are met: the person (1) has a condition that prevents him from working or limits the kind or amount of work he can do, (2) ever retired or left a job for health reasons, (3) did not work in the survey week because of a long-term illness or disability that prevents the performance of any kind of work, (4) did not work in the previous year because he was ill or disabled, (5) is under 65 years of age and covered by Medicare, (6) is under 65 and a recipient of Supplemental Security Income. If one or more of the last four conditions is met, the individual is counted as having a severe work limitation. The survey is administered only to working-age adults, 16 to 64 years of age. See Robert L. Benefield and John M. McNeil, *Labor Force Status and Other Characteristics of Persons with a Work Disability: 1981 to 1988*, Current Population Reports, series P-23, no. 160 (Washington, DC: Government Printing Office, 1989).

4. See Lawrence D. Haber, "Operating Definitions of Disability: Survey and Administrative Measures," in *Disability in the United States*, ed. S. Thompson-Hollman and I. F. Storck (New York: Springer, 1991), pp. 228-41. Haber reports the low estimate—8.5 percent—

from the 1980 Census of Population and similarly low estimates from the March Supplements to the Current Population Survey. Haber notes that the more extensive and detailed health questions in surveys such as the National Health Interview Surveys appear to increase the reported incidence of disability. The highest estimates are from surveys of the Social Security Administration.

5. Ibid. See footnote 3 for a common definition of being severely disabled.

6. Michael Grossman, "On the Concept of Health Capital and the Demand for Health," *Journal of Political Economy*, 80:223-55 (Mar. 1972).

TABLE 1
PERCENTAGE OF WORKING-AGE ADULTS WITH A WORK
DISABILITY, BY GENDER, AGE, AND YEARS OF SCHOOLING, 1990

	Age				
Years of Schooling	16-64	25-34	35-44	45-54	55-64
Males with a work limitation					
Total	9.28	5.98	8.50	12.30	23.05
<12	15.97	11.98	14.22	24.62	44.57
12	9.34	6.76	9.69	12.12	20.23
13-15	7.16	4.35	7.72	10.41	19.65
16+	4.30	2.36	3.15	5.64	11.06
Females with a work limitation					
Total	8.56	5.40	7.12	11.11	21.31
<12	16.20	10.79	16.38	24.66	34.37
12	8.33	6.25	7.36	9.38	17.55
13-15	5.42	3.86	5.65	7.21	14.08
16+	3.93	2.48	3.42	4.57	11.56

SOURCE: U.S., Department of Commerce, Bureau of the Census, Current Population Survey, Mar. 1990.

and other health inputs as well as poorer access to health information. They consequently end up with smaller stocks of health capital, resulting in more disabling conditions. At the other end of the schooling spectrum, highly educated individuals with serious impairments are better able to cope with them because they are, on average, wealthier and usually hold jobs requiring less physical effort.

Disability is largely a product of age. The vast majority of disabled persons acquire their impairments as mature adults. Knowledge of the age at onset is important for at least three reasons. First, individuals of the same age and impairment are likely to perceive different degrees of limitations depending on the age at onset. A 50-year-old woman who has had an arthritic condition for 10 years will have learned how to cope and will thus experience fewer task limitations than a 50-year-old who just became arthritic last year. Second, the earlier the age at onset, the stronger is the incentive to invest in training and vocational rehabilitation. A person who becomes disabled at 55 or 60 years of age may simply choose an early retirement. Third, the kinds of impairment responsible for disabling limitations happen to be related to the age at onset. Orthopedic impairments are, for example, the reasons for 41 percent of work limitations for adults under 45 years of age, but they caused only 23 percent of work disabilities of older (45- to 69-year-old) adults. Circulatory impairments—heart conditions, hypertension, and so on—tend to occur later in life and hence were responsible for only 7 percent of disabled adults under 45 years of age but 25 percent of disabled adults over 45.[7] The efforts to adjust to the onset of a disability and the resulting capacity to work depend both on the severity and nature of the functional limitations and on the impairments causing those limitations.

EMPLOYMENT AND EARNINGS

A majority of all disabled individuals are out of the labor force. Only 30.5 percent of disabled men were gainfully employed in March 1988 compared to 90.1 percent of nondisabled men (see Table 2). The employment-to-population ratio—the odds of holding a job—is lower for less educated and older persons. This pattern is observed for both nondisabled and disabled individuals, but it is more pronounced for the latter. For disabled men, the percentage with a job was 16.4 percent for 45- to 64-year-old high school dropouts, and 62.2 percent for 25- to 44-year-old college graduates; the corresponding figures for nondisabled men were 81.7 and 96.1 percent. When they find work, disabled workers are more likely to be part-year employees. The percentage with year-round jobs was 44 percent for disabled and 80 percent for nondisabled male workers.

Additionally, the annual earnings of disabled workers were only 64.2 percent of the earnings of nondisabled employees (see Table 3).

Older disabled workers suffer a larger wage discount; their earnings ratio was only 52.6 percent for 55- to 64-year-old workers. If the comparison is limited to year-round, full-time workers, the earnings penalty is smaller. The earnings ratio was 80.7 percent for all year-round workers and 68.3 percent for 55- to 64-year-olds. Part-year older disabled employees earned about 70 percent of the earnings of their nondisabled counterparts.[8]

Regular, year-round work and education clearly matter. If we look only at the earnings of high school graduates 25-64 years of age, disabled workers received about 90 percent of the earnings of nondisabled high school graduates. The low earnings of all disabled working-age adults are largely due to the fact that very few find suitable employment.

Survey responses to the work disability questions could produce some classification errors. I believe that the effect of these classification errors on the patterns of employment and earnings differences are small because of the stability of the response patterns across different surveys. The question is, To what extent are the low employment-to-population ratios and the lower relative earnings of disabled persons due to labor market discrimination that might be remedied by the ADA?

---

7. Mitchell LaPlante, "The Demographics of Disability," in *The Americans with Disabilities Act: From Policy to Practice*, ed. Jane West (New York: Milbank Memorial Fund, 1991), pp. 55-77 (hereafter cited as *ADA*).

8. If no adjustments are made for age and education, the annual earnings of part-year disabled workers were 96.8 percent of earnings of nondisabled part-year workers. If age and schooling are held constant, the earnings are around 70 percent of those of similar nondisabled workers.

TABLE 2
EMPLOYMENT AND WORK EXPERIENCE, BY DISABILITY STATUS, MEN 25-64 YEARS OF AGE, MARCH 1988

	Age					
	25-64		25-44		45-64	
Years of Schooling	Disabled	Nondisabled	Disabled	Nondisabled	Disabled	Nondisabled
Proportion of civilian population employed in March 1988 (employment/population ratio)						
All schooling levels	0.305	0.901	0.394	0.919	0.239	0.867
< 12	0.194	0.825	0.252	0.832	0.164	0.817
12	0.325	0.893	0.393	0.911	0.264	0.858
13-15	0.449	0.917	0.529	0.927	0.362	0.889
16+	0.478	0.946	0.622	0.961	0.367	0.913
Proportion of persons with work experience in 1987 working full-time year-round						
All schooling levels	0.440	0.800	0.435	0.794	0.446	0.813
< 12	0.385	0.685	0.350	0.646	0.410	0.731
12	0.443	0.793	0.431	0.784	0.456	0.812
13-15	0.464	0.822	0.449	0.816	0.488	0.837
16+	0.507	0.862	0.653	0.857	0.452	0.873

SOURCE: Robert L. Benefield and John M. McNeil, *Labor Force Status and Other Characteristics of Persons with a Work Disability: 1981 to 1988*, Current Population Reports, series P-23, no. 160 (Washington, DC: Government Printing Office, 1989).

TABLE 3

**ANNUAL EARNINGS IN 1987 OF DISABLED WORKERS
AS A PERCENTAGE OF NONDISABLED WORKERS' EARNINGS,
ALL MEN AND MEN WITH 12 YEARS OF SCHOOLING**

Age and Employment Status	All Men	Men with 12 Years of Schooling
All workers		
Total	64.24	73.24
16-24	82.32	77.91
25-34	63.06	75.18
35-44	59.16	67.92
45-54	60.36	68.91
55-64	52.55	60.49
Year-round workers		
Total	80.68	93.89
16-24	102.43	104.94
25-34	86.78	95.03
35-44	80.43	91.60
45-54	72.57	87.59
55-64	68.25	79.71
Part-year workers		
Total	96.67	95.10
16-24	100.00	108.70
25-34	68.29	79.76
35-44	70.57	83.97
45-54	74.32	72.46
55-64	70.05	72.23

SOURCE: Benefield and McNeil, *Labor Force Status*, tab. 9, pp. 52-57.

DISABILITY ON THE SUPPLY SIDE OF THE LABOR MARKET

Each disabled individual has to decide whether he or she should seek a job or choose to remain out of the labor force. In the received theory of labor supply, the amount of time allocated to the labor market is determined by (1) the individual's tastes, described by a utility function for consumption goods, X, and leisure time, L; (2) his or her market productivity, or the wage, W, that can be commanded in the labor market; and (3) the individual's endowments of nonwage income and time. We can imagine that each of us has a stock of health capital, K, larger values of K indicating better health. The onset of a disability is modeled as a reduction in K.

Disability destroys some health capital, K, putting the person on a lower level of utility. In the process, it can affect the value of leisure time, the amount of consumption, X, that he or she would give up to get another hour of leisure time per week. It seems reasonable to expect that disability raises the value of leisure time, meaning time not allocated to working. A stronger preference for leisure leads to a decrease in the optimum number of work hours supplied to the labor market. It could even result in a complete withdrawal from the work force.

To the extent that functional limitations contract the range of tasks that can be performed, disability will, on average, reduce an individual's market productivity. It need not for some narrowly defined jobs where a disabled person's capabilities can be matched with the requirements of the job. The expectation, however, is that the onset of a disabling condition will generally reduce the wage rate, leading to lower earnings.

Empirical studies support the proposition that higher nonwage incomes from assets, gifts, or public transfer payments expand the demand for leisure time, meaning a decrease in the supply of work hours. Worker compensation, Social Security Disability Insurance (SSDI), Supplemental Security Income, and pensions to disabled veterans are some of the programs that provide income support—nonwage income— for people with disabilities. Some programs require waiting periods to qualify for benefits, and most impose earnings tests. A disabled person who elects to apply for the largest of these programs, SSDI, has to weigh several factors: the estimated earnings loss due to the disabling condition, the Social Security disability benefit levels, the anticipated duration of the disabling condition, the chances of being admitted to the SSDI program, and application costs for medical verification, legal counsel, and the implicit time costs incurred by the applicant. Benefit levels were raised, and qualification standards lowered in 1967 and 1973. The SSDI disability rolls grew rapidly in the 1970s, an outcome that economists attributed to the enhanced work disincentives that attracted some marginally disabled individuals to withdraw from the labor force to obtain the higher SSDI benefits.[9] In addition to disability benefits, the loss in earnings could be offset by greater work effort on the part of other family members.[10]

"Disability" is defined in the ADA as an impairment that substantially limits one or more of the major life activities. I have argued earlier that by focusing on limitations, we overlook a critical characteristic, namely, that disability steals time. All of us get the same calendar time endow-

9. See Donald O. Parsons, "The Decline in Male Labor Force Participation," *Journal of Political Economy*, 88:117-34 (Feb. 1980); Jonathan Leonard, "Labor Supply Incentives and Disincentives for the Disabled," in *Disability and the Labor Market*, ed. M. Berkowitz and M. Anne Hill (Ithaca, NY: ILR Press, 1986), pp. 64-96; idem, "Disability Policy and the Return to Work," in *Disability and Work*, ed. C. Weaver (Washington, DC: AEI Press, 1991), pp. 46-55. But see also John Bound, "The Health and Earnings of Rejected Disability Insurance Applicants," *American Economic Review*, 79:482-503 (June 1989). Bound has challenged the estimated size of the work disincentive effects of the Social Security Disability Insurance program by examining the work experience of individuals whose applications were denied.

10. Walter Oi, "Three Paths from Disability to Poverty" (Technical Analysis Paper no. 57, U.S. Department of Labor, Assistant Secretary for Policy, Evaluation, and Research, Oct. 1978). This result was based on data from the 1972 wave of the Michigan Panel Survey of Income Dynamics. The participation rate for wives of severely disabled men was below that for wives of nondisabled men, which may reflect the need for more care.

ment, 24 hours a day, 168 hours a week. If we deduct the time needed for maintenance of the human agent, we face different endowments of discretionary time. A typical person requires about 9 hours a day for sleep and personal care. People in poor health—physical or mental—need more time for sleep and getting around.[11] Moving beyond the diurnal cycle, individuals with more disabling conditions experience more sick days and devote more time to obtaining medical care. Severely disabled persons make three times as many physician visits a year and purchase four times as many prescriptions in relation to individuals with no activity limitations.[12] A reduction in discretionary time due to the onset of a disability necessarily contracts labor supply and enhances the attractiveness of part-time and part-year jobs. The percentage of employees on full-time, year-round jobs is indeed higher for nondisabled workers (see Table 2).

A survey of vocational-rehabilitation clients lends further support to the proposition that disability mainly steals time. Some 62 percent indicated that they wanted "light work," 47 percent asked for reduced work schedules, and 40 percent expressed a preference for flexitime.[13] Disabled workers are more likely to be self-employed, where they may have more control over the number and timing of work hours; 14.6 percent were self-employed in March 1988 compared to 9.6 percent of nondisabled workers. An Illinois survey revealed that 25 percent of visually impaired persons with a job were self-employed.[14] Some of these may have been forced into self-employment by employer discrimination, but others may have voluntarily selected this option to control their work schedules.

In addition to its impact on discretionary time in a day or a year, disability can affect the length of life. Persons admitted to the SSDI program exhibit substantially higher mortality rates, which are related to diagnostic group.[15] Nearly two-thirds of SSDI beneficiaries with neoplasms—cancers—died within two years of entry to the program compared to a two-year death rate of only 2.5 percent for persons with traumatic injuries. Individuals of the

11. This is suggested in the time-allocation data examined by Frank Stafford and Gregg J. Duncan, "The Use of Time and Technology by Households in the United States," *Research in Labor Economics*, ed. R. G. Ehrenberg (Greenwich, CT: JAI Press, 1980), 3:335-75.

12. Gerben DeJong, Andrew Batavia, and R. Griss, "America's Neglected Health Minority: Working Age Persons with Disabilities," *Milbank Quarterly*, 67(2) supp., pp. 311-51 (1989).

13. Cited in Fredrick C. Collingnon, "The Role of Reasonable Accommodation in Employing Disabled Persons in Private Industry," *Disability and the Labor Market*, ed. Berkowitz and Hill, pp. 196-241.

14. The March 1988 data pertain to male workers and are reported in Benefield and McNeil, *Labor Force Status*, tab. 6, pp. 36-37. The Illinois survey is contained in Corinne Kirchner, Don Harkins, and Robert Esposito, "Issues and Strategies toward Improving Employment of Blind or Visually Impaired Persons in Illinois" (Report, American Foundation for the Blind, Mar. 1991).

15. Barry V. Bye and Gerald F. Riley, "Eliminating the Medicare Waiting Period for Social Security Disabled Worker Beneficiaries," *Social Security Bulletin*, 52:2-15 (May 1989).

same age but different impairments will exhibit different labor supply responses at onset. An impairment that shortens the expected life horizon will encourage an earlier withdrawal from the labor force. In short, disability policy must distinguish different types of disability. At a minimum, we ought to identify the age at onset and the type of impairment responsible for the functional limitations.

The dynamics of the adjustments to disability reveal at least two important facets of the time dimension. First, the vast majority of disabled persons at a point in time became disabled at older ages in the normal course of aging. The disability pushes the individual into a new environment, and acclimating to it takes time. For example, a person who notices that his or her vision is failing is unlikely to seek immediate help. She or he will often wait until the vision loss stabilizes before entering into a training or rehabilitation program, hoping all the time for a reversal in the progress of the vision loss. Second, if the disabling condition is expected to shorten life, the incentive to invest in training for reentry to the work force is greatly reduced. Not all disabled individuals out of work are there because of employment barriers. Supply-side factors account for some voluntary withdrawals from the world of work.

THE DEMAND FOR DISABLED WORKERS

Discrimination can surely depress the employment and earnings of people with disabilities. The ADA is intended to eliminate discrimination by mandating equal employment opportunities.

In an economic model of the labor market, the demand for labor is derived from the demand for final goods and services via the technology that transforms labor and other inputs into output flows. A disabled person is, by definition, substantially limited in at least one major life activity—for instance, walking, lifting, or seeing. These limitations will, on average, reduce the productivity of a disabled person. Variations in the severity of the functional limitations expand the dispersion of productivities across disabled individuals. By the age of 40, most workers have acquired skills and work experience that are specific to a particular firm, occupation, or industry. They know how to sell a bond, sow a field, or skipper a ship. The onset of a physical or mental impairment may not, in some instances, destroy these job-specific skills. A farmer who becomes hearing impaired can continue to harvest her crops, while the loss of a leg may be only a nuisance for an insurance broker. On the other hand, total blindness will compel the farmer to switch jobs and begin anew, undergoing retraining and the arduous task of searching for a new job. When the status of the position that is the aim of the rehabilitation program is approximately the same as the predisability job, there is less reluctance to incur the psychic and time costs of retraining. On the other side of the market, employers resist hiring older workers for jobs that require a lot of on-the-job training. Recall that most disabled workers who are changing occupational pursuits are older. Large firms with structured, internal labor markets may indeed practice statistical age discrimination, which might be confused with discrimination against disabled persons.

It is hard to disentangle the extent to which lower earnings and lower employment-to-population ratios are due to discrimination or productivity differences. Johnson and Lambrinos embraced a methodology wherein wage equations were estimated for separate samples of nondisabled and disabled workers. The difference in mean wages for these two samples can be decomposed into two parts, one due to differences in worker traits such as schooling, work experience, occupation, and so forth, which are determinants of wages, and the other due to different prices received for these wage-generating traits. They concluded that disabled workers received lower prices and hence one-third of the wage differential could be attributed to discrimination.[16]

Most jobs do not call for the capacity to perform all of life's major activities. With appropriate matching and workplace accommodations, a disabled person could be as productive as a nondisabled job applicant. Edward Yelin claims that the increased

consumer demands for services ought to expand the demand for disabled workers because service sector jobs involve less physical effort and more clerical skills.[17] In addition, technological advances in the goods-producing sector have lowered employment barriers, and the Rehabilitation Act of 1973 promoted employment of disabled persons in the public sector. The puzzle is that in spite of these developments, people with disabilities have been, according to Yelin, having more difficulty in finding jobs in the last two decades.

Is there more discrimination against the disabled today than there was a decade or two ago? The allegedly greater difficulty in finding work may, in part, be a consequence of structural changes in the labor market. The U.S. labor market in the last decade has exhibited a sharp increase in the relative demand for highly skilled workers.[18] It will be remembered that the incidence of work disability is concentrated among those with less schooling, the group whose relative and real wages fell during the 1980s. The increased difficulties in finding work may thus reflect the declining demand for less skilled workers rather than more

16. William G. Johnson and James Lambrinos, "Wage Discrimination against Handicapped Men and Women," *Journal of Human Resources*, 20:264-77 (Spring 1985). The validity of their statistical procedure for estimating the discrimination component of the wage difference can be challenged. There are reasons other than employer discrimination that lead to differences in the coefficients of education, work experience, and other explanatory variables in their wage equation.

17. Edward H. Yelin, "The Recent History and Immediate Future of Employment among Persons with Disabilities," in *ADA*, ed. West, pp. 129-49.

18. The results of this shift are reflected in a dramatic change in the structure of relative wages. The ratio of wages for college versus high school graduates as well as the wage ratio for men 45 versus 25 years old were both considerably higher in 1989 than they were in 1980. The studies that analyze these changes can be found in Marvin Kosters, *Workers and Their Wages* (Washington, DC: AEI Press, 1991).

discrimination against people with disabilities.

MANDATING EQUAL EMPLOYMENT OPPORTUNITIES

Having defined "disability," the next step in the ADA is to determine whether the person is a qualified individual with a disability. This determination is to be accomplished in two stages: (1) Does she or he have the requisite skills, education, experience, and licenses for the position? and (2) Can she or he perform the essential functions of the job with or without accommodations? The following excerpt from the Equal Employment Opportunity Commission (EEOC) regulations is informative: "In general, the term *essential functions* means the fundamental duties of the employment position that the individual with a disability holds or desires. The term, *essential functions*, does not include the marginal functions of the position."[19]

If a job is narrowly defined—for example, lifting or proofreading aloud —the task of deciding if the applicant is qualified is simplified. The interpretive guidance accompanying the EEOC regulations contained an example in which an applicant is asked if he has a driver's license because he might be asked to drive in an exceptional circumstance. If driving is a marginal function of the main job, and if there are a sufficient number of employees with licenses among whom any driving chores could be distributed, the employer could not deny the job to an applicant who has no driver's license. The essential functions for any job will be fewer in number, the larger the size of the firm's work force. A clerk at a garden store might occasionally be asked to lift a hundred-pound sack of fertilizer. Lifting would be an essential function of being a clerk at a garden store hiring only 2 clerks, but not at one employing 12 clerks. If a job is described by a work load, such as typing 75 words a minute or standing for eight hours, the employer has to demonstrate that the standard was not set to exclude a disabled person. These examples are helpful, but disputes are sure to arise about what an essential function is.

In addition to essential functions, the determination of "a qualified individual with a disability" has to be evaluated in light of reasonable accommodations: "[Covered] employers are required to make *reasonable accommodations* to the known physical or mental limitations of an otherwise qualified individual unless to do so would impose an *undue hardship*."[20]

Many employers voluntarily make substantial investments in hiring and training a work force and improving the quality of the workplace to raise productivity and morale. According to Becker and Oi, training costs that raise the worker's productivity in all employments—what they call general training—will be borne by the employee who accepts a lower wage during the training period.[21] If

19. The regulations describe seven clauses to define the concept of essential functions.

20. See *Handbook: The Americans with Disabilities Act* (Washington, DC: Government Printing Office, Oct. 1991), sec. 1630.4.

21. Gary S. Becker, *Human Capital* (New York: National Bureau of Economic Research,

training is specific to the firm, however, it is optimal for any costs of training or workplace accommodations to be shared by both the firm and employee.[22] The question of who bears the costs is important in light of the EEOC regulations on what is reasonable.

Reasonable accommodations may include but are not limited to (1) making existing facilities readily accessible and useable, (2) job restructuring, part time and modified work schedules, reassignment to a vacant position, acquisition or modification of equipment or devices, the provision of qualified readers or interpreters, and other similar accommodations for individuals with disabilities.[23]

Under the ADA, employers are responsible for accommodation costs unless they impose an undue hardship.[24] Since small employers can appeal to the undue-hardship defense, the burden of supplying jobs for the disabled will be thrust upon large employers.[25]

This civil rights approach to disability policy encounters at least two serious problems. First, employers are coerced into a satisficing employment strategy wherein all persons meeting the minimum standards have to be treated as equals. A qualified individual with a disability who can perform the essential functions—with or without accommodations—has as much right to the job as any other job applicant. Employers are thus discouraged from searching for the most highly qualified individual. The efficiency losses from such a satisficing policy are small for stock clerks and drill press operators, where there is little dispersion in performance across employees. The losses get larger when the firm is recruiting a highly skilled employee. Second, there is a potential moral hazard because some healthy individuals could improve their chances of landing a job by being classified as disabled.

A POLICY FOR PROMOTING EMPLOYMENT

In her short history of the ADA, Nancy Lee Jones fingered the principal problem with this civil rights approach: "Seldom do race, sex or national origin present any obstacle to an individual when performing a job or participating in a program. Dis-

1964); Walter Y. Oi, "Labor as a Quasi-Fixed Factor," *Journal of Political Economy*, 70:538-55 (Dec. 1962).

22. Masanori Hashimoto and Ben T. Yu, "Specific Capital, Employment Contracts, and Wage Rigidity," *Bell Journal of Economics*, 11:536-49 (1980).

23. See *Handbook: Americans with Disabilities Act.*

24. The advocates claim that most accommodations can be made at little or no cost. This is what was reported in a survey by the Berkeley Planning Associates. See Collingnon, "Role of Reasonable Accommodation," in *Disability and the Labor Market*, ed. Berkowitz and Hill, pp. 196-241. He admitted that if more disabled workers obtained jobs, the average accommodation costs would rise. T. Chirikos criticized the Berkeley study and argued that if the ADA is successful in expanding employment, there will be an even sharper rise in accommodation costs than that suggested by Collingnon. Thomas N. Chirikos, "The Economics of Employment," in *ADA*, ed. West, pp. 150-79.

25. This outcome will lead to a misallocation of resources. See Sherwin Rosen, "Disability Accommodation and the Labor Market," in *Disability and Work*, ed. Weaver, pp. 18-30; Walter Oi, "Disability and a Workfare-Welfare Dilemma," in ibid.

abilities by their very nature, however, may make certain jobs or types of participation impossible."[26]

The ADA presumes that people with disabilities constitute a distinct minority whose members can be identified and counted as members of a race or gender can be. I have already remarked on the absence of a consensus standard among researchers. Additionally, the Social Security Administration has difficulty in deciding who is disabled. Applicants for Social Security disability benefits suffer through long waiting periods, and some incur substantial costs to appeal their cases before administrative law judges and federal courts. In framing the regulations for the ADA, the EEOC passed the buck to the lawyers and administrative law judges by insisting on individual determinations.

[A] case by case approach is essential if qualified individuals with varying disabilities are to receive equal opportunities to compete for an infinitely diverse range of jobs. For this reason, neither the ADA nor this regulation can supply the correct answer in advance for each employment decision concerning an individual with a disability.

Jane West contends that even this "case by case" determination may be inadequate because a case today—meaning an employment decision involving a particular firm and a named individual—could be different from the same case tomorrow. "Unlike race and gender, moreover, disability is often a dynamic and changing characteristic. Furthermore, some disabilities change in their intensity from day to day or week to week and may require different accommodations at various times."[27]

For most cases, reasonable individuals will probably agree on the presence or absence of a work disability, but some marginal cases are sure to be hotly debated.

An assumption that individuals are equally productive is tenable in cases involving race and gender if we are careful to control for personal differences like the quantity and quality of schooling, previous work experience, and so on. The ADA recognized that this assumption has to be modified for persons with disabilities. Someone has to determine who is covered by the law as a qualified individual with a disability. A job has to be redefined in terms of its essential functions, and an assessment made about whether any performance deficits can be remedied by reasonable accommodations. The ADA is vague about sanctions in the event of noncompliance. An employer accused of employment discrimination will be exposed to penalties resulting from legal actions brought by the EEOC or by plaintiffs seeking damages in civil lawsuits. There is ample room for disputes and a possibility for a growth in employment discrimination cases. If punitive and compensatory damages are permitted, the ADA might even reduce the number of disabled workers if successful plaintiffs retire with their settlements. Are the resources devoted to litigation socially wasteful, or will they lead to less labor market discrimination and

26. Nancy Lee Jones, "Essential Requirements of the Act: A Short History and Overview," in *ADA*, ed. West, pp. 25-54.

27. Jane West, "The Social and Policy Context of the Act," in *ADA*, ed. West, p. 8.

hence greater employment and earn-ings for persons with disabilities?[28]

The labor market for people with disabilities may indeed be flawed by discriminatory employment prac-tices, but it also reflects the effects of economic forces. Disabled individu-als are not all alike but differ in im-portant dimensions: the nature and severity of their functional limita-tions, the particular impairments re-sponsible for these limitations, and the age at onset. Not all of them want to work, some are unable to do any work, and others may choose to retire or postpone reentry. Job counseling and vocational rehabilitation have to recognize that individuals have dif-ferent productive capacities and dis-cretionary time endowments.

The costs of workplace accommo-dations should be treated like any other fixed employment cost. When the accommodation is unique to the particular worker-firm match, the cost should be shared. This arrange-ment tends to reduce labor turnover, thereby reducing the cost per period for the accommodation. For special devices that are person specific—for example, a wheelchair that enables the user to approximate a standing position—the employer ought not to be required to incur the cost. If the disabled employee quits or is fired, the employer will have little use for this special wheelchair. The costs should be borne by the recipient, and if she or he lacks the funds, the costs might be borne by a vocational reha-bilitation agency or some other social insurance fund. It is inefficient to place the entire cost of providing workplace accommodations on those employers with deep pockets.

Richard Burkhauser has persua-sively argued that in passing the Americans with Disabilities Act, Congress was trying to do good with-out enlarging the size of the budget deficit.[29] The responsibility for sup-plying work and pay for disabled in-dividuals is shifted to that part of the private sector consisting of firms with 25 or more employees, 15 or more beginning in 1994. The well-being of people with disabilities is not so easily accomplished by ordering these firms to provide them with good, well-paying jobs. I am re-minded of a seminar that I attended many years ago. The economist shifted his assumptions to prove two theorems. When challenged, he re-sponded, "A man wakes up in the morning and shaves himself with a razor. Later, he goes to work and grades a road with a bulldozer. Why should we insist that he use the same tool for both tasks?"

Why indeed? Congress enacted legislation to eliminate labor market discrimination and to obtain equal access to schools and public places for racial minorities. These same rights were extended to women. A civil rights approach worked well for race and gender, but the same tool will not do for the task at hand. Disability defies a neat dichotomous classifica-

28. In Oi, "Disability and a Workfare-Wel-fare Dilemma," I conjectured that resources would be devoted to litigation instead of to producing goods and services. High punitive damages could induce some successful plain-tiffs to choose retirement instead of returning to work. Class-action suits are unlikely, given the case-by-case determination of disability.

29. Richard V. Burkhauser, "Morality on the Cheap: The Americans with Disabilities Act," Regulation, 13:47-56 (Summer 1990).

tion. It is not a simple, black-and-white distinction. Individuals move into and out of being disabled and experience different degrees of limitation. These differences have to be recognized in developing an integrated disability policy that involves income transfers, medical and rehabilitation care, and access to the world of work.

ANNALS, *AAPSS*, 523, September 1992

Positive Action for Women in Britain

By MARGERY POVALL

ABSTRACT: Employers' programs to improve women's opportunities in Britain started in the late 1970s after Equal Pay, Sex Discrimination, and Race Relations legislation had been passed. While equal opportunity is now on employers' agendas, activity is limited to a small number of well-known organizations whose programs often lack specific targets. In this, Britain does not differ much from other European Community countries. Action programs for women in Britain are more common than those for ethnic minorities, despite parallel legislation. Britain leads the rest of Europe, however, in its approaches to racial discrimination. Equal opportunity employers are now starting action programs for people with disabilities, though they are not covered by antidiscrimination legislation. Results are awaited from the strong religious antidiscrimination legislation in Northern Ireland and from European Economic Community attempts to strengthen legislation to assist women.

Margery Povall, an independent organization consultant and researcher, has specialized in equality issues since 1974. She coordinated a pioneering international action research program for women in banking, organized the first British course for women managers, and has acted as a consultant to employers, the European Economic Community, and the International Labor Office. She codirects the Disability Management at Work program at City University, London, and is conducting studies of dual-career families and international mobility, secretarial career development, and small businesses.

UNTIL the late 1970s, employers in Britain had done little to improve opportunities for women. The coming into force of the Sex Discrimination and Equal Pay acts in 1975 led some influential managers to begin to question their practices. Programs designed to influence personnel policies, however, started only in the late 1970s, when externally funded projects stimulated action in some major companies. They set an example later followed by other employers. Parallel activities occurred in some countries of the European Economic Community (EEC), but positive action programs, as they are now known, although highly publicized, are still the exception rather than the rule.

THE BACKGROUND TO EQUAL OPPORTUNITY

The situation of women in the labor market in the early 1970s was anomalous. They formed a growing part of the labor force—36.5 percent by 1971—but job segregation was increasing. Most women were in low-pay, low-opportunity jobs, and their hourly earnings were 63 percent of men's.

Attempts to remedy the situation had in the past fallen afoul of the traditional opposition of British employers and trade unions to any form of employment legislation. True, unions had been making a muted call for equal pay since the nineteenth century, but not, on the whole, because they wanted equality but to avoid "unfair" competition from low-paid women. Nevertheless, sufficient pressure had built up for the Equal Pay Act to be passed in 1970. Five years were allowed for its implementation.

The international obligations of Britain were then, as now, an important factor in gaining agreement to the legislation. If Britain were to join the EEC, it would have to comply with Article 119 of the Treaty of Rome (1957), which laid down the principle of equal pay for equal work. There was also an outstanding commitment for the UK to ratify the International Labor Organization's Convention 100 on equal pay. This called on members to apply the principle of equal remuneration for men and women workers for work of equal value.

By 1970, it was widely agreed that without legislation to improve women's access to better-paid jobs and training, the Equal Pay Act would have limited effect. During the following five years, support for some form of antidiscrimination legislation and for strengthening the ineffective race relations legislation grew in all parties. This resulted in the passing of the Sex Discrimination Act in 1975 and the parallel Race Relations Act in 1976.

THE LEGAL FRAMEWORK

The Sex Discrimination Act covers not only the employment field—recruitment; opportunities for promotion, transfer, or training; and terms and conditions—but also education; the provision of goods, facilities, services, and premises; and discrimination on grounds of marriage. It does not allow compensatory or positive discrimination on grounds of sex to redress past discrimination, except in very limited circumstances relating to training and encouragement to apply for posts or where a person's sex is a genuine occupational qualification for a job, such as in the case of actors and actresses. Most significantly, it does not require employers to take any sort of positive action to comply with the law.

Individuals who feel they have been discriminated against in employment because of their sex can take a case to an industrial tribunal, but redress has been limited and class-action complaints, widespread in the United States, are not permitted.

Although much criticized as ineffective, the act has two potentially powerful provisions. It defines two kinds of discrimination, which have become known as direct and indirect discrimination. Indirect discrimination occurs when a requirement or condition that is applied to men and women equally has the effect of disadvantaging a considerably higher proportion of one sex and cannot be justified.

The power of this poorly understood aspect of the legislation has never been fully realized. Neither have the powers vested in the Equal Opportunities Commission set up under the act.

The commission has two quite distinct and potentially contradictory roles: to promote equality of opportunity, and to enforce the legislation by conducting formal investigations and subsequently issuing nondiscrimination notices. Although the terms of reference for these investigations and the commission's right to require production of relevant information are not restricted, its powers have been little used. It can also support individuals in tribunals and courts and

has done so with effect in the European Court of Justice in Luxembourg.

Legislation enacted in 1977 provided for maternity leave, limited maternity pay to women who met certain conditions, and the right to reinstatement if they return to their employer within six months of their child's birth.

WHY EMPLOYERS
STARTED EQUALITY PROGRAMS

With no legal compulsion on employers to do more than review and possibly revise obviously discriminatory policies or practices, with very few tribunal cases and hardly any formal investigations, there seemed little reason for employers to improve opportunities for women.

One reason for initial programs was, without doubt, the existence of laws and fears of their enforcement.[1] But there were other reasons:

— dawning awareness of the economic and social consequences of failing to utilize the experience and training of women;
— growing union interest in equal opportunity;
— women employees or external women's groups starting to question women's lack of progress;
— a slow realization of the possible commercial advantages of encouraging women to develop their potential;
— shortages of traditional quality male staff;

1. Margery Povall, "Overcoming Barriers to Women's Advancement in European Organisations," *Women in Management Review and Abstracts*, 5(6):26 (1990).

— research findings showing the extent of job segregation in the organization and suggesting that it was within management's power to change this;

— media publicity about the small number of women managers in a particular organization or sector, such as banking; and

— contact with women in North America who, as a result of affirmative action, were competently doing jobs for which, in Europe, they were considered unsuitable or incapable.

Later, two other reasons for action developed. The first was employers' perceived need to keep up with competitors who were adopting measures to attract, keep, and promote women. Equal opportunity policies have become part of good management practice. The second was the so-called demographic time bomb of the late 1980s and 1990s, namely, the drop in the number of school leavers entering the labor market—forecast to be as large as 33 percent—and the perceived need to retain current staff and attract new sources of labor such as women returners, members of ethnic minority groups, and people with disabilities.

THE EXTENT OF PROGRAMS

In Britain in 1992, despite recession, there appears to be a thriving equal opportunity or positive action industry. (Europeans seeking a name for the developing equality programs preferred "positive" to "affirmative" action. This has resulted in ongoing confusion with "positive discrimination.") Equal opportunity initiatives are publicized in personnel journals and the popular press, and a sizable number of consultants and trainers specialize wholly or mainly in equal opportunity work involving women, ethnic minorities, and people with disabilities. Many job advertisements now include a statement that the organization is "an equal opportunity employer," and many organizations have equal opportunity policy statements. However, this appearance of activity is illusory. A survey in Sheffield of all employers claiming in job advertisements to be "equal opportunity employers" revealed that fewer than half had an equal opportunity policy which was developed beyond isolated actions, and few had staff dedicated to implementing the policy.[2]

In the finance sector in 1983, 24 major employers responded to a survey. While 63 percent had issued an equality policy statement, less than half of these had given their managers or recruiters any equality training.[3]

In local government, generally thought to be, with banking, in the forefront of action, only half of the local authorities had an equal opportunity policy in 1986, and many of these policies had not been translated into much action.[4]

2. Pete Gibbon, "Equal Opportunities in Sheffield: Policies and Outcomes," *Equal Opportunities International*, 8(6):11-12 (1989).

3. Margery Povall, *The Finance Sector: Equal Opportunity Developments* (Sheffield: Manpower Services Commission, 1986), p. 18.

4. Margery Povall and Monika Langkau-Herrmann, eds., *Equal Opportunity Developments for Women in Local Government: An Anglo-German Perspective* (London: Anglo-German Foundation, 1991), p. xvii.

Activity is most likely to take place in organizations that already employ many women, but there has also been some activity in largely male industries where there are skill shortages, such as engineering. Most women, however, work in organizations that may not have heard of equality of opportunity, much less taken any steps to improve opportunities for women.

Two kinds of programs

The fact that employers need not achieve specific goals or take specified action in order to comply with the legislation has led to a great diversity of activity; many different views on what constitutes equality; guidance documents from diverse bodies, official and private; some aimless activity; but also some creative actions as people explore the issues and evaluate the results.

Two kinds of programs can be identified: those of local government and those of the private sector, including, in this discussion, central government. They have much in common, but there are some important differences.

Local government initiatives emanate from a political commitment to equality. Formal structures aimed at eliminating inequalities have been developed almost entirely in Labour-controlled local authorities. Activities to lessen job segregation in an organization are usually linked to the improvement of community services. Equality policies in local government have, in theory if not practice, addressed the issues of equality for women, members of ethnic minorities, and people with disabilities and possibly also sexual orientation, age, and trade union membership.

Women working in women's or equal opportunity units have usually been feminists with a strong personal commitment to achieving change and to improving the situation of the most disadvantaged women, such as single parents, black women, and lesbians. Consultation with women has been the cornerstone of some initiatives, links with community women's groups being established.

Results have often been limited. Meaningful support from the politicians who launched the policies has not always been forthcoming. Moreover, resources have been limited, particularly in the late 1980s, when local government budgets were cut by the central government.

Nonetheless, innovations have emerged. Women in low-pay and low-skill manual jobs have received training to increase their earning capacity, job-share policies are common, and some child-care facilities have been established.

A most promising innovation, introducing contract compliance procedures that included equality issues, was nipped in the bud by the Conservative government in 1988. Many attribute this to Mrs. Thatcher's dislike of the equality developments across the Thames at the Labour-controlled Greater London Council, which she abolished in 1986. Some local governments, led by the council, were just coming to grips with both the costs and the potential of contract compliance when it was declared illegal, except in limited aspects of ethnic-minority employment. Many remain convinced from the U.S. experience that this could be the most powerful tool for achieving real change.

Private sector equality initiatives aim to facilitate the movement of "able" women into management, "able" being defined by management. Personal and career development courses for selected women are a common feature and, increasingly, so are career-break schemes, which enable selected women and men to return to an organization at the same level after a break for family reasons of up to five years. Usually, the individual is kept in touch with the organization by various means, typically by returning for two weeks' work each year. Increasingly, provision is made for an initial return on a part-time basis.

PROGRAM FEATURES

Despite the varied political and economic reasons for positive action, the programs of most organizations have common features:

1. Training is provided for managers and supervisors, particularly those involved in recruitment and selection.
2. Training is available for women. Assertiveness courses are common, as are courses to help personal and career development. More rare are courses to provide the skills needed to move into nontraditional occupations.
3. An equal opportunity function is developed. This may be no more than giving one staff member special responsibility for equality activities, along with other aspects of his or her job. A steering group or working party may develop policy. Rarely, a department with many staff members is set up to deal with all aspects of equality policy.
4. There are measures that take account of family responsibilities. Career breaks, enhanced maternity leave, flexible working hours, paternity or parental leave, part-time work, and job sharing are introduced or extended. Exceptionally, childcare facilities or financial help for child care are provided.
5. Personnel policies and practices are reviewed and possibly revised. Recruitment practices are particularly important and selection methods and criteria may be adjusted. But, in spite of a change in the Equal Pay Act that strengthened the concept of equal value, few pay structures and practices have been radically altered. One exception has been local government pay systems for manual workers.

RESULTS

Because few programs have had specific aims, there are few criteria by which one can evaluate results. Implicit in all programs has been the goal of increasing the number of women in higher-level jobs. Anecdotes abound of individual women in jobs they would not have held in the past, but these are frequently not in organizations taking positive action.

In banking, a pioneer in positive action, the number of women in lower and middle-level jobs, but not higher management, has markedly increased. In National Westminster Bank, the proportion of people in junior management grades who were women rose from 9 percent in 1979 to 27 percent in 1989. Similarly, in the Bank of Scotland the proportion of supervisory-grade staff who were female rose from 9 percent in 1980 to 25 percent in 1989. In Midland Bank, the proportion of those in management and supervisory grades who were women was 8.0 percent in 1984 and 17.5 percent in 1989.[5]

No difference is discernible, however, between the record of the banks that were pioneers in positive action and others. This does not invalidate positive action but points to its snowball effect. Organizations, and women who seek to work in them, can react to new employment conditions created by other organizations.

Overall, though women's participation in the work force has grown, positive action has had only minor effects on their concentration in low-paying jobs.

The differential between women's and men's hourly pay narrowed between 1970 and 1975, plateaued, and then narrowed again slowly in the 1980s so that women's pay had reached 77 percent of men's by 1990.

The proportion of managers who are women has risen from 6 percent in 1979 to 11 percent in 1989. That may be called a massive 83 percent rise or only 11 percent of managers. Women's unemployment levels remain high.

5. Margery Povall and Attie de Jong, *Case Study on Developments in Equal Opportunity for Women in Banks in European Countries* (Geneva: International Labor Organization, 1990).

CURRENT ISSUES

The nature and effectiveness of British positive action programs are much debated.

Conflicting policies

Positive action does not exist in a vacuum. The current recession may have affected women's jobs more than men's. Staff cutbacks and organizational restructuring affect traditional career paths. The introduction of new personnel procedures or pay systems without thought to their equality consequences can undo any progress achieved by positive action. Equal opportunity is a concern of some executives, but most corporate decisions disregard it.

Low pay

Antidiscrimination legislation has done little for low-paid women. Unions are starting to bring equal-value cases to tribunals, but with little success. A minimum wage, which the Labour Party has promised to introduce, may address this issue better than further antidiscrimination legislation.

Family commitments

Some early programs addressed women's family responsibilities only peripherally, the implicit assumption being that women would take a break from paid work and then return to work full-time, free of family responsibilities. Child care was not an issue employers took seriously, although unions included it among their demands. Elder care was never mentioned.

Britain has one of the highest percentages of women working part-time in the European Community (the Netherlands has the highest). This is partly related to its scant provision of public child care. Official policy has traditionally been that child care is a personal and private matter, except during the war or for a few families in particular need. Child-care provision has suddenly come to the fore for employers. A major factor was Midland Bank's announcement in 1989 that it would set up 300 workplace nurseries by 1993, possibly in collaboration with other employers. Much discussion has ensued among other employers, along with many feasibility studies, and the provision of some workplace or employer-subsidized facilities. Most child care, however, is still in the hands of family members or untrained and often unlicensed persons.

Black and disabled women

The position of black and disabled women in equality programs is an issue of increasing concern. In some organizations, all equality programs are managed by the same unit; others have separate race and women's units. Women's programs are criticized for ignoring the needs of black or disabled women, and the reverse is true of programs for black people.

Legislative changes

The Conservative government in power since 1979 has resisted calls for stronger legislation. Legislative changes forced by European Commission edict and European Court judgments have been made grudgingly. In the past, Britain met its international obligations with laws that often went beyond Community, U.N., or International Labor Office requirements. For instance, the powers and resources of the Equal Opportunities Commission are envied in other Community countries. In contrast, the stronger Equal Pay Act forced on Britain by the EEC has resulted in provisions so complex that even the responsible civil servants have disagreed about their meaning.

The European Commission's attempts to introduce further regulations or directives to improve women's employment opportunities have been steadfastly blocked by Britain. On the agenda have been the employment rights of part-time and temporary workers, the protection of pregnant women, contract compliance, maternity rights, child care, sexual harassment, minimum wage, equalization of pension and social security benefits, and positive action. Few measures have been adopted, and when they have been, it has usually been in much diluted form. British objections have often been the sole cause of delays and rejections.

Were a Labour government elected, it would be more sympathetic to the foregoing measures.

OTHER EQUALITY PROGRAMS

Women's equality programs have been influenced by and contrast with those relating to race, religion, and disability, as well as developments in other countries.

Race equality

Britain's 1976 Race Relations Act dealt with discrimination and equal opportunity for persons of any race, color, ethnic group, or national origin. Court decisions have ruled that the act covers discrimination against Gypsies, Jews, and Sikhs, because they are separate and distinct communities by virtue of characteristics commonly associated with common racial origin, but not a Muslim, because this is a religious, not cultural, identity.

To implement the act, a Commission for Racial Equality was established with powers similar to those of the Equal Opportunities Commission. It has been much more active than the Equal Opportunities Commission in carrying out formal investigations, related often to discrimination in recruitment. Present race equality programs suffer from the same problems as those dealing with women—inadequate resources, top management support, and focus. But they have lacked the influence that large numbers of able but disadvantaged women in a work force can provide.

Blacks and Asians compose about 4.8 percent of the working-age population (the 1991 census will provide more accurate ethnic information). They are heavily concentrated in industrial and urban areas. The presence of many black or Asian employees has spurred some employers to act, but positive action for women is far more common than for minorities.

Action has too frequently been confined to monitoring the ethnic composition of the work force. Setting up an information system that meets all the objections voiced has taken so much time and energy in some organizations that the information collected has been little used. Ethnic monitoring has on occasion become an end unto itself.

In Europe, however, Britain is thought to be at the fore of race relations activity. The EEC has not, as with gender issues, led the way. Directives about equal treatment for migrant workers entirely ignore the issues facing minorities, particularly black minorities, in such countries as the United Kingdom, Germany, France, and the Netherlands. The latter two countries are addressing race issues in various ways, but in Germany the illusion persists that, for instance, the large, semipermanent population of Turks are temporary migrants.

People with disabilities

British legislation does not protect disabled persons from employment discrimination. The 1944 act requiring employers to employ a 3 percent quota of registered disabled people has not been enforced. Exemption certificates are issued without question. The act was passed primarily to make employment provision for disabled ex-servicemen and -women.

Persons are registered as disabled by disablement resettlement officers in the Department of Employment if they are thought to have a reasonable prospect of obtaining employment—either sheltered or open—and they have an injury, disease, or congenital deformity that substantially handicaps them in obtaining or keeping work. As there is very little advantage—and some potential stigma—to registering, the number of people registering has dropped over the years to well below 3 percent. As disabled people's groups have become increasingly politicized, the call for antidiscrimination legislation has grown. This the Labour Party has promised to introduce.

Employers active in implementing gender and race equality policies have, however, provided a new impetus in recent years as they have begun to address the issues of discrimination against people with disabilities.[6] Disability awareness training for managers and supervisors is perhaps their most visible activity. Some organizations are setting up mechanisms for consulting with employees with disabilities, reviewing access, and adjusting selection procedures. Some local authorities have used the quota requirements to open some job vacancies only for people with disabilities.

Northern Ireland

In 1989, a controversial Fair Employment Act was adopted in Northern Ireland to promote equal opportunity in employment and occupations for persons with different religious beliefs. Its provisions, heavily influenced by American antidiscrimination legislation, are much

6. Michael Floyd and Klaus North, eds., *People with Disabilities: Improving Civil Service Employment Opportunities in Britain and Germany* (London: Anglo-German Foundation, 1991), pp. 61-74; Brenda Smith, Margery Povall, and Michael Floyd, *Managing Disability at Work: Improving Practice in Organisations* (London: Jessica Kingsley; City University, Rehabilitation Resource Centre, 1991), p. 146.

stronger than those relating to sex and race. All public and most private organizations must register with the Fair Employment Commission and submit monitoring reports. A Code of Practice strongly recommends affirmative action, and the commission may impose it on those failing to comply. Critics of the British government's failure to strengthen the race and sex legislation await results with interest.

Britain and the EEC

In many ways the British experience of women's equality programs resembles that of other countries, if only because each country now has legislation and mechanisms to meet minimal EEC requirements. Lack of real political support, ineffective legislation, limited resources, and lack of direction are common to all EEC countries. France has apparently had stronger political support, as it established a Women's Ministry in 1981, but even there women's equality is subject to political vagaries.

Only in Britain are employers beginning to link action on behalf of women, ethnic minorities, and people with disabilities, though the legislative framework differs for each group. But also in Britain—and Ireland, with similar legislation—of the earlier nine-country Community, there seems the least focus on the effort, even if the magnitude of effort may be greater. Confusion about targets and quotas persists, and because the legislation bars quotas or positive discrimination—"reverse discrimination" in the United States—many organizations have not set targets—

"goals" in the United States—either. This is gradually changing as managements realize that they have no way to measure the results of their equality activities. By contrast, in Germany and the Netherlands, organizations serious about equality programs set quotas and actively seek women to fill vacancies.

How much can all the equality efforts of British employers achieve without comprehensive support for families? In France, with plentiful free or cheap child care and extended parental leave, women can more easily stay in paid work and have a better chance to progress up the corporate ladder.

Equality developments for women in Britain—and the rest of the EEC—have been strongly influenced by those in the United States. It is frequently said, "We are 10-15 years behind the U.S." The German Marshall Fund scholarships for Europeans to study American policy and practice proved highly influential in shaping European thinking. The 10-year gap and legal and cultural differences have, however, resulted in some different approaches.

Equality efforts are hampered by the state of the labor markets. The labor markets of the 1960s, with constant skill shortages, have been replaced by unemployment. This has inevitably lessened efforts to attract yet more people into employment and to raise women's aspirations. Britain is not as litigious a country as the United States, and while EEC efforts will no doubt result in more anti-discrimination legislation, the Conservative British government is determined not to swamp employers in equality paperwork and expensive legal structures.

Similarities can be seen between British equality efforts now and those in the United States in the 1960s. A minority of large "good employers" are involved in activity, and the rest are not. But there is one major difference. Child care, maternity provisions, and issues around women's domestic responsibilities have always been on the agenda, particularly trade union agendas, in Europe. Concrete results may be slight, but lessons from the United States are being absorbed.

The question is increasingly raised, How can equality for women in employment be provided that will benefit all women, not just the well educated and childless? The changes in traditional structures and ways of operating would have to be great for this to happen. Most employers will not introduce them without coercion. Employers' positive action must be linked to a government's will to help women win economic independence, enabling them to bear children and provide for their care without sacrificing their job security or career. The European Commission has that will; many national governments do not.

National Bank of Greenwood

By HAROLD ORLANS

ABSTRACT: The affirmative action plan, employment records, and personnel practices of the National Bank of Greenwood, employing 138 persons in the Indiana town of 20,000, were subjected to a grueling inspection by Labor Department staff for more than two years starting in 1979. The staff changed frequently, repeatedly demanded more and different information, and then rejected what it had demanded. "We feel," the bank president said, "that . . . [the Labor Department] has taken over . . . [our] personnel function." Such ordeals have often occurred, especially when contractors were developing personnel records to meet the complex and often unrealistic government affirmative action requirements. Setting aside the manifest incompetence and unreasonableness of Labor staff, the experience reflected the conflicting goals of bank and Labor officials. The bank sought to treat all applicants and employees fairly; Labor, to increase the number of women and minority employees, especially in better-paid jobs.

Harold Orlans, an independent scholar in Chevy Chase, Maryland, has studied higher education and research policy issues at the National Science Foundation, the Brookings Institution, the National Academy of Public Administration, and elsewhere in Washington. He has also written Stevenage: A Sociological Study of a New Town *(1952) and edited* Adjustment to Adult Hearing Loss *(1985) and* The Literary Criticism of T. E. Lawrence *(forthcoming).*

THIS case study summarizes material in part 1 of *Oversight of the Activities of the Office of Federal Contract Compliance Programs of the Department of Labor*, hearings before the Committee on Labor and Human Resources of the U.S. Senate on 29 and 30 July and 22 October 1981. The testimony was submitted by Robert W. Hill, president of the National Bank of Greenwood; Wilson A. Hurrell, vice president and personnel administrator; and Roberts, Ryder, Rogers & Neighbours, an Indianapolis labor relations law firm retained by the bank.

The National Bank of Greenwood is—or was, until acquired by a larger corporation—a local bank with a main office and three branches in Greenwood, Indiana, a town of 20,000 some 15 miles south of Indianapolis. In 1981, the bank had assets of $117 million and employed 138 persons full- or part-time.

From March 1979 to July 1981, when bank officers testified before the Senate committee, the bank underwent a prolonged review of its equal employment opportunity policies and its affirmative action plan and activities by Indianapolis district staff of the Office of Federal Contract Compliance Programs (OFCCP).

The officers believed the bank had been selected at random, since, to their knowledge, no one had ever charged them with employment discrimination. As the banking industry was then being targeted by OFCCP, however, they suspected it viewed them as a model for other banks, since news travels in the industry.

A LONG COMPLIANCE REVIEW

In March 1979, OFCCP notified the bank that a compliance review would be conducted and listed 12 types of records to be examined. During the next two months, two OFCCP staff members examined personnel records and asked countless questions. On 21 June, the bank was informed that its affirmative action plan did not meet OFCCP regulations; half a page of "deficiencies" were cited and administrative action was threatened.

In July, the bank provided information to meet the deficiencies. In August, OFCCP replied that areas of concern remained and another investigation would be conducted. OFCCP staff visiting the bank said the plan could be approved after certain statistical analyses were submitted. In September, however, they mentioned additional problems and requested further information.

On 26 September, the bank's attorney supplied the information, noting that the different statistical instructions were confusing; on 1 October, a modified "availability" analysis with prescribed weighting factors and job groups was submitted.

On 26 November, OFCCP stated that the plan was still not in compliance and itemized three and a half pages of new deficiencies. An official confirmed that the "availability" of women and minorities had been correctly calculated but cited other deficiencies. On 30 November, the plan for handicapped persons and Vietnam veterans was judged unacceptable.

On 28 December 1979 and 3 January 1980, the bank submitted voluminous modifications responding to these communications and again requested approval of its affirmative action plan. OFCCP acknowledged the materials.

Five months later, on 3 June 1980, OFCCP requested much more information about bank employees: their race, sex, date hired, qualifications, initial and current position and salary, and training provided were to be reported in 14 days. The bank complied in 20.

On 22 July, OFCCP announced another investigation and listed 14 types of records to be examined. From 24 to 29 July a new OFCCP representative inspected payroll and personnel records and interviewed employees and supervisors. She said the job groups and availability analysis were incorrect. Told that her predecessors had required that format, she nonetheless instructed the bank to change it. OFCCP then itemized four pages of deficiencies—not previously noted—in the bank's plan. On 14 August, yet more information about employees was requested.

On 28 August, the bank submitted a revised plan. On 25 September, OFCCP declared it unacceptable and specified three pages of necessary changes. On 9 October, the bank made them.

Two days earlier, however, the OFCCP agent had altered her request; this rendered the analysis unsatisfactory, as the bank was formally advised on 6 November. The agent remarked that, with certain modifications, the plan would be approved in "a matter of days." On 10 November, the bank submitted these modifications, yet on 17 November, OFCCP identified further deficiencies.

Two OFCCP letters soon arrived. The first, six pages long, requested much more information about employees, and the second, more information than any previous request since the investigation began in March 1979.

On 12 December 1980, the bank forwarded the information. On 6 April 1981, a new OFCCP official asked for more information.

Ineptitude

Bank officers told the Senate committee they had been

... frustrated by the apparent ineptitude or bumbling of the OFCCP representative handling the investigation. A prime example ... [was] the statistical analysis [of women and minority "availability"]. ... [In] September of 1979, the OFCCP [provided] ... forms. ... Days later, a Bank representative ... was told not to use these ... [but] a different set. ... Within an hour, the OFCCP instructed him not to use the second ... [but] a third set of forms. The Bank completed ... [them and] a listing of jobs in a format requested by the OFCCP representatives.

Six months later when the investigation was turned over to a [new OFCCP] representative ... , two of the primary deficiencies she found were that the Bank's statistical analysis and listing of jobs were not in the proper format.[1]

1. U.S., Senate, Committee on Labor and Human Resources, *Oversight of the Activities of the Office of Federal Contract Compliance Programs of the Department of Labor*, Hearings, 97th Cong., 1st sess., 29 and 30 July and 22 Oct. 1981, pt. 1, p. 614.

Four feet of information

In meeting OFCCP's innumerable requests, the bank provided literally a complete job history of all its employees, past—in some cases, back to 1947—and present: their name, race, sex, and educational level; copies of all job applications; dates of hire and termination; all jobs held and the dates; the minimal qualifications for each job; any changes in these qualifications over the years; training given; wage and salary recommendations; dates and amounts of pay raises; job descriptions and responsibilities; hours worked per week and attendance records. Also included were disciplinary records; the names of all persons transferred or promoted; the dates of these actions; the name and title of the person who made the decision; the basis of the selection; and the names of other employees considered for the position and why they were rejected.

In addition, the bank sent the names of all employees who became pregnant; their job title, pay, and the date and nature of any subsequent change in job or pay; the date each pregnancy was known to the bank; the date pregnancy leave started and ended; whether formerly pregnant employees were still employed; their address and phone.

"About the only thing that the OFCCP has not requested is their hat and shoe size."[2]

To meet these requests, the bank gave OFCCP reports and documents estimated to measure three to four feet high.

Whose personnel system?

By mid-1981, the bank had spent over $100,000 and 4000 man-hours to meet OFCCP regulations and requests. "We feel," the bank president said,

that in a very real sense the OFCCP has taken over the direction of the personnel function of the bank by coming in and telling it what records to keep, . . . where we can recruit our personnel, how to write its job descriptions, what type of interviewing system it should use, what type of salary and wage program should be instituted, what type of job evaluation forms and systems it should use, and what types of personnel decisions should be made.[3]

In July 1981, the bank was directed to

conduct a detailed analysis of job descriptions and specifications by January 1, 1982; utilize specified recruitment sources and contact them by letter, telephone, or personal contact within 30 days of [affirmative action plan] approval; develop a score interview rating form and review the form every 90 days; develop physical and mental job qualifications within 30 days of program approval; develop a skills inventory for all employees within 90 days[;] . . . develop a formal wage and salary program by January 1, 1982; develop a formal career counseling program within 90 days of program approval; and so on and on.[4]

UNDERLYING ISSUES

What employment policies are reasonable? Government and bank officials gave markedly different answers to that question.

2. Ibid., p. 615.

3. Ibid., p. 105.
4. Ibid., p. 108.

Recruitment area

One major issue underlying the dissatisfaction of OFCCP staff with the bank's employment practices, statistics, and plans was the area from which it should recruit. The bank contended it should be eight nearby townships where 98 percent of its employees and 87 percent of its job applicants lived. OFCCP insisted upon the far larger Indianapolis Standard Metropolitan Statistical Area (SMSA), comprising Indianapolis and contiguous counties. In the eight townships, minorities were 1.4 percent of the labor force; in the SMSA, 12.9 percent.

Bank executives thought the estimates of "availability" should be realistic and employment goals, attainable, not so high that they would repeatedly have to explain why their goals were not met and to prove they were acting in good faith. Contrariwise, OFCCP staff sought high goals to increase the employment of minorities and women. To them, statistics indicating that few minorities were qualified or "available" reflected past discrimination and present patterns that, deliberately or unintentionally, perpetuated it, not the true level of equal employability that affirmative action was designed to achieve. One staff member suggested that, for most employees, the statistical areas with the highest percentage of minorities should be used and, for executives, Louisville, Detroit, Virginia, and other states.

Eventually the bank compromised and, under protest, accepted the SMSA for certain purposes.

Computing "availability"

The "eight factor analysis" to compute the "availability" of women and minorities created great confusion and conflict and consumed perhaps more time than any other issue.

"Availability" is defined as "the percentage of minorities or women who have the skills required for entry into a specific [job] group, or who are capable of acquiring them."[5] The eight factors represent statistics on the pertinent number of minorities or females and the total number of persons in a given area, in the area work force, employed, unemployed, with requisite skills, promotable, transferable, or trainable.

The bank bought 1970 census tract statistics on the eight townships from the National Planning Data Corporation of Ithaca, New York. The analysis then proceeded: for each factor, determine the percentage of minorities and women; assign to each factor a "value weight" ranging from a high of .225 to a low of .05, the weights to total 1.0; multiply each percentage by each weight; and add the eight resultant figures to obtain a total "availability percentage."

This procedure was required for each of 12 job groups. With fewer than 150 employees and 12 job groups, many or most statistics generated by this analysis were zero, small fractions, meaningless, unreliable, fanciful, or speculative.

5. U.S., Department of Labor, Office of Federal Contract Compliance Programs, *Federal Contract Compliance Manual* (Washington, DC: Government Printing Office, [1981?]), 1-60.15, p. 1-6.

After the bank accepted SMSA statistics for two factors, the revised analysis was rejected by a new OFCCP agent who said that, because one factor—the number with requisite skills—had the highest proportion of minorities, it should have the greatest weight, .5, far above the maximum previously allowed. Though the bank adopted this weight, its analysis was again rejected because, adjusted for the other factors' lower weights, the final availability figure fell below .5. "The Bank then inquired . . . , why go through the charade of an eight factor analysis when . . . the availability figure should equal the highest percentage . . . among the eight factors. No response was given."[6]

Ultimately, OFCCP prepared its own analysis, with weights as high as .95, which the Bank accepted under protest.

Job groups

Regulations require employees to be classified by job groups. Initially, OFCCP indicated that the "EEO-1" classification—nine categories[7] used by employers to report the number of minority and women employees to the Equal Employment Opportunity Commission—was appropriate. After disagreements about the placement of particular employees, these statistics were accepted.

6. *Oversight of the Activities*, p. 145.
7. The categories were officials and managers, professionals, technicians, sales workers, office and clerical workers, craft workers, semiskilled operatives, unskilled laborers, and service workers.

Later, however, new instructions altered the nine EEO categories to twelve and individual jobs had to be repeatedly reclassified. All told, the job groups were redone eight times before being approved. Each change compelled a corresponding recomputation of the "eight factor analysis."

"Impact analysis"

In July 1981, 27 months into the compliance review, the bank was told to conduct an "impact analysis" of personnel actions: applications, hires, promotions, training, and terminations. Separate analyses were required for minorities and women for each action in each of the 12 job groups. Whenever the minority or female selection or participation rate was less than 80 percent that of whites or males, an explanation and justification was required. "Due to . . . [the] few personnel actions . . . in a year, the Bank felt that such an analysis would be meaningless. Yet the OFCCP required [it]. . . . in 115 of the 120 calculations performed the percentage was 0."[8]

Ringing the changes

The changes in OFCCP staff, requirements, and instructions were the one constant element in the bank's experience.

"We are amazed at the ever changing demands . . . for statistical data, general format, job groups, language, recruitment areas, the eight-factor analysis," Vice President Hurrell testified.

8. *Oversight of the Activities*, p. 147.

For 2½ years it has been like a river, always moving, always shifting, always changing; it never stays the same.

In our last meeting with OFCCP on July 7 [1981] . . . once again we were told to change job groups. We had reached agreement on this matter [in 1980]. . . .

Three employees were shifted . . . affecting five job groups, the work force analysis, the utilization analysis, and . . . the goals and timetables.

. . . 3 days later the specialist who requested that change . . . questioned our resulting statistics. . . . she had forgotten that she had requested the change.[9]

DISCUSSION

In their testimony, bank officers repeatedly stressed their support of equal employment opportunity. But the OFCCP affirmative action regulations and guidelines[10] issued to clarify, implement, and enforce Pres-

9. Ibid., p. 107.
10. Regulations, which must, in theory, be obeyed, are adopted after a public announcement and opportunity to comment. The regulations governing the affirmative action and equal employment opportunity work of OFCCP occupied 112 pages of the *Code of Federal Regulations* in 1989. Guidelines, which usually serve to amplify regulations, need not, in theory, be followed, especially if they conflict with regulations. Except in cases that come before a hearing officer or judge, the distinction can have little practical significance. Rufus Miles, for many years the senior administrative official in the Department of Health, Education, and Welfare (HEW), writes, "In the spring of 1965, [to implement school desegregation under the 1964 Civil Rights Act] HEW issued what were labeled 'guidelines,' a new type of instrument of administration. These guidelines fell short of being formal regulations and yet their sponsors sought to convey the impression that there was considerable force behind them. Their indeterminate status allowed a good deal of flexibility in their appli-

ident Johnson's Executive Order 11246 were not and are not designed merely to ensure fair, equal, and nondiscriminatory employment and promotion opportunities.

Insofar as many blacks and Chicanos, for example, are poor, poorly educated, often unemployed, and unqualified for highly paid jobs, equal opportunity may afford them only the opportunity to remain at the base of the nation's economic and social pyramid. Therefore, OFCCP guidelines press employers to increase their employment, training, and promotion of minorities, women, and handicapped persons especially in upper-level, better-paying jobs where they have been "underrepresented."

Lies and statistics

The vital elements of affirmative action—the present "representation" and future "goals" of employment in each "job group"—are defined, measured, and evaluated by statistics in the employer's affirmative action plan. No matter that there are "lies, damned lies, and statistics"[11]; that available statistics are seldom sufficiently complete, detailed, timely, or applicable to the location, circumstances, and needs of an individual firm; that the fractionation into 10 demographic groups,[12] 9 or 12 job groups, and perhaps eight salary levels renders many detailed employ-

cation." Rufus E. Miles, Jr., *The Department of H.E.W.* (New York: Praeger, 1974), p. 248.
11. Ascribed to both Disraeli and Mark Twain, and borrowed by Michael Wheeler, *Lies, Damn Lies, and Statistics* (New York: Liveright, 1976).
12. White, black, Hispanic, Asian, and Native American males and females.

ment statistics and goals for small and even large firms unreliable or meaningless.

The guidelines require or permit the kind of requests or demands that were made of the bank officers. The bank officers could reasonably object to many features of the compliance review: the frequent turnover of staff, the short time allowed for their response and the long time OFCCP then took to deal with it, the frequent changes in requirements, the excessive volume and burdensomeness of requests. They could object to staff incompetence, arbitrariness, and unreasonableness; to the rote application of a national manual in a local setting where many provisions did not apply.

They could not, however, reasonably object to the staff's doing their job conscientiously. To a varying degree not made clear in their testimony, they apparently objected to affirmative action as defined and prescribed by OFCCP regulations and guidelines.

Recruitment area

Thus, when a firm usually recruits most employees in a geographic area where few minorities live, the guidelines permit or require that the area be broadened to include nearby centers with a large minority population. The bank's situation was that of

a contractor which does not normally recruit in an area broad enough to encompass the greatest availability of minorities or women but whose pay or other features . . . would be likely to attract minority or female applicants from the broader area. . . . Such situations sometimes exist in rural or suburban areas

within commuting distance of an urban center with a significant minority population. In such circumstances, the contractor may be required to include the minority or female requisite skills data for that area in the availability analysis.[13]

"Historical discrimination"

The guidelines warn that old "availability" data such as "1970 Census data being used during 1979," as the bank was doing, may underestimate current availability and, if used to set future employment goals, perpetuate past patterns of discrimination.

Census availability figures may merely be indices of discrimination. For example, blacks or women may have been traditionally excluded from certain kinds of jobs even though they currently possess the ability to perform them. Thus, Census data on the number of blacks or women in those jobs may merely mirror past discrimination.[14]

Hence, in doing the "eight factor analysis," the guidelines state, the factors pertaining to "requisite skills" should be considered "the very 'floor' of availability, above which the contractor's analysis must build by the application of the other factors." The proportion of minorities and women in the area work force is said to be more pertinent than the proportion with requisite skills, since "historical discrimination" may have denied them the opportunity to acquire these skills. "It is reasonable to assume that, absent historical discrimination, the proportion of women and minorities . . . in any job group might

13. *Federal Contract Compliance Manual*, 2-160.5b, p. 2-32.
14. Ibid., 2-160.1d2, p. 2-29.

roughly approximate their percentage of the labor force."[15]

In setting employment goals, OFCCP staff must estimate the future availability of minorities and women. For "job groups for which training is generally obtainable . . . [this] will . . . usually approximate their percentages in the overall labor market area."[16]

This viewpoint may be simplistic. It may require gifts of prophecy. It may attribute present labor force characteristics of minorities and women too much to "historical discrimination" and too little to other factors such as poverty, the large-scale immigration of poorly educated persons from Mexico and Puerto Rico, and the historical absence of many mothers from the work force. The assumption that statistical groups of diverse social composition and culture should, can, or wish to replicate the occupational distribution of a statistical conglomerate of white males belies reason or the contrary assumptions of multicultural diversity.

But it is the viewpoint that permeates OFCCP philosophy and the instructions OFCCP staff sought to implement. The consequences of their diligent efforts for the hapless National Bank of Greenwood were recounted by bank officers.

486 pages of instructions

The *Federal Contract Compliance Manual* setting forth these instructions and providing guidance to firms and OFCCP staff was a 486-page document full of detailed, often complex, definitions, provisions, and forms—replaced in 1990 by a 651-page document. Even a military dictatorship with troops posted in every town would find it impracticable to impose all the provisions equally upon all employers. The judgment of individual staff and the policy emphases of Washington and local officials must govern the enforcement of such prodigious and often artificial procedures.

The bank's experience was doubtlessly exacerbated by the fact that this affirmative action plan was its first, and a first plan often presents more difficulties than succeeding plans. Many universities had similar experiences preparing their first plan in the late 1960s and early 1970s. Like the bank, they had to develop new personnel and employment records and procedures to satisfy the government's insatiable demand for meaningful and meaningless numbers.

The compliance review was initiated during the period when President Carter's administration put renewed emphasis on affirmative action. What bank officers thought inane, government officials may have considered minor pains inflicted for a valuable social purpose.

What would happen subsequently in the administrations of Presidents Reagan and Bush would be another story.

Seeking that story, I asked a bank official to bring it up to date. I believe he would have done so, but the bank has been taken over by a large corporation whose senior vice president deemed silence more prudent than speech.

15. Ibid., 2-160.1f, p. 2-29.
16. Ibid., 2-160.1g, p. 2-29.

After the grueling experience re-counted here, the bank was reviewed twice by OFCCP, in 1988 and again in 1990. The reviews were evidently shorter and more merciful—critics of Reagan and Bush policies might say more perfunctory and toothless—than the earlier investigation.

I also sent this account to Philip Stepteau, head of the OFCCP India-napolis office, requesting his com-ments and corrections. He forwarded the request to Washington, where it went unacknowledged. Telephone calls, apologies by Public Affairs Di-rector Jan Ellis, and a broken ap-pointment finally led to a discussion where a response was promised, as-signed to an official, and not received. Everyone who has dealt with OFCCP staff notes the imbalance between the short deadlines they impose and the long time they take to respond—or not respond at all.

I gained the impression that they are harried, that their tasks are too great for their number, perhaps im-possible for any number. Staff still turn over often, because after the government trains them, industry hires them away to prepare all the statistics the government demands. That may be a just fate or just an-other circle in the perennial cycle of reform.

ANNALS, *AAPSS*, 523, September 1992

Affirmative Action in the Military

By JOHN SIBLEY BUTLER

ABSTRACT: African Americans have fought in American conflicts since colonial days. The segregation practiced during the Civil War endured until abolished by President Truman in 1948. Since the all-volunteer force was established in 1973, the number of African American troops has risen; in 1991, they composed 28 percent of the Army and three-fifths of some combat units. Thus desegregation and affirmative action in the military have been years ahead of that in civilian society. Current policy seeks to increase the enlistment of whites and to ensure fully equal treatment and opportunity and good race relations.

John Sibley Butler is the Dallas TACA Centennial Professor in Liberal Arts and the Arthur James Douglass Centennial Professor of Entrepreneurship and Small Business at the University of Texas, Austin. He received a B.A. from Louisiana State University and a Ph.D. in sociology from Northwestern. His extensive publications include Inequality in the Military: The Black Experience *(1979) and* Entrepreneurship and Self-Help among Black Americans *(1991).*

WHILE most analyses of affirmative action emphasize increasing the number of previously excluded persons, the military has a history of utilizing groups excluded by the larger society. The participation of blacks in military organizations predates the nation's birth, but they were long denied opportunities for advancement. The military has never actively recruited blacks and, on occasions, has sought to keep them out. To understand its affirmative action record, we must understand the uniqueness of this institution.

This article will first consider the meaning of affirmative action for military organizations. It will then review the history of blacks in the military, the structure of the military, and its role in expanding opportunities for excluded groups. Special attention will be given to the rising number of female soldiers following the advent of the all-volunteer force.

THE MILITARY'S EMPHASIS ON BLACK AMERICANS

Current affirmative action policy originated in a series of executive orders by each president from Franklin Roosevelt to Lyndon Johnson, which barred employment discrimination by government contractors. The precise meaning of affirmative action and the measures required of contractors remained problematic, however, until the Department of Labor issued Revised Order No. 4 in 1971.

This order stated that an affirmative action program is "a set of specific and result-oriented procedures to which a contractor commits itself to apply every good faith effort." It specified that

an acceptable affirmative action program must include an analysis of areas within which the contractor is deficient in the utilization of minority groups and women, and further, goals and timetables to which the contractor's good faith efforts must be directed to correct the deficiencies . . . at all levels and in all segments of his work force.[1]

In 1966, while civil rights protests escalated in the country, Charles Moskos observed that the military was the only institution in America where white personnel were often commanded by black superiors.

For the man newly entering the armed forces, it is hard to conceive that the military was one of America's most segregated institutions less than two decades ago. For today color barriers at the formal level are absent throughout the military establishment. Equal treatment regardless of race is official policy in such nonduty facilities as swimming pools, chapels, barbershops, post exchanges, movie theaters, and other more formal aspects of the military.[2]

The same year, in a comprehensive study of racial attitudes, William Brink and Louis Harris reported that blacks perceived the military as more equalitarian than civilian society, with better chances for training and promotion.[3]

In *The American Soldier* (1949), Samuel Stouffer and his colleagues

1. U.S., Department of Labor, Office of Federal Contract Compliance Programs, Revised Order, Number 4, *Federal Register*, 4 Dec. 1971, p. 234.

2. Charles C. Moskos, Jr., "Racial Integration in the Armed Forces," *American Journal of Sociology*, 72:132-48 (1966).

3. William Brink and Louis Harris, *Black and White* (New York: Simon & Schuster, 1966), pp. 162-75.

suggested that black and white soldiers in mixed racial units had more positive attitudes than those in single-race units.[4] This research, conducted as the military was moving rapidly toward desegregation, was reported to the court in the landmark case of *Brown* v. *Board of Education*.

Subsequent research has sustained the basic findings of Stouffer and Brink and Harris.[5] Scholars now view the military as a success story for African Americans and a model for the larger society.[6] Indeed, in the last decade, major attention has been given to decreasing the number of blacks in portions of the military.

HISTORY

African Americans have been involved in all U.S. military conflicts. They participated as militia in the defeat of the Yamassee Indians in 1715. In the French colony of Louisiana, slaves and free Afro-Americans were enlisted to fight the Chickasaw and Natchez Indians. In all four wars of the colonists against the French, African Americans were utilized as scouts and soldiers.[7]

4. Samuel Stouffer et al., *The American Soldier* (Princeton, NJ: Princeton University Press, 1949), 1:459.

5. See, for example, Alvin J. Schexnider, "The Development of Racial Solidarity in the Armed Forces," *Journal of Black Studies*, 5: 414-34 (1975); John Sibley Butler and Malcolm D. Holmes, "Perceived Discrimination and the Military Experience," *Journal of Political and Military Sociology*, 9:17, 30 (Spring 1981).

6. Charles C. Moskos, "Success Story: Blacks in the Army," *Atlantic*, May 1986, pp. 64, 72.

7. Jack D. Foner, *Blacks in the Military in American History* (New York: Praeger, 1974), pp. 43, 4-5.

In the colonists' eyes, the military service of African Americans was necessary rather than desirable. Colonists granted them the privilege of serving but feared that they might turn their weapons on them and try to put an end to slavery. After a slave revolt in 1739, Carolina colonists noted that "there must be great caution used, lest our slaves when armed might become our masters."[8] But the manpower shortage ensured African Americans a role in all colonial conflicts.

The Revolutionary War

During the American Revolution, over 5000 African Americans supported the colonists; many lost their lives. About 20 percent of the colonial population of 2.5 million was black at that time. Nonetheless, at the start of the rebellion, General George Washington issued four orders forbidding free blacks and slaves from joining the Continental Army.

Recognizing that slavery was a divisive issue for the colonists, the British solicited black recruits, offering freedom to slaves who fought for the crown. In 1777, John Murray, earl of Dunmore and royal governor of Virginia, proclaimed

all indentured servants, Negroes, or others, (appertaining to Rebels) free, that are able and willing to bear arms, they joining His Majesty's Troops, as soon as may be, for the more speedily reducing the colony to a proper sense of their duty, to His Majesty's crown and dignity.[9]

8. Ibid., p. 3.

9. *Black Americans in Defense of Our Nation* (Washington, DC: Department of Defense, 1981), p. 4.

Over 200 blacks answered the call. They had "Liberty to Slaves" inscribed on their uniforms and served in a unit called Lord Dunmore's "Ethiopian Regiment."[10]

In response to the British action, General Washington authorized the recruitment of blacks.[11] Washington's army averaged 54 blacks in each battalion; the two races were integrated, fighting side by side. But some colonies, such as Massachusetts and Rhode Island, raised all-black battalions.

When the British were defeated, blacks were not allowed to remain in the military, and slaves who had been promised freedom were sent back to bondage. The needs of war and the promises of freedom were replaced by the conservatism of the constitutional era.[12]

The policies toward blacks after the Revolutionary War began a pattern, which has been called recruit-retain-and-reject, that lasted until the Korean conflict. Blacks would be recruited only when manpower shortages developed, retained during the conflict, and dismissed thereafter.

When the Civil War erupted, Northern blacks responded enthusiastically to the first call for volunteers. Then Secretary of War Edward M. Stanton declared, "This department has no intention to call into service any colored soldiers."[13] Only after the Emancipation Proclamation were blacks allowed to fight against the Confederacy. Nearly 180,000 were formed into separate units called "United States Colored Troops." They fought crucial battles, won 14 congressional medals of honor, and helped to liberate Petersburg and Richmond.[14]

Buffalo soldiers

After the war, Army policy was not to retain or enlist blacks for peacetime service.[15] But in response to tension and battles with Indians in the West, four African American units were created (there had been 120 during the war)—the Ninth and Tenth Cavalry and Fourteenth and Fifteenth Infantry—which played major roles in the Indian Wars from 1870 to 1890.[16]

These units also protected settlers moving west, the mail, and the railroad under construction. For the first time in U.S. history, black soldiers moved freely among the Euro-American population. Despite their protective role, they faced hostility from settlers. In 1881, after several years of conflict with local citizens, African American soldiers posted the following handbill in San Angelo, Texas:

10. Ibid.

11. United States Army, Europe, Race Relations School, "Black Soldier: A Compendium" (Washington, DC: Department of Defense, 1972), p. 1.

12. John Sibley Butler and Malcolm D. Holmes, "Changing Organizational Structure and the Future of Race Relations in the Military," in *Conscripts and Volunteers*, ed. Robert K. Fullinwider (New York: Rowan & Littlefield, 1982), pp. 167-77.

13. Richard J. Stillman, *Integration of the Negro in the U.S. Armed Forces* (New York: Frederick Praeger, 1968), p. 9.

14. Dwight W. Hoover, *Understanding Negro History* (Chicago: Quadrangle Books, 1968), p. 270.

15. Foner, *Blacks in the Military in American History*, p. 127.

16. Stillman, *Integration of the Negro in the U.S. Armed Forces*, p. 11.

We, the soldiers of the United States Army, do hereby warn cowboys, etc., of San Angelo and vicinity, to recognize our rights of way as just and peaceable men. If we do not receive just and fair play, which we must have, someone will suffer; if not the guilty, the innocent. It has gone too far; justice or death. U.S. Soldiers, one and all.[17]

The black soldiers stationed among hostile Euro-Americans fought over a hundred battles with Indian tribes. Their bravery earned them the sobriquet "Buffalo Soldiers" and 18 medals of honor.[18]

The Spanish-American War began when the battleship *Maine* sank in Havana Harbor; 22 black sailors were in its hull. Though African Americans were barred from state militia, North Carolina, Virginia, Illinois, and Kansas permitted them to organize volunteer units. As the war lasted only 10 weeks, few of these units saw action, but established units—the Buffalo Soldiers, Ninth and Tenth Cavalry, Twenty-Fourth and Twenty-Fifth Infantry—were in the heat of battle. The Twenty-Fifth Infantry and Tenth Cavalry fought at El Caney, and the Tenth received honors; the Twenty-Fourth Infantry helped in the assault on San Juan Hill.[19]

Over 200,000 African Americans served in World War I, following President Woodrow Wilson's plea that "the world must be made safe for democracy." Georgia Congressman Frank Park's bill to make it unlawful to appoint blacks as noncommis-

sioned or commissioned officers was defeated, and they served in all ranks. The practice of segregating troops, established in the Civil War, continued, however.

After the war, many black servicemen in uniform were lynched in the widespread race riots of the "red summer" of 1919. The Army instituted a quota system to restrict the number of African Americans to their proportion in the population. By 1940, only 5000 remained, serving in all-black units. They had only five black officers; white officers commanded most black troops as they had done in the segregated army of the Civil War and World War I.[20]

By the time World War II started, African American troops had served under integrated and segregated conditions and won over forty medals of honor; over 15 had earned the rank of general.[21] They did their duty despite frequent insult and hostility. Many of the people they fought later immigrated and became part of "white America."

During World War II, the relationship between African Americans and the military was renegotiated. Civilian social issues were now explicitly tied to their role in the defense industry and the military. African American leaders linked military participation to defense jobs. A. Philip Randolph called for a march on Washington to end racial segregation

17. *Black Americans in Defense of Our Nation*, p. 28.

18. Ibid.

19. Ibid., p. 21.

20. John Sibley Butler, "The Military as a Vehicle for Social Integration," in *Ethnicity Integration and the Military*, ed. Henry Dietz et al. (Boulder, CO: Westview Press, 1991), p. 38.

21. *Black Americans in Defense of Our Nation*, pp. 13-14, 18-19.

in the military and to open defense jobs to blacks.

"We call upon you to fight for jobs in National Defense . . . to struggle for the integration of Negroes in the Armed Forces. . . . This is the hour of crisis. . . . To American Negroes, it is the denial of jobs in governmental defense projects. It is widespread Jim-Crowism in the Armed Forces of the nation."[22]

Discrimination by defense contractors was ended—in principle, if not practice—by President Roosevelt's Executive Order 8802 in June 1941, but military segregation remained. More than 900,000 African Americans served in segregated units during World War II.

Military desegregation

The pressure to desegregate the military continued nonetheless. The emphasis was on desegregation, not on increasing the number of African American troops. Segregation had not always been the norm; in many earlier conflicts, troops were desegregated.

In 1944, Lieutenant General Alvin C. Gillem chaired a board to examine how African Americans might be integrated. Earlier in the war, the military had experimented with integrated units. The Gillem board interviewed over 320 white officers. Its 1945 report concluded that small black units in larger white or integrated units were superior to all-black units in combat readiness, morale, and "moral" discipline. It recommended that African American recruitment be limited to 10 percent of

the Army, however, and that segregated units be maintained. Five years later, a second board, headed by Lieutenant General S. J. Chamberlain, concurred.[23]

Disregarding these recommendations, President Truman issued Executive Order 9981 in 1948, ending military segregation. The order declared, "There shall be equality of treatment and opportunity in the Armed Forces. This policy shall be put into effect as rapidly as possible, having due regard to the time required to effectuate any necessary changes without impairing efficiency or morale.[24]

Integration became a reality during the Korean conflict, and researchers noted that the fighting abilities of African Americans and Europeans were the same.[25] During the Cold War, they pointed to the military, especially the Army, as a model of race relations. One writer declared, "The U.S. Army has solved the Negro integration problem still plaguing much of the rest of the nation."[26] This theme constantly appeared in the literature on race and the military at the time.

The Vietnam war disrupted the prevailing harmonious race relations in the military. A higher proportion of African American troops were en-

22. August Mier, *Black Protest Thought in the Twentieth Century* (New York: Bobbs-Merrill, 1969), p. 25.

23. Butler, "Military as a Vehicle for Social Integration," p. 38.

24. John P. Davis, *The Negro Reference Book* (Englewood Cliffs, NJ: Prentice-Hall, 1971), p. 652.

25. Charles C. Moskos, *The American Enlisted Man* (New York: Russell Sage Foundation, 1971), p. 111.

26. James C. Evans, "Integration, Differentiation and Refinement," *Negro History Bulletin*, Apr. 1960, p. 151.

gaged in this war than in any previous American conflict. In 1968 alone, over 70,000 saw action.

Racial turmoil spilled over from civilian society to the military. In 1964, major riots broke out in Harlem, Rochester, and Philadelphia. On 2 July 1964, the same day that Congress passed the broadest Civil Rights Act in history, the Army issued equal opportunity directive AR 600-21:

Every military commander has the responsibility to oppose discriminatory practice affecting his men and their dependents and to foster equal opportunity for them, not only in areas under his immediate control, but also in nearby communities where they may live or gather in off-duty hours.[27]

In 1965, the upsurge of civil rights protests continued with the march from Selma to Montgomery, the Vietnam war escalated, and formal complaints of discrimination—in military justice, promotions, and treatment—in the Army were made. In the summer of 1969, serious racial incidents were reported at 11 military installations in the United States and at many overseas installations.[28]

During the Vietnam war, African American soldiers tended to stay in the military longer than whites and to volunteer more often for elite units such as the airborne or air cavalry. They bore a disproportionate number of casualties and won twenty medals of honor.[29]

The charges of discrimination and the affirmative measures taken to resolve them marked a new racial era. The former goals of increasing the number of African Americans and integrating them had been achieved. The new goals were to establish and maintain full equality and healthy race relations.

EQUAL OPPORTUNITY AND RACE RELATIONS

The first step the Army took was to develop a course of instruction in race relations. In doing so, it was years ahead of civilian firms, which are still developing programs to "attract minority candidates." By 1970, the Army Infantry School had prepared separate four-hour blocks of instruction entitled "Leadership Aspects of Race Relations" for six grades of troops and officers.[30]

The courses sought to foster an understanding of the basic factors in race relations, the causes of racial tension, and steps that must be taken to promote racial harmony. They included information on the history and achievements of minority groups and individuals, slavery, Army policy on equal opportunity, and the leader's responsibility in race relations.

In 1971, the Defense Department established the Defense Race Relations Institute to train instructors in race relations for military personnel throughout the world and to ensure that racial education programs were fully consonant with departmental and service policy.

27. Peter G. Nordlie et al., *Race Relations in the Army* (McLean, VA: Westgate Research Park, 1972), p. 12.

28. Ibid., p. 13.

29. *Black Americans in Defense of Our Nation*, p. 38.

30. Guy R. Marbury et al., *Race Relations in the Army* (McLean, VA: Human Sciences Research, Champion Press, 1972), p. 25.

The provision of equal opportunities for African Americans required their assignment to all occupations, upward mobility through the ranks, and just treatment. Research clearly showed that, even after controlling for test scores, African Americans were more likely to be assigned to combat than to technical occupations and were promoted more slowly. They were punished more often and more harshly than whites.[31]

REVERSE AFFIRMATIVE ACTION

After the Vietnam war, race relations in the military tended to return to their earlier status, and studies indicated that interracial attitudes improved.[32] The military no longer sought to regulate the number of African Americans, which increased markedly, especially with the switch from the draft to the all-volunteer force in 1973. From 1971 to 1974, their proportion in the enlisted ranks rose from 14.4 to 19.9 percent in the Army, from 11.4 to 17.7 percent in the Marine Corps, from 12.3 to 13.8 percent in the Air Force, and from 5.4 to 8.1 percent in the Navy. The percentage of all enlisted persons who were black increased from 11.4 to 14.9 percent.[33]

A new issue now arose: the overrepresentation of African Americans, particularly in Army ground combat forces. In a landmark paper, Morris Janowitz and Charles Moskos wrote:

Overrepresentation of blacks in the armed forces, while not yet an issue of national debate, can be defined as a problem from several perspectives. Thus some professional military officers and civilian commentators view a large concentration of blacks as exacerbating race tensions and management problems within the services. A few of them are apprehensive about the internal reliability of such a force. Conversely, others, not only blacks, are distressed over the potential disproportions of black casualties in time of war. This paper . . . attempts to reformulate the discussion in terms of representativeness of core institutions and political legitimacy.[34]

By 1980, 27.2 percent of Army enlisted personnel were black. This was due in part to the growing enlistment of women, who composed only 1 percent of the Army in 1960 but 10 percent in the mid-1980s. A rapidly rising proportion of African American Army enlistees have been women: in 1973, 18.9 percent; in 1979, 40.8 percent.[35]

While official Pentagon policy did not restrict the enlistment of African Americans and while the Army was dedicated to equal treatment, scholars and journalists debated the growing black presence in the military. By the time of the war with Iraq, blacks made up 28.9 percent of the Army,

31. John Sibley Butler, "Inequality in the Military," *American Sociological Review*, 41:807, 818 (Oct. 1976); U.S., Department of Defense, *Report of the Task Force on the Administration of Military Justice* (Washington, DC: Government Printing Office, 1972).

32. John Sibley Butler and Kenneth L. Wilson, "The American Soldier Revisited," *Social Science Quarterly*, 59:451, 467 (Dec. 1978).

33. Morris Janowitz and Charles C. Moskos, "Racial Composition in the All-Volun-

teer Force," *Armed Forces and Society*, 1:109, 123 (Nov. 1974).

34. Ibid., p. 109.

35. Charles C. Moskos, Jr., "Symposium: Race and the U.S. Military," *Armed Forces and Society*, 6:587-94 (Summer 1980).

TABLE 1

**PROPORTION OF OFFICERS AND ENLISTEES IN
EACH MILITARY SERVICE WHO ARE AFRICAN AMERICAN, 1991**

Rank	Percentage of African Americans				
	All Services	Army	Marines	Navy	Air Force
Officers*	6.8	11.1	4.5	4.0	5.6
Enlistees	22.6	31.6	20.0	17.7	17.3
Total	20.3	28.6	18.5	15.9	15.1

SOURCE: U.S., Department of Defense, Office of Defense Manpower Documentation Center.
*Warrant officers excluded.

29.9 percent of Army troops in the war theater, and three-fifths of some Army combat units. They were led by four-star General Colin Powell, then chairman of the Joint Chiefs of Staff, the highest-ranking in a long line of U.S. black generals.

As the danger of war rose, the proportion of African Americans in the military became a public issue. Some black leaders argued that black soldiers were victims of an economic draft, forced into the military as a refuge from poverty and crime. Others argued that, historically, blacks have chosen the military for patriotic reasons and, like many other Americans, as a way to obtain technical training and improve their career prospects.[36]

While the news media has discussed the high proportion of African Americans in the military, the academic literature has dwelt on the opposite issue of how to increase the number of white middle-class youths in the all-volunteer force—or, it might be said, how to establish an affirmative action program for white youths.[37]

African Americans constitute a far larger proportion of enlistees and officers in the Army than in the three other services (Table 1). Many black families have identified with the Army since the early days of the nation. The largest service, it offers a wide range of technical training and occupational opportunity. The services have long been an economic refuge for those unable to find stable employment due to discrimination, depression, or inadequate training. Special programs have also helped to educate the children and support the families of enlistees and officers.[38]

36. For an excellent discussion, see "The Battle for Respect," *Newsweek*, 11 Mar. 1991, pp. 54-57. Regardless of race, veterans of all conflicts but Vietnam earn more than comparable nonveterans. Dudley L. Poston, Jr., et al., "The Influence of Military Service on the Civilian Earning Patterns of Female Veterans," in *Women in the United States Armed Forces*, ed. Nancy L. Goldman (Chicago: Inter-University Seminar on Armed Forces and Society, 1984), pp. 152-71.

37. Janowitz and Moskos, "Racial Composition in the All-Volunteer Force," pp. 115-23.

38. John Sibley Butler, "Race and the All-Volunteer Force," *Armed Forces and Society*, 6:594-600 (Summer 1980).

A CLOSED STRUCTURE
AND OPEN MEMBERSHIP

Why did military desegregation predate the 1954 Supreme Court decision on school desegregation and the 1964 Civil Rights Act, which desegregated public facilities and programs?

As Spindler and Freeman pointed out in two significant papers,[39] the military is a relatively self-contained institution that meets its members' needs for food, clothes, and shelter. It promotes its physical and psychological separation from civilian society, especially for new recruits.

Authority in the military is centralized in an integrated series of hierarchical offices vested with powers and privileges. At the apex is the President of the United States, who serves as both chief executive and commander in chief. In this hierarchical structure, patterned on the relationship of command and obedience, decisions are not democratic and do not have to accommodate the personal desires or opinions of military personnel. A presidential order can change a commander or the social composition of the forces.

Thus, in 1972, 1.9 percent of the armed forces were women. The following year, President Nixon ordered an all-volunteer force. By 1976, over 5 percent of the force were women and by 1982, 9 percent. Their numbers were 45,000 in 1972, 108,000 in 1976, and 190,000 in 1982.[40]

These increases were accompanied by major changes in personnel policies, including allowing women to command units composed of men and women; allowing them to enter aviation training and military academies; ending the automatic discharge of pregnant women and those with minor dependents; providing equal family entitlements for married men and women soldiers; and providing access to a wider range of training and to 95 percent of enlisted occupations.[41] The Defense Department and Congress still bar women from combat.

Unlike civilian institutions, which struggled with the utilization of women, the military did not have to worry about the attitudes of servicemen or officers. After the President issued his order, the number of females rose dramatically.

CONCLUSION

Affirmative action emphasizes the increased—or, more precisely, the proportionate—participation of underrepresented groups. It does not preclude discrimination, racism, or sexism. Derogatory acts and prejudices may continue despite the achievement of an armed force or civilian work force that represents—or, indeed, overrepresents—formerly excluded groups. Racial and gender prejudices and inequalities persist in the armed forces and it will be a long time before they are completely eliminated.

39. G. Dearborn Spindler, "The Military—A Systematic Analysis," *Social Forces*, 27:83-88 (1948); Felton D. Freeman, "The Army as a Social Structure," ibid., pp. 78-83.

40. Martha A. Marsden, "The Continuing Debate: Women Soldiers in the U.S. Army," in *Life in the Rank and File*, ed. David R. Segal and H. Wallace Sinaiko (Washington, DC: Pergamon-Brassey's, 1986), p. 42.

41. Ibid.

Nonetheless, the military has rapidly absorbed and integrated large numbers of blacks and women with no loss—indeed, with a gain, if their performance in the Iraq war is a fair test—in operational effectiveness. The services' experience offers lessons to civilian institutions in how a firm policy, equal treatment, and intense training can incorporate previously excluded groups into an effective organization.

ANNALS, *AAPSS*, 523, September 1992

Affirmative Action at Harvard

By JOHN B. WILLIAMS

ABSTRACT: Affirmative action to employ more women and minorities at Harvard consists mainly in efforts to increase the number who apply for jobs. Since the first affirmative action plan was prepared in 1973, the proportion of women employees has risen markedly, especially in nonfaculty positions, but the proportion of black and Hispanic faculty has changed little. The record of the Medical School is particularly poor. Affirmative action is hampered by a lack of vigorous support from Harvard leaders, the decentralized university organization, the often unjustified perception of candidates' weak quality, the opposition of some women and minority faculty, and the shortages of qualified candidates.

John B. Williams, associate professor at the Harvard Graduate School of Education, has an A.B. from Princeton and an Ed.D. from Harvard. As assistant to President Derek Bok from 1985 to 1988, he was the chief Harvard official responsible for affirmative action. He has written Highest Honors: American Public Schools in the 1990s *(forthcoming) and edited* Desegregating America's Colleges and Universities: Title VI Regulation of Higher Education *(1988).*

THE Office of Federal Contract Compliance (OFCCP) at the U.S. Department of Labor (DOL) is currently responsible for implementing the affirmative action program for federal contractors initiated in 1965 by President Lyndon Johnson's Executive Order 11246. OFCCP staff conduct regularly scheduled "desk audits"[1] to determine compliance. They also conduct an audit before a contractor receives a federal contract of $1 million or more.[2] OFCCP audits focus on two kinds of employment issues affecting minorities and women: "underutilization" and "disparate impact."

In their affirmative action plans, colleges and universities must calculate the "availability" of women and minorities—roughly speaking, their percentage in designated job categories such as secretarial-clerical or humanities professors—in a geographical area available to the institution. If the percentage actually employed in a category is below the availability estimate, the institution must set an employment goal and make special efforts to increase minority or female employment in the category over a period of one to five years. In most cases, explanations for failure to meet employment goals are provided, and OFCCP evaluates "good-faith efforts" by the institution and permits it to set new goals and to try again.

1. Conducted by examining institutional reports and records in the OFCCP regional offices.

2. As major research universities receive many contracts of $1 million or more, they complained that they were audited constantly. When notified of a $1 million award, OFCCP now conducts an audit only if none has been conducted for two years.

OFCCP works through the federal court system to initiate and authenticate an official finding of noncompliance under complex bureaucratic and judicial procedures. In the case of egregious violations, most institutions adopt remedies prescribed by OFCCP in order to avoid noncompliance findings by the courts. Seldom, however, has OFCCP clearly established and then vigorously pursued evidence of noncompliance by colleges and universities.

"Disparate impact" occurs when minorities or women are employed or promoted at lower rates, or terminated at higher rates, than white males. In such cases, explanations are sought and a judgment is reached. Findings of disparate impact seldom result in rulings of noncompliance. In most instances, remedies are devised and "good-faith efforts" are monitored by OFCCP.

Over the past twenty years, federal affirmative action policy for higher education has evolved along two related paths, one bureaucratic and the other political. Bureaucratic requirements, policies, and procedures have developed at times cumbersomely. All aspects of the regulatory process, from the specific content of affirmative action plans to the broad evidence and procedures for noncompliance rulings and withholding contracts, have been changed at one time or another.

Politically, successive national administrations have taken different views of the value of affirmative action. At times, universities like Harvard have received little regulatory attention. At other times, the regional OFCCP office in Boston has audited any institution due to receive a $1 million federal contract—which happens frequently at Harvard or the Massachusetts Institute of Technology. At times, its small staff, reduced by low funding, could give little attention to higher education. At other times, expanded staffing permitted audits at a reasonable number of New England institutions.

During the Reagan administration, the Boston staff promoted a new approach. They offered incentives for compliance, publicizing awards for special accomplishments. Unlike corporations, few colleges or universities competed for these awards. In higher education, substituting incentives for sanctions amounted to watering down compliance. Moreover, competing for awards determined in unknown ways engages universities in politics they ostensibly attempt to avoid.

Harvard regularly receives large sums for research from federal agencies. DOL gave the university one of the first awards for exemplary affirmative action, supposedly for its initiative in establishing a New England "higher education liaison group." In the 1970s, DOL had promoted liaison groups to keep contractors abreast of rapidly evolving affirmative action requirements. In the 1980s, it began a program of awards in an attempt to rejuvenate these groups.

By that time, the Harvard staff who had helped to organize the New England group had departed. When the award was conferred, no liaison group existed and I—who was then the Harvard affirmative action officer—was not, as DOL announced, its

chairman.[3] When other university leaders attempted to form a group, they had little success. Most colleges and universities gained little from participation; some corporations with exemplary affirmative action records enhanced their chances of receiving government contracts.

While the definitive history of federal affirmative action policy remains to be written, it appears that the rules became clearer as political pressure to enforce them dissolved. The requirements are clearer today than ever before. Institutions routinely undergo audits, identify underutilization, measure disparate impact, and promise "good-faith efforts" to improve. Upon finding adequate "good-faith effort," OFCCP routinely lets them off the hook and experiences little pressure to do otherwise.

In earlier years when the requirements were uncertain, it was difficult for OFCCP either to demand strenuous or to allow pro forma compliance. While the Boston office now conducts desk audits more regularly, the requirements are sufficiently streamlined to permit pro forma reviews. The 1990 Harvard review will be described subsequently.

ENROLLMENT

Biennially before and annually after 1990, all 3700 colleges and universities report their enrollment by

3. When one editor of this *Annals* issue visited the OFCCP Washington headquarters in November 1991, he was told that the New England group was a good example of liaison groups and that John Williams, the Harvard affirmative action officer, was its chairman.

TABLE 1

PERCENTAGE OF AFRICAN AMERICAN AND ASIAN AMERICAN
STUDENTS IN SELECTED HARVARD FACULTIES, FALL 1980, 1985, 1990

| | Percentage of Students Who Were | | | | | |
| | African American | | | Asian American | | |
Faculty	1980	1985	1990	1980	1985	1990
College	6.8	6.0	7.7	4.7	8.9	14.8
Graduate school	2.0	1.9	2.3	2.1	2.6	3.6
Business	3.9	5.0	6.1	1.6	2.4	3.7
Law	7.4	9.5	10.4	1.9	2.6	5.8
Medicine	10.5	8.3	7.8	4.8	9.2	19.7
Total university	5.7	5.3	6.0	3.3	5.6	8.8

SOURCES: Harvard University, Office of Budgets, "Fact Book, 1980-81," mimeographed (Cambridge, MA: Harvard University, Office of Budgets, 1981); idem, "Fact Book, 1985-86," mimeographed (Cambridge, MA: Harvard University, Office of Budgets, 1986); idem, "Fact Book, 1990-91," mimeographed (Cambridge, MA: Harvard University, Office of Budgets, 1991).

minority status and sex to the Department of Education, which makes the data public.

The Office for Civil Rights at the department investigates complaints of discrimination in admissions and conducts periodic reviews of admission practices. Recently, for example, the Office of Civil Rights investigated charges that several institutions, Harvard included, had systematically discriminated against Asian applicants. It found that Harvard had not.

Overall enrollment of minorities at Harvard rose from 13 percent in 1980 to 20 percent in 1990. From 1980 to 1985, African American enrollments dropped, however, especially at Harvard College and the Medical School. Their numbers rebounded afterward in most faculties but not in the Medical School. Hispanic enrollment also fell at the Medical School, though not in the university as a whole. The number of Asian American students rose markedly, particularly in the College, Law, and Medicine (Table 1).

In graduate departments of arts and sciences, the primary source of future faculty, only 11 percent of the students were minorities in 1990-91. Arguably, the enrollment of all minorities except, perhaps, Asian Americans should be increased in all faculties, particularly the graduate school.

In 1990, 41 percent of Harvard undergraduates were women. Over the 1980-90 decade, the proportion of women rose in every faculty, even the Business School, with by far the lowest proportion—27 percent. In Education, Divinity, and Public Health, a majority of students are now women and, should recent trends continue, in another decade that will also be true of Law (Table 2).

EMPLOYMENT

Harvard's first affirmative action plan was approved in 1973. Until

TABLE 2

TOTAL ENROLLMENT AND PERCENTAGE OF WOMEN IN HARVARD FACULTIES, FALL 1980, 1985, 1990

Faculty	Total Enrollment			Percentage of Women		
	1980	1985	1990	1980	1985	1990
College	6,561	6,568	6,622	36.5	41.3	40.9
Graduate school	2,402	2,485	3,237	31.9	33.1	36.9
Business	1,614	1,635	1,654	22.2	24.4	27.4
Dentistry	85	152	158	35.3	36.2	37.3
Design	336	476	482	29.8	37.2	38.4
Divinity	264	456	484	42.6	52.9	59.7
Education	963	1,041	1,233	61.8	62.2	68.3
Government	635	635	717	30.4	33.4	37.8
Law	1,753	1,796	1,755	28.1	34.7	42.3
Medicine	673	649	670	29.1	36.2	39.9
Public Health	412	408	554	44.2	53.7	51.8
Total	15,698	16,301	17,566	35.0	38.9	41.6

SOURCES: Harvard University, Office of Budgets, "Fact Book, 1980-81"; idem, "Fact Book, 1985-86"; idem, "Fact Book, 1990-91."

then, uncertain directives about government requirements had emerged from Washington. Events leading to the first plan have been satisfactorily chronicled.[4] Through the years, the plan has evolved in response to changing federal requirements and the university's changing capacity to meet them.

The 1990-91 plan describes the university "as a confederation of its various Faculties . . . with a Central Administration. Decisionmaking is decentralized, and high degrees of responsibility for governance are vested in its various academic units." The Harvard system for implementing affirmative action involves urging the ten university faculties and six central administrative divisions to devise their own means of elimi-

4. See John E. Fleming, Gerald R. Gill, and David Swinton, *The Case for Affirmative Action* (Washington, DC: Howard University Press, 1978), pp. 158-77.

nating discrimination and increasing the employment and promotion of women and minorities.

The 10 faculties are the Faculty of Arts and Sciences; the Graduate Schools of Business Administration, Design, and Education; the Schools of Dental Medicine and Public Health; the John F. Kennedy School of Government; and the Divinity, Law, and Medical schools. Five central administrative divisions are headed by vice presidents for administration, alumni affairs, finance, government, and legal affairs; the sixth is the President's Office.

Currently, no faculty unit is headed by a woman; one administrative unit is. The only woman dean in Harvard history, Education Dean Patricia Graham, resigned in 1991. No minority member has been a dean or vice president, but in 1991 an African American, Joseph Henry, was acting dean of the Dental School.

The 1991 plan states, "The effectiveness of equal employment policies . . . is enhanced when flexibility is given each Faculty to develop its own . . . processes and procedures. . . . However, appropriate elements of the University-wide affirmative action policy are interpreted, monitored and reviewed centrally." Those with universitywide responsibility are the president, his assistant for affirmative action, the universitywide Equal Employment Opportunity Committee, the head of the Office of Human Resources, the secretary of the university, and the general counsel.

In this system, affirmative action policies and procedures vary somewhat among faculties and administrative units. For the most part, they focus on assembling and increasing pools of potential applicants for vacant positions. Individual deans and supervisors have, on occasion, adopted additional strategies.

In most instances, standard search procedures are followed: organizing a search committee with members of diverse ethnicity and sex; posting vacancy announcements in public media; interviewing minority and female applicants; and providing explanations for each decision not to hire or promote them. Such searches, with special efforts to include minorities and women in the applicant and sometimes in the interview pool, constitute affirmative action at Harvard.

OFCCP requires the establishment of goals and timetables in "underutilized" job categories but does not specify what must be done to remedy underutilization. It does not even require search committees, though they are now considered a standard

means of compliance. Harvard has seldom adopted stronger methods.

In the 1970s, Dean Henry Rosovsky authorized the fifty-odd departments in the Faculty of Arts and Sciences to identify highly qualified minority and female candidates even when no position was vacant. He then provided funds for the department to hire the candidate. The policy was successful in increasing the number of junior female faculty.

Revived in the late 1980s by President Derek Bok and Dean Michael Spence to increase minority faculty, this policy had little success. Only one or two departments used the opportunity to make a minority appointment.

Another approach was the creation of an Administrative Fellows Program in 1989 to increase the number of senior minority administrators. In two and a half years, 25 minority administrators received one-year training fellowships; 16 were offered and 8 accepted permanent positions. In 1991-92, 6 new fellows were appointed.

Few other significant affirmative action programs have been introduced.

EMPLOYMENT TRENDS

Harvard's employment profile has changed little over the past ten years.

During the 1980s, three-fifths of nonfaculty employees were women (Table 3). Only in service, maintenance, and skilled crafts were women a minority. From 1982 to 1990, the proportion of women among faculty in ladder positions rose from 13.4 percent to 18.6 percent; in tenured positions, from 3.6 percent to 7.4 percent (Table 4).

TABLE 3

**NUMBER AND PERCENTAGE OF WOMEN AND MINORITY
NONFACULTY EMPLOYEES BY JOB CATEGORY, 1982 AND 1990**

Job Category	1982*		1990	
	Number	Percentage	Number	Percentage
Executive[†]				
Total	1,112	100.0	1,881	100.0
Women	559	50.3	1,105	58.8
Minority	74	6.7	173	9.2
Professional				
Total	1,579	100.0	1,890	100.0
Women	783	49.6	1,124	59.5
Minority	157	9.9	197	10.4
Technical[‡]				
Total	547	100.0	596	100.0
Women	298	54.5	322	54.0
Minority	60	11.0	101	17.0
Secretarial[§]				
Total	2,711	100.0	3,008	100.0
Women	2,315	85.4	2,410	80.1
Minority	342	12.6	452	15.0
Skilled craft				
Total	262	100.0	248	100.0
Women	4	1.5	12	4.8
Minority	43	16.4	28	11.3
Service[‖]				
Total	1,176	100.0	1,180	100.0
Women	411	34.9	410	34.8
Minority	269	22.9	483	40.9
Total	7,387	100.0	8,803	100.0
Women	4,370	59.2	5,383	61.2
Minority	945	12.8	1,434	16.3

*Academic centers and auxiliary units omitted.
[†]Executive, administrative, managerial.
[‡]And paraprofessional.
[§]And clerical.
[‖]And maintenance.

With year-to-year fluctuations, minority employment rose moderately from 1982 to 1990 in most nonfaculty job categories. In professional positions, the increase was negligible but in executive and technical positions, greater; unfortunately, it was greatest in service and maintenance jobs (Table 3).

Minorities constituted 5.3 percent of tenured faculty in 1982 and 6.8 percent in 1990; of ladder faculty, 8.1 and 8.4 percent, respectively, after a drop to 7.7 percent in 1986 (Table 4).

TABLE 4

**NUMBER (AND PERCENTAGE) OF WOMEN AND MINORITY
FACULTY, BY TYPE OF APPOINTMENT, 1982, 1986, AND 1990**

| | | | | Nonladder | | |
| | | | | | Medical | |
	Total	Tenured	Ladder	Nonmedical	Annual	Training*
1990						
Total	12,551	980	2,453	1,588	3,645	3,885
Women	3,538	72	456	437	1,247	1,326
	(28.2)	(7.4)	(18.6)	(27.5)	(34.2)	(34.1)
Minority	1,700	67	206	290	308	829
	(13.5)	(6.8)	(8.4)	(18.3)	(8.5)	(21.3)
1986						
Total	6,758	942	2,189	704	2,923	
Women	1,442	53	347	172	870	
	(21.3)	(5.6)	(15.9)	(24.4)	(29.8)	
Minority	496	56	168	72	200	
	(7.3)	(5.9)	(7.7)	(10.2)	(6.8)	
1982						
Total	5,476	856	1,782	640	2,198	
Women	927	31	238	136	522	
	(16.9)	(3.6)	(13.4)	(21.2)	(23.7)	
Minority	394	45	144	53	152	
	(7.2)	(5.3)	(8.1)	(8.3)	(6.9)	

SOURCES: Harvard University, Affirmative Action Plan, 1983; ibid., 1990.
*Interns, residents, and postdoctoral fellows; not counted in 1982 and 1986.

Asian Americans accounted for most of the increase. The proportion of African Americans probably declined; in 1990, they were only 1.9 percent of tenured and 1.1 percent of tenure-track (ladder) faculty (Table 5).

EMPLOYMENT GOALS

The Affirmative Action Plan includes hiring goals for each faculty and administrative division that "underutilizes" women and minorities (employs proportionally fewer than their availability). Table 6 summarizes the 1990-92 hiring goals for female and minority faculty and other employees.

Of all the faculties and administrative divisions, the Medical School has clearly done the poorest job of affirmative action over the past two decades. Employing two-fifths of all junior faculty, it was supposed to hire 224 women and 46 minorities for tenure or tenure-track positions in 1990-92. Medical School leaders offer various explanations for their poor record: the preference of minority and women physicians for clinical practice; the shortage of qualified candidates with the required specialties; and the fact that hiring at several associated hospitals is not controlled by Harvard.

TABLE 5

**NUMBER AND PERCENTAGE OF WOMEN AND MINORITY
FACULTY AND OTHER EMPLOYEES IN SELECTED POSITIONS, 1990**

Position	Total*	Women	Minorities Total[†]	Asian	Black
			Number		
Faculty[‡]	12,551	3,538	1,700	1,193	208
Tenured	980	72	67	36	19
Tenure-track	2,453	456	206	141	26
Training	3,885	1,326	829	622	73
Research	717	180	213	172	17
Other employees[‡]	8,802	5,383	1,434	268	923
General office	2,316	1,958	319	56	222
Academic managers	1,271	830	105	20	63
Custodial	589	193	360	19	270
Librarians	358	232	28	18	7
Research	240	140	32	19	8
Total	21,353	8,921	3,134	1,461	1,131
			Percentage		
Faculty[†]	100.0	28.2	13.5	9.5	1.7
Tenured	100.0	7.3	6.7	3.7	1.9
Tenure-track	100.0	18.6	8.4	5.7	1.1
Training	100.0	34.1	21.3	16.0	1.9
Research	100.0	25.1	29.7	24.0	2.4
Other employees[†]	100.0	61.2	16.3	3.2	10.5
General office	100.0	84.5	13.8	2.4	9.6
Academic managers	100.0	65.3	8.3	1.6	5.0
Custodial	100.0	32.8	61.1	3.2	45.8
Librarians	100.0	64.8	7.8	5.0	2.0
Research	100.0	58.3	13.3	7.9	3.3
Total	100.0	41.8	14.7	6.8	5.3

SOURCE: Harvard University, Affirmative Action Plan, 1991.
*Includes men.
[†]Includes Hispanics and Native Americans.
[‡]Includes positions not detailed below.

The hiring goals for women in nonfaculty positions are relatively low, reflecting the substantial growth in their numbers. The Faculty of Arts and Sciences and central administration had the highest goals, or rates of underutilization.

The hiring goals for minority faculty are low because the number of qualified candidates is quite small. Government regulations require no increase in employment when the proportion already employed is similar to the proportion available.

The highest goals—or the poorest records—for employing minorities in nonfaculty positions were set by the faculties of Arts and Sciences, Medi-

TABLE 6

HIRING GOALS FOR WOMEN AND MINORITIES, 1990-92

Faculty or Unit	Faculty		Other Employees	
	Women	Minority	Women	Minority
Faculty	271	63	135	174
Arts and Sciences	12	3	71	91
Business	11	4	10	22
Dentistry	3	—	—	2
Design	4	1	3	1
Divinity	2	1	7	3
Education	1	—	4	9
Government	3	2	5	8
Law	3	—	8	3
Medicine	224	46	24	29
Public Health	8	6	3	6
Administrative unit			106	116
President's Office			4	21
Administration			65	74
Alumni			—	—
Finance			16	9
General Counsel			19	12
Government			2	—
Total hiring goals	271	63	241	290

SOURCE: Affirmative Action Plan, 1991.

cine, and Business, the division of Administration, and the President's Office.

OFCCP AUDIT

The results of the OFCCP January-September 1990 audit provide further insight into Harvard's affirmative action problems and progress. OFCCP asked the university, especially the faculties of Arts and Sciences and Medicine, to set a two-year goal of hiring three Native American faculty. There had been six in 1989, but only one remained in 1990.

OFCCP required Harvard to undertake regular monitoring and adverse impact analysis of its employ-ment searches and position reclassi-fications, terminations (particularly in underutilized job groups), the effects of reorganizations, job postings, and the reasons for waivers for strong internal candidates. Reviews were to be conducted of salary equity on the bases of race, sex, and age; special affirmative action recruitment efforts; programs for persons with disabilities; discrimination complaint processes; and training and career development programs and benefits. OFCCP also asked Harvard to undertake analyses of its recruitment and training needs as a step toward remedying its underemployment of minorities and women.

The foregoing bureaucratic procedures, now routine in federally enforced affirmative action programs, have been adopted more slowly by colleges and universities than by corporations. OFCCP's directives for Harvard are not harsh. The monitoring it requests is routinely required of all institutions. Some measures are specified, and others are clearly implied in its regulations.

Arguably, some of the procedures, or portions of them, already exist at Harvard. At times they have been followed more assiduously and at times less. Apparently, OFCCP encountered enough evidence to rule that Harvard does not engage in discrimination, even though the foregoing procedures were not implemented at the time of the audit.

Interpreted less generously, the findings suggest that Harvard officials did not take affirmative action seriously enough to engage in fairly routine and widely accepted procedures to monitor progress and help identify problems. If they had, but had not liked federal procedures, they would have substituted or added procedures of their own.

The OFCCP requirement that the university evaluate its recruitment and training needs suggests a finding of minimal "good-faith effort" in remedying underemployment. Essentially, the finding is that Harvard's affirmative action program is fairly weak. Its major strategy is to compile information on women and minority candidates for potential job searches. This strategy is neither consistent nor persistent throughout the university. In 1990, OFCCP seems to have urged Harvard to move beyond unsystematic recruitment strategies toward more substantial affirmative action beginning with more aggressive needs analysis and monitoring.

HARVARD AND COMPARABLE INSTITUTIONS

Since 1987, the affirmative action office has compared Harvard's employment profile with that of comparable institutions. The 1991 Affirmative Action Plan reported that, among 17 comparable institutions, Harvard ranked fifteenth and ninth, respectively, in its percentage of tenured female and minority faculty— 8.5 percent and 7.7 percent—excluding medical faculty. In nontenured faculty, it ranked tenth in its percentage of both women—28.7 percent— and minorities—11.8 percent—again excluding medical faculty.

Among the 13 medical schools at these institutions, Harvard ranked eleventh and tenth, respectively, in its percentage of tenured women and minority faculty—5.1 percent for both—and eleventh and eighth in nontenured women and minorities— 16.0 percent and 7.5 percent. Harvard ranked third among the 17 institutions in the proportion of executives who were women—58.8 percent—but tenth in the proportion of minorities—9.2 percent.

These data suggest that Harvard's record in hiring and promoting women and minority faculty has not been outstanding; it has done better with nonfaculty women but not minority employees. The reasons for the different performance of prominent institutions have not been systematically and convincingly explored.

BARRIERS AND PROSPECTS

OFCCP has audited Harvard many times and always found it in compliance. Successive "conciliatory agreements" concluded after audits have had the effect of moving the university to monitor and report its employment activities more explicitly, but this has not led to markedly higher employment rates of women and minorities, particularly in many faculty positions.

Aside from the OFCCP requirements, no standards exist for judging the university's accomplishments. Most Harvard leaders agree that more tenured women and minorities are needed, but neither the university as a whole nor its autonomous components have established a strong affirmative action policy that transcends government requirements.

At times, often by student action, attention gets drawn to affirmative action problems, and ad hoc remedies are undertaken. During the years 1989-91, for example, students engaged in protests to force the Law School to appoint an African American female tenured professor. There has never been one; indeed, only three African American women have ever held tenured Harvard positions.

Minority faculty eventually got involved and, in a widely publicized protest, Law Professor Derrick Bell has taken a leave of absence until a minority woman receives a tenured position. To date, the dean has refused to make such an appointment, arguing that to do so would compromise the school's mission and academic standards.

Clearly, the OFCCP requirements do not amount to much. Since they are linked to the availability of qualified candidates, a university need only show that availability is low to maintain its low employment rate for women and minorities. The regulations require little change in faculty hiring until the number of qualified candidates increases. The same is true of other employees, but to a far lesser extent. The government's view is simply that institutions cannot hire unqualified people and, particularly where faculty are concerned, the standards for determining qualifications are left to the institutions.

Statistics of qualified candidates do not take into account Harvard's special advantages, however. Because of its reputation as, arguably, the premier—and certainly the richest!—university in the country, its capacity to recruit faculty is great, even if its standards are uniquely demanding or specialized. OFCCP regulations and compliance reviews do not consider this point.

Until recently, OFCCP has audited any institution due to receive a federal contract of $1 million or more. The audit was to be completed within 30 days of OFCCP's being notified of an agency's intent to award such a contract.

In 1986, the National Institutes of Health awarded the Medical School a large contract for research on acquired immune deficiency syndrome, and OFCCP undertook the required audit. For many reasons, it took more than three months. Despite the school's poor record in employing women and minorities, was it likely that research on such an important health problem would be delayed even if the audit found evidence of egregious discrimination?

DOL's authority to compel other federal agencies to comply with its findings of discrimination is backed by the courts. With sufficient evidence and determination, it could have asked the federal district court for a "show-cause" order to stop the award until the court could rule. Evidence of employment discrimination is seldom crystal clear, however, and, in such a situation, political forces determine the outcome. Clearly, there is much less political support for affirmative action today than when it was launched.

Presidents Reagan and Bush have opposed affirmative action as a national employment policy. Perhaps as a consequence, its grass-roots support has eroded substantially. Absent clear evidence of discrimination that increasingly conservative federal courts will accept, the Labor Department's options have been reduced.

Ironically, this has occurred when its administrative capacity to conduct compliance reviews and establish meaningful standards has increased considerably. Over the past twenty years, its investigative and monitoring work has become much more clear and precise. Its basic problems in improving affirmative action results are political, not analytical and administrative.

On campus, the most difficult dilemma of Harvard leaders is to reconcile the university's high-quality standards with perceived weaknesses in the quality of the minority and female work force. Even those who support affirmative action most energetically and persistently respond with great difficulty to the widely held beliefs that selection should be based solely on merit and that this leads unavoidably to the disproportionate selection of white males.

Many explanations are offered for perceived weaknesses in minority and female candidates: past discrimination, lack of equal educational opportunity, lack of motivation to meet Harvard's standards. Clearly, many of these perceptions are unjustified. Minority and female applicants are often compared to the best, not the average or worst, white male staff. Indeed, some of the best Harvard faculty and administrators are not, and many of the poorest are, white males.

Choosing the appropriate quality standards in personnel decisions is a serious problem for Harvard leaders under pressure to hire more women and minorities. Few convince their critics that zealous affirmative action does not inevitably produce a poorer work force. And few can discard the mind-set that Harvard always chooses the very best. (A work force of 21,000 cannot all be the best.) Consequently, a major barrier to effective affirmative action is the lack of unequivocal and sustained support from Harvard leaders.

Another barrier is the lack of support and even opposition by some women and minority faculty. A number question the basic principles and potential benefits of affirmative action. Some fear it diminishes their independent accomplishments. Many disavow its assistance and seek recognition as scholars, not women or minority scholars. The most naive and distinguished place scholarly standards above all other standards in all circumstances, expecting this to enhance their careers. However, when appropriate, some distinguished white scholars criticize them for possessing insufficient race identity.

Harvard's highly decentralized system also weakens organized support by minority and women employees. Needs and aspirations vary widely from one unit to another, and presenting a unified position may be difficult. For example, some black faculty respectfully criticized Derrick Bell's action; black administrators disagree over the relative importance of increasing their numbers or their chances of promotion.

Harvard's performance is hampered by the inadequate supply of qualified women and especially minorities. Some shortages are dramatic. From 1979 to 1987, the number of doctoral degrees awarded to African Americans fell from 1056 to 767, while the number awarded to Hispanic Americans rose from 464 to 619. Thereafter, the trends were reversed, African Americans earning 811 doctorates in 1989 and Hispanics, 570. The degrees awarded to Asian Americans rose steadily from 428 in 1979 to 621 in 1989.[5]

Qualified minority faculty are in short supply in most fields, as are women in mathematics, the natural sciences, and related disciplines. Harvard needs faculty in highly specialized fields. Merely increasing the number of Ph.D.'s will not in the short run greatly change its employment profile.

5. Deborah Carter and Reginald Wilson, *Ninth Annual Status Report: Minorities in Higher Education* (Washington, DC: American Council on Education, 1991), p. 34.

Report of the Board of Directors to the Members of the American Academy of Political and Social Science for the Year 1991

MEMBERSHIPS AND SUBSCRIPTIONS
AS OF DECEMBER 31

Year	Number
1981	9,874
1982	9,536
1983	8,904
1984	6,564
1985	5,704
1986	5,606
1987	5,151
1988	4,674
1989	4,903
1990	3,932
1991	4,378

PUBLICATIONS
NUMBER OF VOLUMES OF THE ANNALS PRINTED
(6 PER YEAR)

1981	69,313
1982	74,211
1983	68,236
1984	52,154
1985	52,800
1986	53,201
1987	43,629
1988	53,497
1989	40,269
1990	39,000
1991	37,246

FINANCES
SIZE OF SECURITIES PORTFOLIO
MARKET VALUE AS OF DECEMBER 31

1981	351,886
1982	390,119
1983	485,809
1984	384,312
1985	369,389
1986	373,320
1987	387,997
1988	345,634
1989	284,732
1990	139,451
1991	164,537

NUMBER OF VOLUMES OF THE ANNALS SOLD
(IN ADDITION TO MEMBERSHIPS AND SUBSCRIPTIONS)

1981	5,884
1982	7,562
1983	5,877
1984	5,230
1985	5,910
1986	5,119
1987	5,314
1988	13,283
1989	4,802
1990	5,005
1991	3,766

STATEMENT OF INCOME AND RETAINED EARNINGS
FOR THE YEAR ENDED DECEMBER 31, 1991

Income
Royalty—Sage Publications	$110,002
Sales of review books	1,264
Royalties and reprint permissions	1,708
Miscellaneous	21,843
Total Income	134,817

Operating Expenses
Salaries	84,295
Payroll taxes	6,533
Pension expense	7,222
Employee benefits	9,091
Depreciation	10,862
Insurance	5,357
Postage	3,058
Repairs and maintenance	7,578
Professional and contracted services	11,593
Book review costs	8,677

Supplies	2,645
Utilities	13,772
Miscellaneous	4,300
Total Operating Expenses	174,923
Loss from Operations	(40,106)
Other Income (Expenses)	
Investment income (net)	5,661
Gains (loss) on sale of investments	(2,854)
Grant administration overhead	15,285
Total Other Income (Expense)	18,092
Net Income (Loss)	(22,014)
Retained Earnings—January 1	121,884
Retained Earnings—December 31	99,870

Report of the Board of Directors

During 1991, the six volumes of THE ANNALS dealt with the following subjects:

January   *Japan's External Economic Relations: Japanese Perspectives,* edited by Solomon B. Levine, Professor Emeritus, University of Madison, Wisconsin, and Koji Taira, Professor, University of Illinois, Urbana-Champaign

March   *Electronic Links for Learning,* edited by Vivian M. Horner, Senior Vice President, SkyPix Corporation, Seattle, Washington, and Linda G. Roberts, Senior Associate, Office of Technology Assessment, U.S. Congress, Washington, D.C.

May   *American Feminism: New Issues for a Mature Movement,* edited by Janet K. Boles, Associate Professor, Marquette University, Milwaukee, Wisconsin

July   *Foreign Investment in the United States,* edited by Michael Ulan, International Economist, U.S. Department of State, Washington, D.C.

September   *New Directions in U.S. Defense Policy,* edited by Robert L. Pfaltzgraff, Jr., President, Institute for Foreign Policy Analysis, Cambridge, Massachusetts, and Washington, D.C.

November   *Resolving Regional Conflicts: International Perspectives,* edited by I. William Zartman, Jacob Blaustein Professor of International Organization and Conflict Resolution and Director of African Studies, School of Advanced International Studies, Johns Hopkins University, Washington, D.C.

The publication program for 1992 includes the following volumes:

January   *China's Foreign Relations,* edited by Allen S. Whiting, Professor and Director, Center for East Asian Studies, University of Arizona, Tucson

March   *World Literacy in the Year 2000,* edited by Daniel A. Wagner, Professor and Director, National Center on Adult Literacy, University of Pennsylvania, and Laurel D. Puchner, Doctoral Candidate, University of Pennsylvania, Philadelphia

May   *Drug Abuse: Linking Policy and Research,* edited by Eric D. Wish, Acting Director, Centr for Substance Abuse Research, University of Maryland, College Park

July   *The Future: Trends into the Twenty-First Century,* edited by Joseph F. Coates, President, and Jennifer Jarratt, Vice President, Coates & Jarratt, Inc., Washington, D.C.

September   *Affirmative Action Revisited,* edited by Harold Olans, an independent scholar in Chevy Chase, Maryland, and June O'Neill, Professor and Director, Center for the Study of Business and Government, Baruch College, City University of New York

November   *Political Islam,* edited by I. William Zartman, Jacob Blaustein, Professor of International Organization and Conflict Resolution and Director of African Studies, School of Advanced International Studies, Johns Hopkins University, Washington, D.C., and Charles E. Butterworth, Professor, University of Maryland, College Park

During 1991, the Book Department published over 170 reviews. The majority of these were written by professors, but reviewers also included university presidents, members of private and university-sponsored organizations, government and public officials, and business professionals. Over 600 books were listed in the Other Books section.

Twenty-eight requests were granted to reprint material from THE ANNALS. These went to professors and other authors for use in books in preparation and to non-profit organizations for educational purposes.

MEETINGS

The ninety-second annual meeting was postponed from 1990 to 1993.

OFFICERS AND STAFF

The Board reelected the following officers: Marvin E. Wolfgang, President; Richard D. Lambert, Vice President; Anthony J. Scirica, Secretary; Elmer B. Staats, Treasurer; Henry W. Sawyer, III, Counsel. Reappointed were: Richard D. Lambert, Editor, and Alan W. Heston, Associate Editor.

Respectfully submitted,
THE BOARD OF DIRECTORS

Elmer B. Staats
Marvin E. Wolfgang
Richard D. Lambert
Lloyd N. Cutler
Henry W. Sawyer, III
Anthony J. Scirica
Frederick Heldring

Philadelphia, Pennsylvania
18 December 1991

Book Department

INTERNATIONAL RELATIONS AND POLITICS

LEPGOLD, JOSEPH. *The Declining Hegemon: The United States and European Defense, 1960-1990.* Pp. 225. Westport, CT: Greenwood Press, 1990. No price.

SOLO, ROBERT A. *Opportunity Knocks: American Economic Policy after Gorbachev.* Pp. 205. Armonk, NY: M. E. Sharpe, 1991. $34.95.

Joseph Lepgold's book, *The Declining Hegemon*, is a serious study of U.S. nuclear and defense policy in the North Atlantic Treaty Organization (NATO). Robert Solo's book, *Opportunity Knocks*, is a more polemical critique of America's domestic and international economic policy.

Lepgold begins by observing that from 1960 to 1980, U.S. power declined, yet U.S. commitments in NATO did not. He asks why. His answers are that dominant powers—hegemons—such as the United States resist decline by knowingly over-extending themselves, both because potential physical threats increase and because psychological concerns about reputation, both their own and that reflecting the weakened resolve of allies, make retreat inadvisable. Thus the United States never wavered from its commitment to use nuclear weapons (first, if necessary) to defend Europe, even as the Soviet Union acquired a retaliatory capability against the United States that made first use of nuclear weapons in Europe suicidal and even as the allies became stronger and more capable of mustering a conventional defense that might have alleviated, if not effectively eliminated, the need to resort to nuclear weapons. Instead, the United States accepted the risks of a growing gap between its commitments and capabilities and pressured the allies to accept greater defense burdens or face reductions of American conventional forces in Europe.

Thus, from 1961 to 1965, the United States introduced the strategy of flexible response to maintain its commitment to use nuclear weapons but now at an undefined level of conventional conflict and hence capabilities, in effect fuzzing the gap between commitments and capabilities. In addition, American policymakers badgered the Europeans to accept more of the costs of defense (the offset arrangements with Germany) and the dollar (loans to support the U.S. balance of payments). From 1966 to 1973, the United States extended its commitments further in Vietnam and Asia, straining resources and relations in Europe even as the Soviet Union embarked on an unprecedented military buildup in Europe. For the rest of the 1970s, then, the United States made valiant efforts to reinforce NATO against the Soviet buildup in Europe—especially the deployment of Soviet SS-18 missiles. It did so in particular by manipulating nuclear policy, which was less vulnerable to pressures from Congress—for example, emphasizing limited nuclear options and counterforce targeting strategies.

Lepgold's account suggests that, as hegemons decline, they have more ways to adapt than traditional power theories allow. Hegemons monitor and then finesse critical constraints. But the constraints Lepgold examines are still largely physical—resources, technology, and the like. He says little about the definition and evolution of threat. Ultimately true to power perspectives, he does not consider the ideological constraints that divided the United States and Soviet Union and bred the distrust and reciprocal arming of the superpowers after World War II. Now that the ideological divide is narrowing, mutual suspicions are waning. Rather than increasing and leading to overextension, threats are receding, and the United States, although a "declining hegemon," faces no need to overextend. Decline theories come up short because they consider only power and not the sources of threat (except to equate power with threat).

If Lepgold says little about the threat in Europe and how it changed over the postwar period, Solo says bluntly that there never was a Soviet threat. For decades, he argues, America squandered its resources on a chimera. Now, thanks to Gorbachev, who suddenly made clear that the Soviet Union was never a threat, "opportunity knocks" to put American resources back to work to achieve full employment and price stability.

The policies that Solo recommends to accomplish this, however, are also chimerical, if not quixotic. He calls for a resurrection of deficit-based spending which does not divert resources from private spending and which is financed by a Federal Reserve System that purchases U.S. Treasury bonds without charging any interest. At the same time, a new Agency for Industrial Management, patterned after Japan's Ministry of International Trade and Industry, would intervene to constrain the power of corporations, which are responsible for inflation, pollution, and depressed wages. This agency would also

monitor performance, industry by industry and great firm by great firm, and . . . in the face of poor performance . . . force the replacement of corporate management and . . . support financially a restructuring of the organization and an upgrading of the technology under the new management (p. 64).

As if that were not enough, central government would also control all foreign exchange transactions, prevent all international cash and portfolio financial flows—only "real" investment permitted—and balance all trade transactions (because imbalances are inherently mercantilist and zero-sum). The world would abandon global free trade and form trade blocs that are sufficiently large to capture the requisite economies of scale.

Why America needs more deficit spending after two decades of budget busting is unclear. How the government can run deficits that do not decrease private savings—remember, according to Solo, deficits cannot divert resources from private spending, so they must come from private savings—yet also do not require inflows of foreign savings—remember, international financial flows other than real investment are prohibited—is equally unclear. Also not evident is why one would want to abolish the Federal Reserve's monetary policy role, as Solo recommends (because the Fed causes high interest rates), when one of the main accomplishments of U.S. policy in the 1980s was to regain control of monetary growth and hence inflation. The whole scheme seems poorly reasoned, ill-advised, and often intemperately argued—for example, according to Solo, Bush is a "shyster" (p. 5), and as a mechanism to allocate resources, "Wall Street would be the choice of an imbecile" (p. 111).

Lepgold's study is well argued and carefully researched within the theoretical framework of traditional power perspectives, but this framework is increasingly found wanting as a good part of the world moves beyond interstate power politics to greater domestic community based on pluralistic institutions and competitive markets. Solo's book is a warning that, in a world of reduced threat, not every set of new ideas is likely to be helpful in exploiting the opportunity for prosperity and peace, especially when those ideas ignore the experiences and lessons of the past.

HENRY R. NAU

George Washington University
Washington, D.C.

AFRICA, ASIA, AND
LATIN AMERICA

CHEHABI, H. E. *Iranian Politics and Religious Modernism: The Liberation Movement of Iran under the Shah and Khomeini*. Pp. xiv, 342. Ithaca, NY: Cornell University Press, 1990. $29.95.

The Iranian revolution of 1978-79 has had an unintended salutary result—a virtual flood of works in English of extraordinarily fine quality on modern Iranian history and politics by Iranian scholars now living abroad, works that would probably never otherwise have been written. H. E. Chehabi's book is one of these.

The book deals with the history of the Liberation Movement of Iran (*Nehzat-e azadi-ye Iran*), the political organization that, with its forerunner organizations, Chehabi credits with the responsibility for laying the political and ideological foundations for the Revolution.

The hero of the book is Mehdi Bazargan, born in 1907 and still alive and active as a political figure at this writing. Bazargan's personal biography comprehends virtually a complete history of Iranian politics in the twentieth century. He was the prime minister of Iran under the Khomeini regime, though only of a provisional government that lasted a scant six months. Though a revolutionary leader, Bazargan is a political moderate. The book shows this as one of the reasons for his eventual removal from central power in the post-Shah regime.

Chehabi masterfully shows all of the intertwinings of religious and secular inspiration that underlay Bazargan's own personal philosophy of government and revolution. The National Liberation Movement is seen by Chehabi as a religious modernist movement—an Iranian instance of a widespread phenomenon known to anthropologists as a revitalization movement. Movements of this sort involve the invocation of a strong set of religious precepts as a base for political and moral conduct, to rescue a social system seen as under attack from internal or external force.

The sources for the Iranian Revolution are extraordinarily broad, including the nineteenth-century religious reformer Jalal al-Din Asabadi (al-Afghani); the relatively unknown French intellectuals Alexis Carrel and Pierre Lecomte de Noüy; the revolutionary prime minister of the 1950s, Mohammad Mossadeq; the postwar sociologist cum religious/political philosopher Ali Shariati; and the major clerical leaders of the twentieth century such as Ayatollah Sayyid Mohammad-Hosein Borujerdi and Ayatollah Ruhollah Khomeini. This collection of individuals constitutes an array of figures almost unknown in the West. Yet it was their combined influence that overthrew the Shah and changed Middle Eastern politics perhaps forever.

Eventually Bazargan's fate was to be turned out as head of the revolutionary government and serve as head of a "loyal opposition" to the clerical government.

Chehabi's treatment is replete with detail drawn from many primary sources. His tone in assessing the philosophy and contributions of Bazargan and other members of the Liberation Movement of Iran is admirably neutral. He neither approves nor disapproves but presents the facts as they seem best evidenced in the historical record. The result is a book that will be much appreciated by supporters of the former monarchy, by supporters of the new regime, and by those who support neither. Those who are familiar with the volatile world of Iranian politics know how hard a task this has been.

WILLIAM O. BEEMAN

Brown University
Providence
Rhode Island

MOSHER, STEVEN W. *China Misperceived: American Illusions and Chinese Reality.* Pp. ix, 260. New York: Basic Books, 1990. $19.95.

The gap between ordinary life in the People's Republic of China and the various illusions that Americans have projected upon it is, overall, probably the most important fact that the American public can learn from the opening of China after Mao. Steven Mosher's book is a good place to begin.

In 1979, as a graduate student in anthropology, Mosher went to live for a year in a southern Chinese village and was shocked. He found daily life onerous and driven by hard-bitten self-interest; rulers and the ruled were separated by a rift filled with resentment and fear; things got done through bribery and personal connections, while the language of socialism, when relevant at all, was but a tool for bringing leverage in the pursuit of private advantage.

Mosher grew indignant—not just at the suffering of ordinary Chinese but also at how Americans had for years been misled into accepting false accounts of Chinese daily life. How could normally savvy Western journalists, in the 1940s and 1970s alike, fall prey to the organized mendacity of a Communist regime? How could scholars spin imaginary fluff from wishes and theories that had more to do with their own minds than with Chinese facts? Why do U.S. government officials even today speak and act as if "China" were a synonym for the very small group of atypical Chinese who rule the country?

While doing well at identifying general problems, Mosher is less convincing when he tries to assign blame for them. In attacking Western correspondents for their failure to perceive the reality of the Communist movement in the 1940s, he neglects to mention that many Chinese, especially among the intellectuals, were similarly naive in those years and now face, more painfully than does any Westerner, the problem of how to re-understand what happened. Mosher satirizes American student radicals in the 1960s for their idealistic fantasies about China, yet many of these same people, after learning more about actual Chinese conditions, have turned their idealism toward a denunciation of Communist rule that resembles Mosher's own. In his anger, Mosher labels Harvard historian John K. Fairbank a Maoist—a mistake that will do more harm to Mosher's credibility than to Fairbank's reputation.

Mosher lofts more accurate arrows at the China experts who move among university political science departments, State Department service, and posts in between. Although widely credited in government and in the press as having deep knowledge of China, generally—there are exceptions—these experts know the Chinese language poorly if at all, have not lived in ordinary-life contexts in China, and have only superficial understandings of Chinese history and culture. Their specialty is China relations, but they perceive only dimly the ways in which foreign relations—or all of official culture in China, for that matter—are but part, sometimes only a tiny part, of a much more complicated fabric of Chinese life. Mosher is way ahead of the experts on these scores, and his criticisms of them are well worth heeding.

PERRY LINK

Princeton University
New Jersey

SCHNEIDER, RONALD M. *Order and Progress: A Political History of Brazil.* Pp. xvi, 486. Boulder CO: Westview Press, 1991. $55.00.

This political history of Brazil, focusing on elite-military interactions, is the result of many years of research and is replete with interesting detail on political breakdown and transitions. Schneider is particularly effective in dealing with the breakdown of monarchy and transition to the Old Republic, military maneuvering during the Vargista period, the internal politics of the military regime (1964-85), and Sarney's stewardship.

Schneider's modernization approach does not link the considerable economic information supplied throughout the book with the politics that he so skillfully depicts. He considers economics an autonomous rational realm best separated from the political. Thus there is no analysis of the structural problems of the Brazilian miracle, which collapses, according to both Schneider and the Brazilian military, because of Organization of Petroleum Exporting Countries pricing. The relation between the miracle and subsequent hyperinflation is not explored, because growth of the gross national product is considered a good in itself. This bias accurately reflects Brazilian elite authoritarianism, which separates mass politics from policy decisions but shows a lack of critical depth.

Schneider betrays conservative biases in what is excluded from the text: the Brazilian people play no role except as demographic variables and as voters in rigged elections. The Canudos war ends, Schneider writes, with the loss of "at least 15,000 humble hillbillies," the 1964 coup crushes "an immature radical Left equipped with mouths much bigger than their real appetite for a fight." Popular movements, including the complex party left, the Catholic Church, Partido dos Trabalhadores (Workers Party), and the massive Direitas Já mobilization, are ignored or presented as intrusions by the extras on the prerogatives of elite players. These movements, for all their deficiencies, motivated the 1985 democratic transition. Also excluded from consideration is the persistent U.S. role in the destabilization and overthrow of Brazilian governments and in facilitating dirty war, widespread torture, and the takeover of Brazilian resources and markets by multinational corporations.

The amazing assertion on page 372 that "material aspects of living have been improving for a very large proportion of Brazilians" is a function of Schneider's reliance on official statistics and his lack of concern for the 80 percent of Brazilians who remain impoverished victims of progress.

The reader is left with mixed feelings. The book is a tour de force, a mine of valuable information. But its representation of the posturings of one of the world's most irresponsible and brutally corrupt elites as normal politics and valid developmental policymaking shows an unfortunate lack of compassion for the Brazilian people. The book should be read, but it cannot stand alone.

N. PATRICK PERITORE

University of Missouri
Columbia

EUROPE

FRIEDLANDER, JUDITH. *Vilna on the Seine: Jewish Intellectuals in France since 1968*. Pp. xv, 249. New Haven, CT: Yale University Press, 1990. $27.50.

The Jewish community in France is today the largest one in Europe. Most of its members are postwar immigrants from Eastern Europe, northern Africa, and the Middle East and their children. In *Vilna on the Seine*, Judith Friedlander is primarily interested in the first of these groups and especially in the immigrants from Lithuania. While Friedlander pictures Lithuania ("Lite" in Yiddish) in maps and through the descriptions of its former inhabitants, Lite ceases to be a geographical area only. It becomes a metaphorical place as well, symbolizing both Jewish religious learning and secular Jewish thought. Jewish Lite no longer exists—the YIVO Institute for Yiddish Studies in Vilnius (formerly Vilna), prob-

ably reinstituted after the completion of Friedlander's book, has to assume a museum's position. Despite the sense of nostalgia that Friedlander shares with many of the subjects of her book, her study is guided by the question of whether anything has been, or could be, recovered from the past.

At the beginning of her first chapter, Friedlander quotes an anecdote by Isaac Bashevis Singer about a Jewish man who went to Vilna and who found the Jewish people there remarkable:

"I saw a Jew who all day long was scheming how to get rich. I saw a Jew who's all the time waving the red flag calling for revolution. I saw a Jew who was running after every woman. I saw a Jew who was an ascetic and avoided women." [His friend replied,] "I don't know why you're so astonished. Vilna is a big city, and there are many Jews, all types." "No," said the first man, "it was all the same Jew" (p. 5).

For Friedlander, prewar Lite poses a counterexample to a postwar France that had proclaimed to be "one nation within one state." Jewish life in Lite enjoyed a certain freedom of expression, and it may suggest that different nations and ways of life can coexist within one state. In France, Friedlander sees attempts in recent years to define a notion of nationhood that would allow for a multicultural experience. But Singer's anecdote is used by Friedlander to point to another story as well. As her title suggests, Friedlander is particularly interested in the "generation of 1968," in former student activists who disregarded any Jewish tradition but who have, in later years, joined Jewish reading groups, Yiddish courses, or the Strasbourg Yeshiva. Friedlander's first story takes each view expressed in Singer's tale as one that would be representative for a particular group. Her second story returns the anecdote to that of a single person and adds a historical perspective. Friedlander becomes the writer of biographies: biographies of participants in the 1968 student revolution as well as of their past and/or present teachers and intellectual idols.

As Friedlander's stories unfold, problems and contradictions become obvious. She points, again and again, to maps of Lithuania and France and names the region or county after every place name mentioned, even if geography has no further relevance for her argument. Instead of contributing to a historical understanding, Friedlander's tight grip on the geographical reality appears as a means to avoid defining that other sense of Lite, which may be much more difficult to describe. Friedlander feels the need, moreover, to mark each individual under discussion as Jewish. Even in a brief reference to Henri Bergson's philosophy, for example, Friedlander is eager to state his "Jewish origin." While the reader may not be sure about Friedlander's distinction between "Jews" or persons of "Jewish origin," she sees it necessary to apply ethnic markers in a study that has to question any fixed definition of the Jew. She does not seem to be aware of the danger of this procedure, either, and of the historical antecedents of this separation between the French and the (French?) "Jews."

Many persons discussed in these pages—the former student activists Alain Finkielkraut, Benny Lévy, and Shmuel Trigano, for example—have never been to Lite; others who had been there—like the philosopher Olga Katunal—have changed their views of Judaism greatly since their early youth. While Friedlander is eager to trace the whereabouts of her characters, their families, and their teachers, Lite ceases to be the example of different forms of Jewish life and becomes the "rationalistic Lithuanian tradition." Neither this "rationalism" nor Friedlander's move to this reduction is explained. It is, moreover, unclear whether Lite's example should serve a multinationalism in France or a Jewish multiculturalism. When Fried-

lander refers to the generation of 1968, it seems as if there existed nothing but a Jewish France, and even Jean-Paul Sartre cannot escape becoming a member of a Jewish circle. Furthermore, Friedlander changes the statement of "one nation within one state" into "one nation (culture) within one state" and therefore blurs the general political issues that rest on the relationship of nation to culture. The histories and agendas of the different French institutions are hardly described, and it remains unclear to what extent their views of Judaism have shaped—or been shaped by—the official government positions.

While Friedlander's subjects claim to have found their interpretations of Judaism via the study of religious or secular texts, Friedlander deals with these texts via secondhand summaries and evaluations only. Reduced to biographical data, Friedlander's description has to remain a voyeuristic account. And this account slips at times into the realm of hearsay, as Friedlander hints at unacknowledged sources, avoids explanation, refers to nameless students, generalizes, and even speculates what a person might have done had he or she lived longer. In an appendix, Friedlander offers a list of French Jewish intellectuals whom she would still count within her group under investigation but who were not included in her biographical account.

Friedlander does not explain her choice of biographical subjects nor the rounding-up of additional names that appear simply as a gesture of identifying French intellectuals as Jews (Daniel Cohn-Bendit, one of the most prominent student leaders, obviously counts as German and/or non-Jewish). The question of why many Jews felt the need to join the 1968 student uprising—and why some did not—is never posed, and the reader does not learn about those former students who continued to be disinterested in Jewish affairs. Friedlander's subjects all return to Judaism. Their new interest in Yiddish or Jewish religion or culture coincides, however, with an increased interest in Jewish matters among members of the same generation in England or the United States. Singer, quoted at the outset, was an American, and Rachel Ertel, a teacher of Yiddish and one of Friedlander's subjects, is a professor of American studies in Paris; her assistant Nancy Green is an American scholar. Does perhaps America, as an immigrant country, provide yet another model for a multicultural state that has served as an example for the recent French debate?

Friedlander's book is neither a study of French politics or political institutions nor an intellectual history or philosophical inquiry. It thrives on the anecdotal, and it answers Singer's tale with its own. Perhaps, however, one is in need of such anecdotes to assess what meaning Judaism after the Holocaust could possibly assume. In her acknowledgments, Friedlander hints at the autobiographical impulse that made a Jewish American anthropologist study contemporary Jewish intellectuals in France. Friedlander's book is in many ways a case study of self-exploration, but it may also serve as a self-exploration for its readers, American and French alike.

LILIANE WEISSBERG

University of Pennsylvania
Philadelphia

KAMINISKI, BARTLOMIEJ. *The Collapse of State Socialism: The Case of Poland.* Pp. xiv, 264. Princeton, NJ: Princeton University Press, 1991. No price.

VERDERY, KATHERINE. *National Ideology under Socialism: Identity and Cultural Politics in Ceauşescu's Romania.* Pp. xvi, 406. Berkeley: University of California Press, 1991. $39.95.

Western scholars are finding themselves abruptly obliged to examine the reality of "really existing socialism" in Eastern Europe as a historical failure. Knowing now, as we did not before 1989, that no reform could save the Communist regimes of Eastern Europe, we can properly turn from our preoccupation with the course of attempted or advisable reform to the search for fatal flaws. Such a search informs the admirable new studies of Poland's political economy by Bartlomiej Kaminski and of Romania's cultural politics by Katherine Verdery. Both monographs concentrate on the 1980s, the last decade of Communist rule, but provide enough background from the earlier postwar period to support solidly their arguments that the party's political control of scarce resources in a command economy—in Poland—and culture—in Romania—put ultimately unbearable burdens on both regimes, while helping to sustain them in the short term.

Kaminiski outlines his charges in a model introduction. State socialism's lack of economic success and record of political and social decay follow directly from a government whose powers are nowhere separated. The result is a "fused," rather than a mixed, economy, where all economic decisions are politicized and the individual's only independent power is to withdraw.

Subsequent chapters detail the failures of the Gierek regime in the 1970s and particularly Jaruzelski's period of martial law during 1981-88 to overcome the institutional constraints of a politically managed, supposedly monolithic economy. Lacking the information and even the power needed for micromanagement, central planners found themselves forced to "compromise with local preferences to the point of becoming their prisoners." Enter the special political vulnerability of Poland's Communist regime, forced to compromise with the Catholic Church hierarchy and peasant smallholders as early as 1956. These multiple compromises left Gierek's import- and loan-led strategy for saving planned modernization to founder after 1976 on irresistible demand for consumer imports rather than investment goods. Jaruzelski's crisis management could not reconcile the contradictions between the state system's investment and import biases and the demands of workers for wage increases and of Western creditors for an export surplus.

The number of Poles exiting the system, in Alfred Hirschman's phrase, climbed sharply during the 1980s. Some emigrated, others entered a private sector whose income share jumped by one-half, and all but 7 percent of young people—ages 18-29—were avoiding Communist Party membership by 1986. Kaminski concludes his convincing if relentless indictment with a plea for competition and separation of state powers as the only way to bring such people into a new post-Communist Poland.

Katherine Verdery does not deal with the intellectuals who withdrew from Romanian cultural politics during the last Ceaușescu years. She concentrates instead on those who did take open stands on the overriding issue of Romanian national identity. Unlike Kaminski, Verdery traces the origins of this obsession to the pre-Communist period and also pays it more respect than he does the economics of state socialism. We see her honestly wrestling at length with just how much respect to pay and in the end arguing briefly for the need "to reduce the national idea to a manageable size" if the 1990s are not to resemble the 1930s. Previous chapters proceed from the historical, theoretical, and political context to two case studies—the 1984 bicentennial of the Horea uprising and the "cultural missionarism" of the philosopher Constantin Noica.

Both are studies well chosen to illustrate her main thesis, that the debate over national identity disrupted any Marxist discourse and helped to destroy the party's limited legitimacy. The crisis of Marxist legitimacy liberated a marginal field like philosophy enough for disciples of the non-Communist Noica to be heard by the 1980s. But party historians' corruption of a 1784 peasant uprising into a national revolt that foretold the French Revolution makes her argument most clearly. The perverted "protochronist" approach of Ștefan Pascu and others maintained that Romanian events preceded—and thus presaged—rather than followed Western trends from Baroque art forward. This indigenist line admittedly helped its proponents to win greater control over the scarce resources of legitimacy. Their centralization Verdery explicitly identifies as a feature of Romania's command economy. This was a Pyrrhic victory, however. The distortions of the historical record it demanded laid the groundwork for Romanian intellectuals to protest by the late 1980s; such primitivism only separated them from a European scholarly heritage that they are still struggling to reestablish.

                                  JOHN R. LAMPE

Woodrow Wilson International
    Center for Scholars
Washington, D.C.

University of Maryland
College Park

LEVINE, HILLEL. *Economic Origins of Antisemitism: Poland and Its Jews in the Early Modern Period.* Pp. xiii, 271. New Haven, CT: Yale University Press, 1991. $30.00.

More than half of the nearly 6 million Jews who perished in Nazi Germany's Final Solution came from Poland. One result of that fact has been renewed interest in the history of Polish-Jewish relations. Hillel Levine, professor of sociology and religion at Boston University, makes an immensely valuable contribution to this field by exploring the precarious position of Polish Jewry from 1648 to 1795.

While Levine neither underestimates the power of religiously based anti-Semitism in Poland nor underplays how Jewish culture developed there in distinctive ways during this period, his well-placed emphasis falls on economics and specifically on the effect that Poland's failure to modernize its socioeconomic order had for Polish Jews. The effect was that Polish Jews became, in a word, "nonpersons." Two centuries later, that insidious status would prove devastating by helping to inflame passions to rid Europe of Jewish life.

The ratification of the Polish constitution on 3 May 1791 is a pivotal event in Levine's account. Although it also took inspiration from the Western Enlightenment, which produced the Declaration of the Rights of Man and the American Bill of Rights, Poland's reforming constitution differed fundamentally. While the former elements helped to establish a basis, albeit an imperfect one, for including Jewish participation in the modern world, Poland's May Constitution excluded Jews. "Abrogating rights they had enjoyed for six centuries," Levine explains, "half the world's Jews, at that moment residing in Poland, were now left out of public law and were legislatively defined as nonpersons."

Although the May Constitution did not last long—partitioned for a third time, independent Poland disappeared in 1795—its precedent of nonperson status for Jews remained. More than anything else, Levine believes, changing socioeconomic circumstances created an unfortunate condition. Brilliantly detailing how that process developed, Levine sums up the plight of Polish Jewry by suggesting that it was trapped by a logic that pokes out a group's eyes and then blames that

group for not seeing. That logic took on a life of its own in Poland as the following scenario unfolded.

Largely untouched by the economic modernization that accompanied the Protestant Reformation, Catholic Poland during the early modern period, says Levine, was "the most anticommercial country of Europe." Poland, however, was not isolated from the rest of Europe. The Polish elite, for example, learned to crave the goods that modernized economies could produce but that Poland's still feudal estates could not provide. These Polish interests found Jews useful. As Jews worked in their service—Levine stresses especially how they did so by producing and distributing grain-based intoxicants—they were important sources of revenue.

Crucial though they were as middlemen, that status did little to endear Jews to the Poles with whom they did business. In addition, if "useful" Jews were utilized by some Polish interests to prop up a declining economic system, other ascending interests—also influenced by the Western Enlightenment—did not see Jews as "useful" at all. To the contrary, these groups—some reformist, others simply self-interested—resented Jews as unproductive hindrances that had contributed to Polish backwardness. As the sociopolitical ground shifted, Jews were blamed increasingly for Poland's economic malaise. The extent of the blame became apparent when the May Constitution relegated Polish Jews to nonperson status.

Early on in this book, Levine mentions his teacher, Joseph Levenson, who liked to distinguish between what is "merely" of historical significance and what is "truly" of historical significance. *Economic Origins of Antisemitism* clearly belongs in the letter category. Looking ahead to the fate of Polish Jewry during the Holocaust, Levine calls the history he has traced "the beginning of the end." His study of "the failed modernization of Poland" is telling. Its insightful economic and sociological analysis not only illuminates pre-Holocaust history but also entails post-Holocaust warnings about how people may always be put at risk when they are economically unwanted.

JOHN K. ROTH

Claremont McKenna College
California

UNITED STATES

JORGENSON, JOSEPH G. *Oil Age Eskimos*. Pp. xix, 401. Berkeley: University of California Press, 1990. No price.

Alaskan Eskimos, including Inupiaq and Yup'ik societies, have never led simple lives, contrary to Western myths of primitive culture. But Eskimo lives have never been more complicated or threatened than since the enactment of the Alaska Native Claims Settlement Act (ANCSA) in 1971. ANCSA formally terminated the rights of Native Alaskans to 400 million acres in exchange for 44 million acres of land and $967 million. Furthermore, all previous agreements, including establishment of federal land trusts such as the one at St. Lawrence Island, were dissolved. The administration of the funds and land settlement was made through village and regional Native corporations, who were to bankroll local industry to create as much economic self-sufficiency as possible. In 1991, the Native corporations, including the surface and subsurface rights to their land, were to become public. Alaskan Native peoples' future will be determined in the next few years, as they battle with government and non-Native corporate interests over control of resources.

Jorgenson's timely book asks the question of how ANCSA has changed Eskimo communities in the last twenty years. Three unique communities, Gambell,

Unalakleet, and Wainwright, are compared in terms of history, political economy, ecology, and social organization. This ethnological approach prepares the reader to interpret the effects of ANCSA and to evaluate Jorgenson's speculations about Native Alaskans' futures. The value of this book is not simply its timeliness but also the presentation of current social and economic data on Alaskan Eskimos within the context of their ideologies. Most research in the north is contracted by industry and government and rarely sees the light of mainstream publication. In his more widely available book, Jorgenson has taken great efforts to present his data on Alaskan Natives in an understandable way, sympathetic but not romantic. The reader receives a realistic view of the effect of Alaska's political order on Eskimo life; no single factor is responsible for the poverty of Native communities.

Major factors exposed in this work include problems inherent in ANCSA, especially the undercapitalization of Native corporations. Most of the corporations are bankrupt today, not because of Native mismanagement but because they were never sufficiently capitalized. This is especially true of ventures in renewable resources, such as commercial fishing at Unalakleet, and community services, such as the development of small businesses including stores and small industries in Gambell. Economic development remains regulated by state and federal agencies and laws that often favor non-Native interests. Lack of adequate jobs for Natives is especially painful when so many of the community's jobs in government, education, and construction go to outsiders at generous wages, including a hardship allowance. The problems of lack of adequate cash flow and economic development were exacerbated by the tremendous cuts in transfer payments and public funds during the Reagan years.

Of most concern to all three communities, however, have been the continued environmental threats to subsistence by nonrenewable resource extraction, especially from oil companies. Exxon's irresponsible action during the *Valdez* spill only confirms what Eskimos have suspected all along: wildlife and Native people will suffer from poorly regulated oil development, and the oil companies will not be held responsible for damages.

Additional impediments to economic independence exist within the modernized communities themselves. Internal problems for Eskimo communities include rapid population growth; insufficient health and education resources, especially for women and children; and problems of alcohol abuse and domestic violence. The high costs of transportation and goods in the north are constant factors.

My criticisms of this work are few but significant. Readers unfamiliar with Alaska politics will not clearly understand ANCSA and all its ramifications for Native people. A list of definitions for acronyms and flow charts of government organizations would aid an understanding of how agencies are interrelated. Although a history of the communities is summarized at the beginning, I would have preferred to see more historical depth in the economic and social-organization chapters. Native economies have always been adjusting to external forces, be they climatic, social, or political. Knowing how harvesting patterns, costs of hunting outfits, sources of capital, and household structure have changed since 1950 would offer insight into the tenacity of the subsistence economy over time.

The chapter on ideology I find most lacking. Eskimo ideology is much more complex than a set of shared values, Christian ethics, and spiritual connections to land. Individuals, as well as societies, spiritually thrive on the meanings they develop through subsistence production and resource distribution. For example, the richness of hunting rituals within these communities is not revealed. A description of the ritual action of the hunt and the distribution of the animals would re-create the strength of the significant meanings Jorgenson briefly discusses. No quantitative study of harvesting or formal study of social organization has meaning until these facts and figures are brought to life with the voices of the Native hunter and his family.

Despite these problems, the overriding significance of this book is in its value to the nonspecialist who seeks to understand contemporary Alaskan Native societies. Environmentalists and energy specialists must read this book if they are to work with Native people. Jorgenson has provided an important lesson in development. No one today would think of Native people as heathen, stupid savages; now no one can think of Native people as little children that just need education and a chance. Native Alaskans are human beings with dreams, a sense of place and time, plans, and a special knowledge that is both spiritual and practical. Yet they have little power to protect their children's future. Whether or not they will be able to control sufficient resources to have choices remains to be seen. The hope is that non-Natives, their governments, and their businesses will allow Eskimos their right to self-determination in the next decade.

KRISTEN BORRÉ

Dickinson College
Carlisle
Pennsylvania

YANKELOVICH, DANIEL. *Coming to Public Judgment: Making Democracy Work in a Complex World.* Pp. xiv, 290. Syracuse, NY: Syracuse University Press, 1991. $34.95. Paperbound, $16.95.

Daniel Yankelovich has written *Coming to Public Judgment* to protest a widening gap between the American public and its leaders that is creating a host of impending social and environmental crises. Arguing that our decision-making processes are dominated by a culture of technical control that considers objective facts the only valid form of knowledge, he marshals an eclectic blend of survey research findings, lessons from his experiences as a corporate director, and insights from the discipline of philosophy to urge that we incorporate the normative wisdom contained in public judgments into the governance of society. He offers prescriptions for improving the quality of public judgment and for overcoming resistance to public judgment as an important form of knowledge.

The philosophical underpinnings of his arguments rest on a faith that the essence of human reason compels people of goodwill to work together in pursuit of common goals. I use the word "faith" because there is disagreement among political philosophers, ancient and modern, that such an assumption is warranted. If humans are instead essentially selfish beings who use the political process to dominate others in order to achieve private ends, the concept of a common interest is severely limited, as is the practicality of Yankelovich's vision. This philosophical debate is most material to his presentation of rules for resolution, which outline what leaders can do to promote a democratic society—here I was reminded of Plato's conclusion that his utopia could only be realized when philosophers became kings, or kings became philosophers.

Yankelovich characterizes his vision as "actively conservative" in the sense that he believes we need to reclaim a lost democracy. Unable to identify a time in the past when a majority possessed the power of self-governance, I find his vision actively radical. If realized, it would mean a transformation in structures of political and socioeconomic stratification that have dominated human societies throughout history.

If we are, however, entering a new age of true democratization, the converging crises besetting our country may soon give our population the incentive and the will that Yankelovich identifies as the first requisite to dealing with our problems. In such a context, it is exciting to know that Yankelovich and his colleagues are creating the means that are the second requisite to solving those problems and achieving a democratic society. The techniques and strategies offered in *Coming to Public Judgment* could be of tremendous value to humankind.

EMMIT B. EVANS, Jr.

California Polytechnic
    State University
San Luis Obispo

SOCIOLOGY

LASCH, CHRISTOPHER. *The True and Only Heaven: Progress and Its Critics.* Pp. 591. New York: Norton, 1991. $25.00.

Christopher Lasch has written another provocative book. The author of *The Culture of Narcissism* and *The New Radicalism in America*, among other works of importance, this time critically focuses upon progress and its critics. For him, "the true and only heaven" may not rest only with the advocates of unbounded progress but with the espousers of lower-middle-class culture as well.

While Lasch recognizes that petit bourgeois values sometimes can be narrow and provincial and on occasion have produced racism, nativism, and anti-intellectualism, he contends that liberals sometimes lose sight of what is valuable in such a mind-set. Its moral realism, its understanding that everything has its price, its skepticism about progress, and especially its respect for limits may prove a tonic for American society. Moreover, by discussing thinkers such as Jonathan Edwards, Emerson, Carlyle, William James, and Reinhold Niebuhr, Lasch reveals that such values are not simply the monopoly of Joe Sixpack, if they are his at all.

The study begins with what Lasch terms a deceptively simple question: "How does it happen that serious people continue to believe in progress in the face of massive evidence that might have been expected to refute the idea of progress once and for all?" Lasch's attempt to explain this anomaly—"the persistence of a belief in progress in a century full of calamities"—led him back to the eighteenth century. If liberals such as Adam Smith argued the positive aspects of the insatiability of human wants, which required indefinite economic expansion, then creeping, if not galloping, consumerism with all of its attendant social ills had an early start in our nation. With such an engine driving American society, it is not surprising that we sometimes have gone off course.

Much of the volume revolves around Lasch's implicit and explicit consideration of the tension between limits and hope. His is a wide-ranging appraisal. A concluding chapter on right-wing populism and the revolt against liberalism concerns contemporary cultural cleavages and clashes. The nature of class in modern America, the issues of abortion and busing, neoconservatism, permissiveness, and consumerism all receive attention.

This is no narrow case study; rather, it is a sweeping interpretation of where we are and how we got here by a leading historian and social critic. While one might not agree with all of the author's broad generalizations, they are boldly stimulating and intellectually entangling.

BRUCE M. STAVE

University of Connecticut
Storrs

ORFIELD, GARY and CAROLE ASHKINAZE. *The Closing Door: Conservative Policy and Black Opportunity*. Pp. xx, 254. Chicago: University of Chicago Press, 1991. $22.50.

In this elucidating book, Orfield, a professor of political science and education, and Ashkinaze, a journalist, examine the relative progress of black and white residents of Atlanta in the 1980s. Atlanta should be the perfect test case for the conservative policies of the Reagan and Bush era. If the economy expands sufficiently, conservatives and neoconservatives have confidently predicted, everyone benefits, even those at the bottom of the social system, through what in the early 1980s was rather inelegantly called a "trickle-down theory." Atlanta has a large black professional community, it has black political leadership, and it has experienced extensive growth as corporations fled the cold, unionized northeast for the warmer, antiunion Sunbelt. If things were going to "trickle down" to everyone's benefit anywhere, it should have happened in Atlanta.

It has not. It has not because the market economy has not dealt with the ongoing racial barriers in Atlanta. As Orfield and Ashkinaze's detailed analysis demonstrates, the gap between black and white residents of Atlanta has widened, and many of the hard-fought gains of the civil rights era have been lost. Continued patterns of residential segregation, even in the new suburbs to which black and white middle-class Atlantans have fled from the inner city, are central to understanding the increasing chasm between black and white residents of Atlanta in the quality of education, the quality of housing, the availability of jobs, and income level.

One of the casualties of the Reagan years was research on questions related to race. As Orfield and Ashkinaze state, when the Reagan administration took over, there was a decline in the collection and dissemination of data about racial problems and, instead, "a continuous high-pitched ideological attack by government officials on social programs and civil rights policies."

This book is an effort to focus, once again, on racial issues. The authors draw on a series of working papers by a team of researchers working on the Metropolitan Opportunity Project, an ongoing effort to examine the same set of questions in five American cities—Atlanta, Chicago, Houston, Los Angeles, and Philadelphia.

Orfield and Ashkinaze are not nearly as successful as they could have been in converting the original working papers into a smoothly flowing narrative. The quality of the writing varies considerably from chapter to chapter. Some things are repeated. Other things are alluded to prior to being explained. Some chapters have footnotes and others do not; references are provided throughout, but the format changes. In one case, the authors carelessly leave in a reference to the current work as a "paper" rather than the chapter it has become.

Still, there is an immense amount of important information in the book. It is a sobering and valuable assessment and analysis of the damage done to inner-city blacks during the 1980s.

RICHARD L. ZWEIGENHAFT

Guilford College
Greensboro
North Carolina

ROSENFELD, MICHEL. *Affirmative Action and Justice: A Philosophical and Constitutional Inquiry.* Pp. viii, 373. New Haven, CT: Yale University Press, 1991. No price.

Affirmative action is a battleground for competing notions of justice. In part 1 of this book, Rosenfeld examines libertar-ian, contractarian, utilitarian, and egalitarian approaches to justice, and the derivative approaches to affirmative action, concluding that none of these approaches can mediate the disputes over preferential affirmative action policies. Part 2 examines the Supreme Court's affirmative action rulings, concluding that the Court has not articulated a coherent rationale for or limits to affirmative action. These discussions provide the backdrop for the provocative effort in part 3 to mediate disagreements between proponents and opponents of affirmative action. Rosenfeld draws on Kohlberg and Habermas to develop a moral decision-making process he calls the "principle of justice as reversibility": moral agents should put themselves in the shoes of those with whom they disagree in order to empathetically and accurately reverse their perspective and thereby understand the other. When parties to disagreements embrace this decision-making process, views will converge, or, at least, common understandings will make compromises possible. When applied to affirmative action, Rosenfeld argues, the process of justice as reversibility leads to the conclusion that preferential affirmative action is morally permissible. For Rosenfeld, the judiciary is ideally suited to arbitrate the disputes over affirmative action through the process he recommends, empowered as it is "to undertake the dialogical task of harmonizing a chorus of genuine but antagonistic clamoring voices."

The book is a valuable contribution to affirmative action debates. Unfortunately, most of its discussion will be accessible only to specialists. Although Rosenfeld discusses fairly the merits of the major arguments about affirmative action, sometimes with striking insights, he is needlessly repetitive and excessively verbose. The most lucid discussion examines Court rulings explicitly dealing with affirmative action policies. This legal analysis, however, almost completely ignores how antidiscrimination law, not just affirmative action law, promotes affirmative action. As a result, Rosenfeld fails to discuss crucial rulings based on antidiscrimination law that have promoted affirmative action practices, such as *Griggs* v. *Duke Power* (1971)—which was subsequently overturned in *Wards Cove* v. *Atonio* (1989)—leading to the recent, contentious debates on quotas.

The major contribution of the book is Rosenfeld's constructive effort to provide a theoretical basis for what is arguably the heart of the moral life—the intuitive and imaginative quest to walk in the shoes of the other. Rosenfeld well argues that the recommended process would move the Court to endorse preferential affirmative action. Unfortunately, the ideological cast of the Court provides little hope that the nine people who most ought to read this book would be receptive to its deliberative method.

BRON R. TAYLOR

University of Wisconsin
Oshkosh

ECONOMICS

BHAGWATI, JAGDISH. *The World Trading System at Risk.* Pp. viii, 156. Princeton, NJ: Princeton University Press, 1991. $16.95.

This book has much to commend it: brevity; wit ("Gertrude Stein could have said: A tariff is a tariff is a tariff"); and slant—it favors free trade and the General Agreement on Tariffs and Trade (GATT). Its clear prose clarifies many of the issues leading up to the stalemate at the Uruguay Round of GATT talks— managed trade, aggressive unilateralism, unfair trade, and rising regionalism. And it lambastes the aggressive uni

lateralism of American trade policy on a number of grounds, some of which are solid.

Unfortunately, however, what is missing from Bhagwati's approach is critical for the policy positions he would advocate: the national perspective that makes it in a country's interest to support protectionism at certain developmental phases. Thus he facilely criticizes the flip-flops of Keynes on trade policy without linking those policy changes to the British national interest that Keynes was usually directly or indirectly articulating. He writes of the residues of national strategies incorporated in trade policies —the short-term aggressive unilateralism of the United States, the trader mentality of Japan, and the protectionism of India—without sufficiently indicating the stage of development of each of these countries in the world economy, which would serve to explain their policy positions. His lumping together the positions of developing countries in his GATT policy prescriptions, seeking to put them in a quantitative, time-bound straitjacket for the sake of effective most-favored-nation treatment in the service area, for example, is another telling illustration.

Moreover, at times his style slips into self-absorption and self-citation to the point that he gets in his own way, making his arguments less persuasive than they might otherwise be. His attack on the "culturalists"—picking a mere journalist, James Fallows, as the straw man—does not persuade the reader that he understands much about the sophisticated cultural intricacies of Japanese strategy, which he spends a good deal of time defending. The role of the *sogoshosha* as resurrected *zaibatsu* is ignored, as is the role of multinational intracompany trade in general.

Bhagwati makes one good suggestion that might help resolve ongoing GATT disputes: strike a bargain within categories of goods rather than seeking trade-offs between new and old sectors and issues. In addition, he is very perceptive on the origins and implications of the rise of regional blocs—the European Community and the U.S.-Canadian-Mexican free-trade pacts—for the health and efficacy of the GATT regime.

Bhagwati's book is an important overview made up of sharp propositions on critical contemporary trade issues, but in circling so high above the forest of trade, many of the trees are overlooked. In the process, Bhagwati may succeed in persuading only GATT administrators and academic economists, not policymakers in real countries, whether developed or underdeveloped.

ROBERT ISAAK

Pace University
Pleasantville
New York

BROWN, CHARLES, JAMES HAMILTON, and JAMES MEDOFF. *Employers Large and Small*. Pp. 109. Cambridge, MA: Harvard University Press, 1990. $19.95.

This compact study attempts to counter the conventional wisdom that small businesses create the majority of new jobs and that they lack political power in Washington. By utilizing data from other studies, Brown, Hamilton, and Medoff convincingly conclude that this misconception has influenced policy and regulatory decisions for the past decade. The general populist view and bias against large corporate entities have created a distrust of bigness that has given to small businesses political power and exemptions from numerous regulations. The myth that small businesses represent Ma and Pa shops and that helping these firms is an egalitarian policy in reality perversely redistributes income as the owners of small firms have income and assets several times the average levels.

The key conclusion of the study is that small firms are not the major source of job generation that they have often been portrayed and that this sector has not become more important over the last decade, as has often been concluded. This impression comes from the number of births of new firms and jobs, but it neglects the disproportionate number of deaths of businesses and jobs as well as the instability of the sector. To grant tax benefits and regulatory relief in hopes of job generation is not supported by the evidence. This "small is beautiful" myth also overlooks the fact that jobs in small firms offer lower wages and more meager benefits than do larger firms. The job security and training opportunities are also less prevalent in smaller firms, given quit-rate and other objective data rather than impressions. The indirect testing of job satisfaction by union representation election results shows that employees of small firms are more likely to vote to unionize. Similar data show that union sentiment and activity are greater in small firms even though small firms fight unionization more fiercely and illegally as indicated by rates of labor practice violation by small firms.

The political punch of small firms is hidden because there is not a single voice for small firms as there is for labor; however, the collective political action committees and their strength in numbers result in more staffers for small firms than for large firms and labor unions combined. The underdog image and press favoritism magnify the political power of the sector. The result of the power has created regulatory exemptions to the extent that there are two work forces, one protected and well paid and the other unprotected and underpaid.

W. E. SPELLMAN

Coe College
Cedar Rapids
Iowa

BRUYN, SEVERYN T. *A Future for the American Economy: The Social Market Economy.* Pp. viii, 424. Stanford, CA: Stanford University Press, 1991. $45.00.

Severyn T. Bruyn, a sociologist at Boston College, has written a timely and thoughtful analysis of what he terms the central contradiction of the American economy, that between government control and market freedom. He provides a provocative contribution to the debate over the shape of post-Cold War capitalism.

At a time when world events—from Ronald Reagan's evocation of the "magic of the marketplace" in his address to Latin American heads of state in Cancún, to the recent dismantling of socialism in Eastern Europe and the Soviet Union—suggest a near total victory for market ideology, Bruyn seeks to examine the role of social and institutional factors in reconciling the contradiction between market and state. Placing himself between those advocating unfettered markets and those who see government as an essential mediator between private and public interests, Bruyn argues that a market economy could function more productively and more humanely, with less government regulation, if markets were restructured to transfer "the essence of the modern democratic state—its capacity for self-governance"—to the market.

At first glance, Bruyn's arguments might appear to be little more than a restatement of Adam Smith's arguments for the "invisible hand," the process by which competitive forces lead an individual's pursuit of self-interest to "promote that of society more effectually than when he really intends to promote it." Bruyn, however, contends that the public interest will be best promoted only when private markets are structured to promote increased cooperation, as well as competition. The ability, for example, of domestic firms to meet the challenge of foreign competition requires cooperative arrangements made possible through trade associations. Similarly, the traditional antagonism between the interests of labor and management must give way to the more cooperative structure of the self-managed firm. Government's principal role in this new market structure, which Bruyn characterizes as the "social market economy," should be to support business in organizing a market that regulates itself.

In order to create the social market economy, Bruyn appeals to social scientists to reclaim the study of the economic system from economists. If, as he argues, the economy is grounded primarily in a societal order, then social and economic influences must be studied together to understand the changes taking place in the market. Yet, while the construction of the social market economy requires new forms of analysis and deep changes, Bruyn emphasizes that the seeds for these changes have already been planted and many are taking root. Case studies from Europe, Japan, and the United States are used to demonstrate the ways in which corporations today are already cooperating and how they have developed self-regulatory norms for introducing societal values into the marketplace. These changes, however, will not flourish and mature without new economic indicators that measure cooperation as well as competition and without supportive public policies. Global issues, and their potential to influence changes in the domestic economy, are discussed in a (regrettably) brief appendix.

DAVID W. SCHODT

St. Olaf College
Northfield
Minnesota

SUMMERS, LAWRENCE H. *Understanding Unemployment.* Pp. xxiv, 360. Cambridge: MIT Press, 1990. $27.50.

If all one knew about unemployment were that the rate of unemployment was 8 percent, then none of these statements could be ruled out:

1. Every worker takes a month vacation each year over and above the holiday arranged with his or her employer by resigning from one job and picking up another a month later.

2. Jobs are intrinsically short term. Each job lasts about six months, and, once laid off, a worker has to search for a couple of weeks to find a new job.

3. For a variety of reasons—to become a housewife or househusband, to further one's education, to retire, to build a house, to become a hobo—about 1 out of every 12 workers quits the labor force each year, calling himself or herself unemployed to become eligible for unemployment insurance.

4. In any given month, every employed worker has a 1 percent chance of losing his or her job and every unemployed worker has a 12.5 percent chance of finding a new job. Thus, just by chance, some workers remain unemployed for a long time. Of the 8 percent of the work force unemployed today, 20 percent—equivalent to about 1.5 percent of the labor force—have been unemployed for up to a year.

5. Every year, 1 of 25 workers loses his or her job and must search for a couple of years to find another. The long-term unemployed experience great hardship, loss of property, deterioration of skills, and loss of self-respect, though the hardship is mitigated to some extent by unemployment insurance.

6. Of all workers, 80 percent hold secure jobs and the other 20 percent hold risky jobs. Holders of secure jobs are never laid off. Holders of risky jobs bear a 5 percent chance per month of losing their jobs. A dismissed worker needs eight months to find a new job.

Suitably generalized, each of these statements is true in the sense that it

accounts for part of the observed unemployment, and each is false in the sense that it is less than the whole story. Determination of the relative magnitudes of the different kinds of unemployment encapsulated in these statements is of the utmost importance for the assessment of the effects of public provision of unemployment insurance on the welfare of workers. Insofar as statements 1, 2, and 3 are valid, unemployment insurance is a great foolishness, running money through the public sector in a way that yields little or no net benefit to anybody except, possibly, the administrators of the system. Insofar as 4, 5, and 6 are valid, unemployment insurance alleviates the effects of misfortune that strikes workers at random, though with greater frequency and higher cost to some workers than to others. *Understanding Unemployment* attempts to sort these matters out.

The book reprints 10 essays by Lawrence Summers and several collaborators. A major concern in these essays is with the magnitude of hard-core as distinct from transitory employment. Other writers had asserted that almost all unemployment is transitory, as exemplified by cases 1 and 2 above. From a subtle statistical analysis of the data on unemployment in the United States and elsewhere, Summers concludes that such an interpretation is a misreading of the data and that the common view, according to which much of unemployment is hard-core and therefore burdensome, is essentially correct. A second major concern is the intriguing question of whether unemployment feeds upon itself, whether a person's experience of unemployment unfits him for work or makes him more prone to unemployment in the future than he would otherwise be, and whether society's experience of unemployment causes institutions to develop in ways that make subsequent unemployment more likely.

The essays were written for professional journals of economics. Though uncommonly clear, straightforward, and accessible—by the standards of contemporary economic literature—the essays should really be read together with other papers on the subject that are cited but not summarized as they would be in an integrated text. The book would serve well as supplementary reading in a graduate course in labor economics. It should, and no doubt will, find its way onto the shelves of social scientists and officials who are professionally concerned with understanding unemployment.

DAN USHER

Queen's University
Kingston
Ontario
Canada

OTHER BOOKS

AUGUSTINOS, GERASIMOS, ed. *Diverse Paths to Modernity in Southeastern Europe: Essays in National Development.* Pp. 176. Westport, CT: Greenwood Press, 1990. $39.95.

BELLUSH, JEWEL and DICK NETZER, eds. *Urban Politics, New York Style.* Pp. x, 467. Armonk, NY: M. E. Sharpe, 1990. $24.95.

BOWLES, SAMUEL et al. *After the Waste Land: A Democratic Economics for the Year 2000.* Pp. xv, 269. Armonk, NY: M. E. Sharpe, 1990. No price.

BRYNEN, REX, ed. *Echoes of the Intifada: Regional Repercussions of the Palestinian-Israeli Conflict.* Pp. 314. Boulder, CO: Westview Press, 1991. Paperbound, $36.50.

DENISOFF, SERGE and WILLIAM ROMANOWSKI. *Risky Business: Rock in Film.* Pp. xi, 768. New Brunswick, NJ: Transaction, 1991. $39.95. Paperbound, $29.95.

DONELAN, MICHAEL. *Elements of International Political Theory.* Pp. 212. New York: Oxford University Press, 1990. $59.00.

FLANAGAN, WILLIAM G. *Urban Sociology: Images and Structure.* Pp. x, 390. Needham Heights, MA: Allyn & Bacon, 1990. No price.

GOLDSCHEIDER, FRANCES K. and CALVIN GOLDSCHEIDER, eds. *Ethnicity and the New Family Economy.* Pp. xvii, 200. Boulder, CO: Westview Press, 1989. Paperbound, no price.

HEPWORTH, MARK. *Geography of the Information Economy.* Pp. xix, 258. New York: Guilford Press, 1989. $30.00.

HUDSON, VALERIE, ed. *Artificial Intelligence and International Politics.* Pp. viii, 422. Boulder, CO: Westview Press, 1991. $55.00.

JACOBY, SANFORD M. *Masters to Managers.* Pp. ix, 249. New York: Columbia University Press, 1991. No price.

KLEINBERG, ROBERT. *China's "Opening" to the Outside World: The Experiment with Foreign Capitalism.* Pp. xiv, 277. Boulder, CO: Westview Press, 1990. $36.50. Paperbound, $14.95.

LEE, CHONG-SIK. *Korea Briefing, 1990.* Pp. viii, 175. Boulder, CO: Westview Press, 1990. $35.85. Paperbound, $14.85.

LITTLE, DANIEL. *Varieties of Social Explanation: An Introduction to the Philosophy of Social Science.* Pp. xiii, 258. Boulder, CO: Westview Press, 1991. $55.00. Paperbound, $19.95.

MILLER, J.D.B. and R. J. VINCENT, eds. *Order and Violence: Hedley Bull and International Relations.* Pp. 220. New York: Oxford University Press, 1990. $55.00.

NADER, LAURA. *Harmony Ideology: Justice and Control in a Zapotec Mountain Village.* Pp. xxiii, 343. Stanford, CA: Stanford University Press, 1990. $37.50.

QUETEL, CLAUDE. *History of Syphilis.* Pp. 342. Baltimore, MD: Johns Hopkins University Press, 1990. $35.95.

SALINGER, PIERRE. *Secret Dossier: The Hidden Agenda behind the Gulf War.* Pp. viii, 241. New York: Penguin, 1991. Paperbound, $9.95.

SHLAIM, AVI. *The Politics of Partition: King Abdullah, the Zionists and Palestine 1921-1951.* Pp. xiv, 465. New York: Columbia University Press, 1991. Paperbound, $15.00.

TOCH, HANS and KENNETH ADAMS. *The Disturbed Violent Offender.* Pp. xx, 183. New Haven, CT: Yale University Press, 1991. $25.00. Paperbound, $16.00.

INDEX